New Developments in Film Theory

Patrick Fuery

First published 2000 by
MACMILLAN PRESS LTD
Houndmills, Basingstoke, Hampshire RG21 6XS
and London
Companies and representatives
throughout the world

ISBN 0-333-74490-X hardcover
ISBN 0-333-74491-8 paperback

A catalogue record for this book is available
from the British Library.

This book is printed on paper suitable for recycling and
made from fully managed and sustained forest sources.

10   9   8   7   6   5   4   3   2   1
09   08   07   06   05   04   03   02   01   00

Printed and bound in Great Britain by Creative Print and Design (Wales), Ebbw Vale

Typeset in Great Britain by Aarontype Limited, Easton, Bristol

---

 Published in the United States of America by
ST. MARTIN'S PRESS, INC.,
Scholarly and Reference Division
175 Fifth Avenue, New York, N.Y. 10010

ISBN 0-312-23617-4 (cloth)
ISBN 0-312-23618-2 (paper)

For **Kelli**, whose generous and selfless love inspires more than words can say; for **Morgan**, who always makes me smile; and for **Martin** (1963–97), a brother's love worth remembering

Contents

Contents

Acknowledgements

Many kind and generous people contributed a great deal to the writing of this book.

All the people at the publishers were supportive of this project. In particular, Catherine Gray was unfailingly helpful, good humoured, and offered considerably more than editorial advice. Her intelligent suggestions for design, structure, and style were always welcome.

Many friends and colleagues offered support and encouragement, but I would especially like to thank the following: Stella Bruzzi, whose knowledge of film is something to behold – her kindness over coffee and in emails contributed a great deal; Tom Burvill, who always has time, and always gives so much; Joan Kirkby, inspiring and generous, a pleasure to be with; Horst Ruthrof (who must be getting tired of being mentioned in these pages), who always offers the best advice, at the best moment, with such modesty; Sam Tarlington and Robin Burgess, for their irrepressible spirit and friendship (especially at that time late in June); Linda and Paul Wilkins, and Bryan Wilkinson, and my mother, who all suffered my choices of films with such fine humour – and always offer friendship and a solid base of return; and my family, Kelli and Morgan, who bring to my life brightness, laughter, and much love. How does one ever repay that?

Finally, part of this book's dedication is to my brother, Martin, whose love of cinema will always be a precious memory for me.

PATRICK FUERY

Introduction

Film and Theory

Deleuze concludes his two volumes on cinema with a short reflection on the relationship between film and theory. He argues that 'a theory of cinema is not about cinema, but about the concepts that cinema gives rise to and which are themselves related to other concepts' (Deleuze 1989: 280). In this brief statement we find a comment that summarises one of the most significant turns that film theory has taken in recent times. These theoretical developments have become more focused on the idea that what resonates in cinema is far more than the elements of the films themselves, and to understand what cinema is, and how it operates, we must turn to these wider issues.

This is the first major development in recent film theory – the recognition of the vastness of the scope of both the material and the theories. To understand film, that is, to theorise it, position it within different contexts (including the cultural, philosophical, political, etc.), and to develop analytic models, necessarily moves the points of discussion beyond the celluloid. The theories dealt with in this book, that is, the dominant theoretical models of poststructuralism and postmodernism, are vital to the study of film because it is through the complex ideas of these theories that we might come to better understand the nature of the cinematic apparatus.

Another key development is related to this, and in one sense it is an inversion of the relationship between film and theory. Cinema (both the various theoretical models of film studies as well as the texts themselves) has come to be seen as an essential part of a complex set of theories that have grown out of a number of different disciplines, including philosophy, psychoanalysis, women's studies, cultural studies, gender studies, deconstruction, and semiotics – in short, the sweep and turns, factions and fragments, of poststructuralism and postmodernism. Film has become essential to the development of many of these critical movements, not simply as a textual example, but as a direct contributor to the theoretical operations and concepts. One of the consequences of both these developments is that it has become increasingly more important for us to engage in a range of

1

theoretical issues, and to acknowledge the vitality of these issues to the development of film theory. This is one of the aims of this book; not to attempt to map out all of the developments that have taken place in film theory, but to consider how film and the wider issues of critical theory have come to change each other. The result is not simply hybridisation, but the continued growth of a series of new disciplines. From this point on, the relationship between cinema and different theoretical projects has become entwined. The 'new developments' indicated in the title of this book refers to this dynamic process between film and theory. What this challenges is the idea of film studies/film theory as something only to do with film.

Part of the relational context of film to theory is how cinema itself has come to be a space and praxis for the analytic processes and issues. Cinema is the one textual form that has developed specifically within the theoretical contexts of structuralism, poststructuralism, and postmodernism. It is a form that has continually been surrounded by a devising of self-reflexive theories, many of which have directly challenged the established ways of looking at the world and how we operate in it. Gone is a sense of certainty, wholeness, resolution, and completion. They have been replaced by restless signs, driven by certain passions towards a status of the question and absence, rather than answers and presence. Of course other textual forms (literature, painting, music, etc.) have also shifted within these theoretical developments, but cinema's role has a certain uniqueness because it is the one born in the time of these theoretical challenges.

If film needs theory, just as critical theory needs and enjoys cinema, we are then led to ask what does this relationship produce? The intellectual projects of poststructuralism and postmodernism, such as the interpretation and re-evaluation of topics such as subjectivity, culture, meaning, gender, power, discourse, pleasure, language (to name but a few), represent a profound shift in the climate of Western thought. It would be a sleight of hand to simply argue that these same sorts of issues are part of film's subject-matter, and therefore we need theory to work through them. We should always treat such a simple equation with suspicion, even if there are often specific cases where this is precisely what is taking place. What is more interesting – and this is what Deleuze is getting at in his summation of theory and film – is to examine how film itself can be read as a theorising of these issues. So we move away from the usual interpretation of films as representations of certain themes, and then theory is applied to the texts to 'extract' such concepts, and towards a model that argues that theory and film perform the same sorts of tasks. What we are interested in here is the idea that the critical concepts of poststructuralism and postmodernism are themselves part of the film process. This includes the films, the act of watching them, the socio-cultural contexts, as well as the systems of interpretation.

To consider these issues and relationships a number of the major issues of critical theory have been selected here. These topics have been selected in part because of their centrality to the critical developments, and in part because they offer fresh perspectives on how we might go about analysing the cinematic text. The book is divided into four sections, each consisting of two chapters. Ostensibly these four sections map out some of these issues of critical theory, notably subjectivity, discourse, culture, and meaning. However, there are a number of inflections given to these topics, in part to work as illustration, and in part to push certain lines of thought in different directions. By this we mean that the discussions of both theory and film are directed at offering different perspectives on these key themes and ideas.

The first section considers the issue of the gaze, initially from the perspective of the formations of subjectivity, before moving on to examine cinematic aspects that cannot be held within a relationship of the spectator to image. Fundamental to this is the idea that the spectator's position and relations to the cinematic image tell us something about the larger issues of the formation and operation of subjectivity, textuality, and the social order. Four different concepts are employed to offer a range of approaches to this idea of the gaze and the subject. These are masochism, identification, phantasy, and the *punctum*. These four engage in ideas from psychoanalysis, feminism, gender studies, and semiotics, allowing us to consider how the gaze is part of the construction of a certain type of subject position. Chapter 2 considers this relationship of the spectator to the image from a more detailed perspective. Broadly speaking it deals with how certain ideas from Lacan's psychoanalytic theory and Derrida's theories of deconstruction might be employed in the analysis of film, and how film might be used to explore these ideas. What organises these two models is the idea of the excess and beyond of the image as it is constructed by, and constructs, the spectator. This analytic strategy is adopted throughout the book: the connections between theory and film as they aim for the same purpose, and the use of film to explicate theoretical points.

The next section – on discourse – commences with a consideration of different theories on discourse, before focusing on some key ideas from Foucault and their cinematic potential. The first part of Chapter 3 considers some of the key ideas from semiotics, in particular Kristeva and Barthes. The idea of intertextuality is explored in depth, considering the movement from a simple textual referencing, to the more complex ideas developed by Kristeva. This leads to a point where discourse is seen as an unending roll of textual orders, where pluralism dominates. The second half of the chapter considers Foucault's ideas on discourse, particularly in terms of constructions of power and knowledge. What this means for film is that its discursive practices are diverse, heterogeneous, dynamic and invested with a particular type of knowledge.

This is followed up in Chapter 4 by a more specific set of issues, particularly how we might engage in the discourses of cinema in terms of the body. This is more than the representation of the body in film, instead arguing that film has devised a discursive practice that is driven by the body and its various parts. This chapter on the flesh and body also considers how different aspects of poststructuralist and postmodernist theories might be utilised to produce a theory of film discourse. These include Lacan's readings of the body and Lyotard's ideas on postmodernism, before returning to Foucault to re-evaluate some of his particular notions of discourse in terms of cinema. Of primary concern is the idea that we might speak of a formation of a cinematic knowledge that operates within and through film discourse.

Chapters 5 and 6 are concerned with the relationship of film to social contexts and processes. Chapter 5 considers these issues through the example of love, arguing that in order to understand better the cultural contexts of cinema, we can investigate how it treats a particular social phenomenon. The pervasive, yet heterogeneous, representation of love in cinema makes it an ideal example. Two specific examples are taken up – the kiss and true love – to investigate how there is a cultural process in such representations, and yet at the same time there are resistances in any sense of shared interpretation. Put another way, one of the issues is how there is an interplay between cultural orders (such as love) and the challenge to how we might read them. Both the kiss and true love are common elements in film, yet they both offer problems in reading them.

If both the kiss and love are part of a recognisable cultural order (and set of representations within film) Chapter 6 extends the examination of how cinema both fits into and resists social orders. This is film as it utilises both themes and structures to disrupt, challenge and sometimes even escape the rigours of social patterns and processes. At one level this chapter deals with overt representations of social disruption, in particular the idea of the carnivalesque. This idea is then taken up in terms of realism. By considering both the role cinema plays in disrupting social orders, and the disruptions within its own discourse, this chapter moves towards the idea that these disturbances actually have a positive, creative effect. This is traced through Lyotard's idea of the *dispositif* and Kristeva's study of the carnivalesque.

Chapter 7 considers how films produce and operate within a sense of meaning. This chapter takes phenomenology as a primary example of a critical model of meaning, before turning to other ideas, including psychoanalysis and deconstruction. This is not simply how a film might come to be seen as meaningful, or as having meaning. Rather it is a consideration of how meaning can even begin to exist in cinema, and what cinema has done to expose a certain attitude towards meaning. The final chapter of the book – on seduction – is not meant to act as a point where all that has come before is distilled into a resolved form. Rather it is a sometimes circling back over what has been considered in these earlier sections, as well as provocation of all that has been left unsaid. Seduction also becomes the metaphor for how meaning is always figured as a beyond in this theorising of film. We are seduced towards a sense of meaning, only to be drawn elsewhere. That is to say, that no matter how much we might try to resolve, what remains in both cinema and theory is the seduction towards another point.

Lacan, in negotiating the Reality Principle and the Pleasure Principle, makes the following statement: 'That whole organism seems designed not to satisfy need, but to hallucinate such satisfaction' (Lacan 1992: 28). We can adapt this description to say that cinema is not about satisfaction (of needs and demands, but also of the analytic questions themselves), but the hallucination of such satisfaction. This is not to lessen the power of the cinematic drive, but rather to illustrate the force of cinema in our subjectivities, our cultural orders, and our psychical processes. Part of what defines cinema is its role as a meeting place for all these processes. The hallucination of satisfaction that cinema provides allows it to hold contradictions, splits and doubles without necessarily having to attempt to resolve them or even acknowledge difference.

A Note on the Films and Some Terms

A great many films are referred to throughout this book – more than 200 are cited as examples – and of these some are returned to and discussed in detail. The strategy behind this is that the interrelationship between film and theory is best handled across a great many examples. The critical concepts become clearer if we see them in different contexts, and the films are potentially enlivened by being approached from different critical perspectives. Similarly the concepts discussed shift according to what issue is at hand. Sometimes it is important to utilise the films to work through the critical theories, and other times the theories are there to offer analysis of the films. This fluidity between theory and film is also one of the key developments in film studies in recent times.

1

The Gaze: Masochism, Identification and Phantasy in the Spectator

What I look at is never what I wish to see.
(Lacan)

On the Gaze

The primary concern in this chapter, and the following one, is the gaze as it has been theorised in terms of film, and what some of the implications of these readings are. In order to do this we will take up some of the key points of film studies in the last thirty years, and then offer alternatives to some of these. In one sense what is being set up here is the idea that we can never fully articulate the processes of the gaze in film, simply because the complexity of what is involved constantly moves the issues beyond description and analysis. No longer is the gaze just a term for perception, but now includes issues such as subjectivity, culture, ideology, gender, race, and interpretation. This chapter will tend to locate such issues, rather than explicate any single one, for what is of primary concern here is how the theory of the gaze fits into so many of these other issues and concerns.

To work towards an understanding of what the gaze means in film – what can possibly be meant by it, what its interpretative gestures are – we shall consider certain conceptual points of operation: masochism, identification, phantasy, and the *punctum*. What links all these together is the idea that the gaze is fundamentally about the formation of certain relationships between the spectator and the film. In other words to theorise the gaze is to engage in the interplay between cinematic textual systems (diegesis, montage, *mise-en-scène*, intertextuality, etc.) and the act of viewing, as well as the competing, dynamic and heterogeneous processes involved between the two. As these processes enfold, we witness the theoretical formation of the spectating subject – that is, a type of subjectivity primarily defined

6

through the act of spectating. Many of these issues originate from the point of the relationship between the spectator and the film text, but this is a far from simple interaction. To consider key aspects of this relationship we can take our lead from one of the major theories dealing with these matters – psychoanalysis.

A considerable number of the connections between psychoanalytic theory (in particular Freud and, more recently, Lacan) and film studies can be traced to a very specific set of issues and ideas that developed in the mid-1970s. As with most sorts of histories, there seems to have been a mixture of some design and some accident that shaped this relationship. (Why, for example, were certain passages from Freud taken up and not others? and why did Lacan's interpretations and influences come on to the scene so much later – even given the travails of translation?) This section will map out in broad terms these histories and issues, and then, in the following chapter, we will explore some alternatives to these perspectives. That said, it is important to recognise the major influence that these ideas, drawn from interpretations of psychoanalytic theory, have had on the development of film theory; not simply as an approach to the analysis of film, but also the broader issues of how film itself might be utilised in the examination of a wide range of concepts, and how film studies contributed to the development of critical theory in general. In short, as with a great many of these theories, what we find in the psychoanalytic approach is of relevance to a radical shift in the studies of texts, culture, constructions of meaning, interpretations of ideology, etc. This upheaval in the humanities was greatly empowered and influenced through developments in film studies. The point of origin for this particular paradigm in film theory was the formation of a poststructuralist and postmodernist concept of the gaze.

What is essential to recognise from the outset is that for poststructuralism and postmodernism (largely via psychoanalysis) the gaze is not simply about perception. It is not about the mechanics of viewing or the processing of the image in some physical manner – although both of these aspects may be part of the overall concern. The conceptual field of the gaze covers both the act of looking, and the act of being watched; of perception and interpretation; of things going before one's eyes, and things entering and leaving that optic/subjective domain. So when Lacan urges his audience to contemplate optics, as he does in, for example, *The Four Fundamental Concepts of Psychoanalysis*, he is doing so to encourage a much wider perspective and sweep for the concept of the gaze via psychoanalysis. And it is no coincidence that when many of the initial utilisations of psychoanalytic theory in the analysis of film focused on the gaze, they immediately found themselves involved in much larger issues. There was, for example, a critical concern with feminism and the representation of women, and the ways in which the gaze could be seen as masculinised – an issue we shall return to shortly.

Through its very definitional processes and theoretical premises, a psychoanalytic approach necessarily returns us to issues caught up with the idea and operation of the unconscious – such as, desire, pleasure, repression, and drives. In doing so, something like the operation of the gaze is actually stitched up to the fundamentals of subjectivity itself. In other words, for psychoanalysis, when we analyse the gaze we are also examining the structures, functions, and operations of ourselves as subjects (both conscious and unconscious beings) within socio-cultural and historical contexts. This is an extraordinary project, an undertaking of sometimes breathtaking proportions, and perhaps this is part of the reason why there is always a passion in the arguments both for and against this approach.

Masochism

To some extent the legacies of Mulvey's article 'Visual Pleasure and Narrative Cinema' have been both a blessing and a burden. Quite rightly, this piece is positioned as a key work in the development of a psychoanalytic approach to film. Written at a time (1975) and in a culture (British academe) that was not uniformly receptive to psychoanalytic ideas, Mulvey's article blended ideas from Freud with a feminist perspective in an attempt to analyse the relationship between the film text, the act of looking, and the operation of the subject. To understand what was involved in this strategy, and then to offer some alternatives, we need to briefly consider Freud's ideas on scopophilia.

In what has become an increasingly significant article, Freud (1987) in 'Trieb and Their Vicissitudes'[1] outlines his theory on the creation, function and operation of drives. What concerns us here is the relatively short section midway through the piece. It is at this point that Freud develops the relationship of the self-reflexive subject to him/herself, to others, and to the external world order. As is consistent with Freud, he details a set of common (that is, both individual and cultural) developments in order to discuss what happens when such processes collapse. In this particular discussion Freud is concerned with the scopic drive (which has come to be seen as a fundamental part of the gaze) and its relationship to formations of subjectivity in terms of exhibitionism (the pleasure of being looked at) and scopophilia (the pleasure of the gaze). The first of these is the passive, looked-at position; the latter the active, looking position. Such a binarism is misleading, and these attributes of active and passive have often been taken out of context. In Freud's theories there is always a sense of the active in the passive, and vice versa. This entwining is significant to the notion of the agency of the subject to the self and the outside world.

For Freud, we all commence with a self-reflexive sense of the gaze: 'For the beginning of its activity the scopophilia instinct is auto-erotic; it has indeed an object, but that object is part of the subject's own body' (Freud 1987: 127). Later this changes to an emphasis on an object outside of the body. This shift is important for a number of reasons, not the least being the interplay of what Freud sees as displays of sadism and masochism, and the formation of active and passive subject/object relations. What this means, in the simplest of terms, is that we are continually negotiating sites of the active and passive, subject and object, scopophilia and exhibitionism, through our processes of the scopic drive. This is our scopic and subjective intervention on the world, and the world's intervention on us as subjects. Freud himself sums this up when, turning to love of all things, he states:

> our mental life as a whole is governed by three polarities, the antitheses
>   Subject (ego)–Object (external world),
>   Pleasure–Unpleasure, and
>   Active–Passive.
> The antithesis ego–non-ego (external), i.e. subject–object, is ... thrust upon the individual organism at an early stage. (Freud 1987: 131)

In an extremely important couple of sentences Freud states that in this whole development of the active and passive, of scopophilia and exhibitionism, and of the changes from the early auto-erotic to the relationship of the subject to others, none of the stages are negated, but continue to coexist, and exert an influence on the psychical operation of the subject.

The significance of this is that it makes it impossible to simply say that we are active lookers or passively looked at; or that there are categories of subject formations that make us driven totally by scopophilia or exhibitionism; or that there is a masculine/active/sadistic gaze and a feminine/passive/masochistic gazed at. For Freud, the point is not a binarism of masculine and feminine, active and passive, but an interplay between the two, with each depending on the other to form a relational context. Given that much of Mulvey's work hinges on her reading of the pacification (read masochistic attributes) of the feminine gaze in terms of a binarism to the masculine active gaze, we need to look a little further into this area. To follow this line we can note some of the points from Freud's 'The Economic Problem of Masochism',[2] as it is from the Freudian source that Mulvey, and others, have drawn their points of departure and conclusion.

In this essay Freud speaks of three different forms of masochism: erotogenic, feminine, and moral (Freud 1987: 415). What is significant to note is that even in the type designated feminine, Freud very clearly states that it is not gender specific and begins his discussion with the example of men.

The fact that Freud designates this as 'feminine' should not be misread, although of course there remains the potential problems with such a term. However Freud is specifying a cultural type premised on a phallocentric order, where the masculine is privileged and the feminine position is located as other. In other words, the idea of feminine masochism is more about cultural positioning than it is about gender as a formulating process. This particular type of masochism, Freud explains, is 'entirely based on the primary, erotogenic masochism, on pleasure in pain' (Freud 1987: 417). A couple of film examples will help illustrate this, and lead us back to the idea of the gaze.

Perhaps one of the most striking films to depict such classic Freudian interpretations of (feminine) masochistic phantasies is Buñuel's *Belle de Jour* (1967). The opening scene represents what seems to be a sadistic beating of a woman; the abrupt cut, however, reveals that this is in fact a daydream that the woman is having. Initially we are left with what appears to be the only viable reading, which is one of feminine masochism. The depicted scene parallels Freud's classic description of such phantasies, representing: 'the manifest content of being gagged, bound, painfully beaten, whipped, in some way maltreated, forced into unconditional obedience, dirtied and debased' (Freud 1987: 416). During the film we witness Severine/Belle in all of these situations, sometimes in phantasy and sometimes in reality (and various surrealistic combinations of the two), and yet there is always an aspect running counter to this. Just as Freud describes the holding together of the oppositional elements of the passive and active, pleasure and unpleasure, Severine's phantasies contain both masochistic loss of control, and a subject who produces the self for the self in very specific ways.

In these terms it is important to note that for Freud the twisting of sadism back to the self is a consequence of 'a cultural suppression of drives' (Freud 1987: 425) (translation modified). This echoes what Freud describes in his work on narcissism, and in particular its feminine manifestations. His argument is that narcissism is in part a result of the social repression of women's desires.[3] Severine's desires, repressed and denied, become manifested in these masochistic phantasies which also contain elements of narcissism. Parallel to this is the viewer's own masochistic (and sadistic) feelings for watching such scenes, and the narcissistic inflection of the self watching the self.

In such a scenario what happens to us as spectators? Returning to that first scene (and it is very much part of a primal scene as Severine is shown to be sexually repressed), we as viewers are caught in a painful situation. There can be no pleasure (except a forbidden, antisocial and ruthless one) in witnessing this seeming rape, beating and subjection of a women to cruelty, yet who continues to demonstrate her love for her husband throughout. However, when it is revealed that the construction of this phantasy is by the woman, then questions as to how the gaze is operating are raised. Freud would argue that out of the guilt (the guilt of the spectator for watching such a spectacle, as well as Severine's guilt for thinking it) comes the third masochistic type, that of the moral. And *Belle de Jour* plays with this morality (out of guilt) entirely throughout its narrative, right up until the closing scene. Here Severine is seen as having complete control, almost in a sadistic manner, over her husband, who, along with the other men, stands as a synecdoche for the phallocentric order. In this sense there is a confirmation that throughout the film it is Severine who is in control. In all these scenes (but the closing and opening ones in particular) the idea of a binarism of the controlling, sadistic gaze and the passive, masochistic gazed at, is manipulated, contorted and challenged. From the moment the viewer is forced to reread the opening scene as a phantasy (and in particular a sexual phantasy) he/she is made aware of the tenuous nature of narrated events and the problematics of defining the gaze as some sort of uniform and homogeneous act.

Of course the alternate reading to this is that *Belle de Jour* in fact demonstrates perfectly the controlling processes of the masculine gaze, causing the feminine to be located within a masochistic and passive position: that it is a masculine construction of a sexual phantasy about a woman who has masochistic phantasies for this male gaze. But this would be to miss entirely the function of the viewer in the construction of the diegesis. The act of spectating, the role of the gaze, is continually active, even when there seems to be a restrictive and limiting textual formation. The gaze in *Belle de Jour* is located simultaneously within Severine and outside of her. It is always both a sadistic and masochistic gaze, shifting from being controlled to controlling. And this is entirely in keeping with the psychoanalytic model of the subject and his/her interaction with the external world and the internal psychic apparatus. Like Severine, the film's viewer takes pleasure in the exchange between a lack of control and a sense of total control. This raises one of the problems of Mulvey's approach. Her investment in the idea of a Freudian feminine masochism doesn't take into account fully the points Lacan makes when he is analysing the gaze and the drive. For Lacan the idea of feminine masochism has been misinterpreted: 'It belongs to a dialogue that may be defined, in many respects, as a masculine phantasy. There is every reason to believe that to sustain this phantasy would be an act of complicity on our [i.e., psychoanalysis] part' (Lacan 1986: 192). Such a reading makes the whole idea of female masochism a deeply problematic one not only for psychoanalytic theory, but for any approach that wants to premise itself on such an idea. Later we will consider how Foucault handles such a situation, but for the moment let us take a look at another example.

In the film *Les Diaboliques* (Clouzet 1955) the struggle out of masochism is presented in a curious fashion. Christina Delasalle is in a masochistic relationship with her husband, Michel, but she attempts to emerge from it through the seductive and irresistible urgings of Nicole Horner's plan to murder him. In one sense this is a classic *noir* triangle (compare, for example, *The Postman Always Rings Twice* (Garnett 1955 and Rafelson 1981)) with the position of the other male being taken up by Nicole Horner. The twist in the plot means that Christina escapes one masochistic relationship for another.[4] Her attempt to resist the patriarchal order fails in part because of this swapping of one submissive relationship for another, and in part because of the morality invested in these different relational orders. Freud argues that moral masochism leads to a sexualising of morality which in turn leads to a playing out of the Oedipus complex (Freud 1987: 424).[5] In these terms Michel is the father who has to be overcome, but the seeming immorality of the act of killing the father in order to 'have' the mother becomes entwined in the fact it is the arche-figures of daughter and mother, that is two women.

The viewer, in true *noir* style, is denied the psychological motivations behind Nicole's acts until the end of the film, and our knowledge matches that of Christina. Once more, it would seem, the viewer's gaze is tied up to a masochistic site of passivity and limited information. However, just as in *Belle de Jour*, we must go beyond this straightforward reading and consider how Christina's, and our own, gaze are controlling processes as much as they are manipulated. It would not be enough to simply say that the spectator and Christina hold the morally correct position, and that Nicole and Michel are caught and punished at the end. Perhaps one way out of this paradox is to consider how the spectator of films willingly allows for a certain type of manipulation to take place. In this sense *Les Diaboliques* is as much about ways of spectating and interpretation as it is an exercise in (European) *noir* cinema. For in Christina the audience finds a figure who represents precisely the masochistic positionality of the spectator. She lacks knowledge and control over the events, is manipulated and deceived, but she also usurps this situation by working counter to many of the textual devices. Put another way, the diegetic processes offer a site of viewing, some of which are taken up in the act of viewing, whilst others are resisted and denied. What is certain is that the gaze is never uniform in such constructions and operations.

Herein lies one of the key problems with Mulvey's article. She concludes with the following summary: 'the female image as a castration threat constantly endangers the unity of the diegesis and bursts through the world of illusion as an intrusive, static, one-dimensional fetish. Thus the two looks materially present in time and space are obsessively subordinated to the neurotic needs of the male ego' (Mulvey 1986: 209). There is much psychoanalytic force here, driving the argument as well as informing it. But the problem is that in Mulvey's view of narrative cinema (Classic Hollywood in particular) there is no space (or time) for the female spectator. Everything is restrictive and negating; women's image has 'continually been stolen' (Mulvey 1986: 209). But such an argument denies the subversive potential of the spectator, with the implication that the act of reading for women is necessarily a pacified one. It is undeniable that in classic narrative cinema the representation of women as passive and men as active is a recurring one, but this is not a watertight and compulsive representation which offers a homogeneous viewing position. Nor is it possible (or analytically wise) to speak of such a uniform site of spectatorship based entirely on gender. What is central to this debate is the idea of identification.

Identification

One of the major contributions to the theorising of identification in film is Christian Metz's *The Imaginary Signifier: Psychoanalysis and Cinema* (1985). It is a book heavily influenced by Lacan's theories, demonstrating a sharp (and somewhat understandable) turn towards psychoanalytic theory after the largely semiotic based *Language and Cinema* (1973). The connection between the two works is subtle but significant. When, for example, Metz speaks about Barthes's work in an earlier volume *Film Language* (Metz 1974: 267–71) he does so within a context of the spectator's/reader's participation in the creation of the text. It is, to use a Barthesian term, a writerly rather than a readerly process.[6] Such an approach is quite in keeping with the issues and debates raised in *The Imaginary Signifier*, with its emphasis on what we do when we read a film (which necessarily includes watching, analysing, responding to, interpreting and constructing the film text).

Another specific example of this early blending of the semiotic with the psychoanalytic approaches is to be found in the section on syntagmatic and paradigmatic formations (chapter 8 of *Language and Cinema*). Metz's theorising of these filmic structures is often premised on the role and function of the reading of the film, and the film's textual processes as influencing the act of reading/spectating. In such an argument the reader of the film is firmly positioned as a creative agent not simply in the formations of meanings, but the actual structure of the film itself. For Metz, following the semiotic line, it is the paradigmatic which is 'missing' from the film, and which must be supplied through the act of viewing. In doing so the spectator becomes an active part of the textual formations of the film. Even at the syntagmatic level, Metz indicates that the spectator participates in their operation.

To give an example, Metz speaks of inter-codical syntagms (Metz 1974: 181–3), by which he means the combinations of codes as they operate within the textual system: codes of one type (lighting, for example) combine with another (montage, sound, etc.) to construct possible meanings or referential systems of interpretation. So, for example, a dimly lit scene with the low, steady sound of a heart beat, utilises inter-codical syntagms of light and sound within particular code structures. But for such an inter-codical syntagm to operate, the spectator must firstly make the connection, and then construct possible meanings. Such connections and meanings may be presented by the film (in this case the most likely being tension, fear, suspense, or even passion and pleasure), but many other, equally valid, ones may not. Metz points out the potentially disruptive quality of the meta-cinematic, that is, when a film makes it apparent that it is making references to itself, for itself. We have come to expect it in films by, for example, Godard, such as *A bout de souffle* (1959) which construct inter-codical syntagms based on montage and narrative – the jump-cut reflexively reveals the syntagmatic code of editing, and in doing so disrupts the narrative process. However when films purposefully set up disruptive inter-codical syntagms we often find a particular generic field in operation, such as, broadly, comedy, or more specifically parody. When one of the Spice Girls, at the end of *Spice World* (Spiers 1997), argues that she would like to utter 'We're not from London' during the film, two inter-codical syntagms operate: the positing of an extra-diegetic paradigmatic (the utterance is never actually made in the body of the film); and an intertextual reference to Richard E. Grant's (who plays their manager) earlier film *Withnail and I* (Robinson 1987), where exactly just such an exclamation is made. Both such coding syntagms rely on the spectator's participation, and, at a further level, a formation of identification. This latter phenomenon is derived from the breaking of the tradition that characters do not address the audience, or make extra-textual references.

Such an idea leads us to one of the issues at the heart of *The Imaginary Signifier*, where we find Metz exploring the issue of identification with a sustained vigour. Part of the aim of this project is to analyse and categorise different strata of identification, devised largely from Lacan's theories of the subject.[7] The influence of Lacanian theory operates at a number of levels in Metz's theories, and one of these is to allow for a differentiation between semiotic, narrative and psychoanalytic approaches to cinema in a manner that is often as much strategic as it is analytic. For example, Metz discusses the viewer's identification with characters but is able to dismiss it on the grounds that it is 'only valid for the narrative-representational film, and not for the psychoanalytic constitution of the signifier of the cinema' (Metz 1985: 46–7). Because Metz defines his project as being concerned precisely with this psychoanalytic signifier, he is able to exclude such identifications from the central issues of his analysis. Similarly, he excludes the viewer's identification with actors because it is at a secondary level, with the camera, the image, and, perhaps most significantly, with oneself. Metz's strategy is a good one, even if it does not always come off. By acknowledging that actor and character identification are prevalent and common processes (often working in combination), but also stressing that they yield little in the understanding of the psychoanalytic processes and issues at hand (including the explication of this psychically constructed cinematic signifier), Metz makes a significant contribution to an understanding of the processes of the spectator (but of course at the cost of not analysing these other variations and manifestations).

If these two most apparent forms of identifications are to be placed to one side, what is left? For Metz himself points out that comprehension of the film depends on the process of identification, which in itself necessarily includes all formations. Metz is concerned with a truly Lacanian project, which includes the analysis of the positioning of the subject in relation to the cinematic signifier. This leads him to the theme of the mirror, and specifically to Lacan's theory of the mirror stage.[8] Metz's theorising (at times via Jean-Louis Baudry) on how identification operates, and for what reasons, commences with a comparative positioning of the spectator of a film and the formation of the subject through the mirror stage. The self-reflexivity of the mirror stage becomes the self-consciousness of the film spectator as he/she negotiates the position of the self in terms of the film and meaning. This idea allows Metz to make the conceptual leap that identification for the film spectator is actually a self-identification: 'the spectator identifies with himself, with himself as a pure act of perception . . . as the condition of possibility of the perceived and hence as a kind of transcendental subject, which comes before every *there is*' (Metz 1985: 49). This is a Metz who designates both structure and meaning/interpretation as part of the psychic processes of the spectator. Nothing, according to such a position, can make sense without the caveat of the self-reflexive/self-reflecting subject. This is the absent/present status of the spectator which leads Metz to state: 'At every moment I am in the film by my look's caress' (Metz 1985: 54). In short, the identification which takes place in the spectator's relationship to the film is one of self-identification. This is entirely in keeping with Lacan's own theorising of the mirror stage, for at one point he states: 'As I have often underlined, the mirror stage is not simply a moment in development. It also has an exemplary function, because it reveals some of the subject's relation to his image' (Lacan 1988a: 74). The idea of the gaze, in these terms, is as much a confrontation to the spectator, as it is a way into the film. In terms of the previous ideas on masochism, it may well involve such an inflection, but the self-reflexive turn is not necessarily masochistic in design or intent.

It is important to realise that Metz's ideas on identification are based on a sense of cultural phenomena; it is a model constructed to define the cinematic signifier, that is, a designated process unique to spectatorship and film. This cinematic signifier, Metz argues, is 'not only psychoanalytic', it is 'more precisely Oedipal in type' (Metz 1985: 64). It is this because it positions the viewer in a secretive, almost impossible site, like the child who observes the 'amorous play of the parental couple' (Metz 1985: 64). But how far can such a connection be made? This designation of the Oedipal moment presents a number of problems, not the least being the conflict of the primal scene, and the emergence of the self into the social world order. The first of these Metz attempts to resolve by linking elements from Freud's theory to the act of watching a film (the child/spectator as voyeur; the parents/filmic text as unknowing objects of being watched, or who is watching; the solitude of the child/spectator, etc.).[9] However, this does not allow for the fundamental issue of the conflict within the child that such an observation creates.

The other difficulty, this time with the comparative link to the Oedipus complex, is similar. To describe the cinematic signifier as Oedipal means that it does not simply represent this process, but reflects and perhaps even reiterates it (even Metz would stop short of saying it causes it). However, the Oedipal complex, especially for Lacan, is part of the fragmentation process of the mirror stage. It is the forceful positioning of the subject in terms of language (the signifier and the vast complexity of chains of signification) as it forms the Symbolic order. Clearly not all cinema performs such a complex task (perhaps only a few films at all can do so), so the question arises as to how Metz can claim such a force as a defining point of the cinematic signifier. The answer lies in part in a separate, but closely linked, psychoanalytic reading of phantasy.

Phantasy

So far the two main readings of the gaze we have considered have taken up the issues of masochism and identification. A concept that can be seen to connect the two is the idea of phantasy,[10] which continues this theme of the subject's relationship to that what is 'observed' (that is, either literally through the gaze, or in the operation of dreams, daydreams, and phantasising). This was an important concept for Metz and Baudry, both of whom continually attempted to match aspects of the cinema and the act of watching with psychoanalytic concepts such as the unconscious. In these terms, if the idea of masochism insists on a sexual differencing of the filmic spectator, and identification with a positioning of the spectator in a referential status to the self via the text (this curious act of mirroring), then phantasy, it can be argued, through the theories of phantasy (especially Freud's), ties the two together by positing the notion of a psychic reality. By considering this aspect we witness a further theorising of the gaze.

It is in *The Interpretation of Dreams* (1986) that Freud struggles constantly with his attempts to distinguish a psychical reality (a reality of unconscious wishes and desires) from a material reality (the 'outside' world order) or a reality derived from immediate conscious thoughts. What quickly becomes apparent when we introduce the spectator of the film (and its order(s) of reality) into this schema is where he/she might be located. The most obvious reading is that the filmic text represents a reality which is derived from all three sources, with the addition of its own textual world order. Such a reading of the heterogeneity of the filmic reality accommodates the interplay of active/passive acts of reading, as well as certain dimensions of identification. When we watch a film we see certain images which relate to an interpretation of a material world order; we consciously negotiate the similarities and differences with our own experiences (both in the world and through other texts, including films); and we contribute a phantasising quality to the filmic world through our dreams, desire and unconscious drives.

There is much to be said about such a neat, symmetrical order; however there are also a number of difficulties, especially if one continues to follow Freud's ideas on phantasy. Laplanche and Pontalis, in their influential essay 'Fantasy and the Origins of Sexuality', make the following point: 'phantasy is not merely material to be analysed, whether appearing as fiction from the very start (as in daydreaming) or whether it remains to be shown that it is a construction contrary to appearances (as in screen-memory), it is also the result of analysis, an end-product, a latent content to be revealed behind the symptom' (Laplanche and Pontalis 1986: 14). What such an interpretation suggests is that if phantasy is to be located within the act of viewing a film, then consideration must be made of the relationship between the construction of a phantasy beyond the heterogeneous realities, and their various combinations. This is the production of a something else, beyond the phantasies as they appear on the screen, or are reconfigured in the psychic reality of the spectator. Furthermore, as Laplanche and Pontalis point out (for example, Laplanche and Pontalis 1986: 19–20), the relationship between primal phantasy (those of the unconscious) and a second order of phantasising (such as daydreams) must be made distinct in order to understand how they differ in their relationship to the world out there and to the subject's internal world of the unconscious.

The key point for us here is how Freud attempted to resolve this dilemma over what began, early in his career, as a difficult theory to sustain – that of the scene of seduction. This was an early version of what would later be incorporated into Freud's theories on sexuality.[11] We do not need to be too concerned with the finer points here, but the relevant part is how Freud resolves the issue of events that may or may not have actually taken place in childhood (for his concerns) but have a currency and psychic reality. This is Freud's *Urphantasien* or primal (original) phantasy.

Significantly, Freud's theories on phantasy insist on a type of enfolding between phantasy and structure, so that the initial 'moment' of the phantasy becomes an integral part of the organising of representational structure. In other words, the way the phantasy is manifested is linked to the actual material of the phantasy itself, and the context in which it was initially encountered. Freud's earliest mention of primal phantasies recounts the story of a patient who believes she is being photographed by others under the instructions of her lover: 'Lying partly undressed on the sofa beside her lover, she heard a noise like a click or beat. She did not know the cause, but she arrived at an interpretation of it after meeting two men on the staircase, one of whom was carrying something that looked like a covered box. She became convinced that someone acting on instructions from her lover had watched and photographed her during their intimate *tête-a-tête*' (Freud 1984: 154). Such an image is seductively cinematic in its story and composition and lends itself to these points of comparison. It is particularly relevant to the ideas on the formation of the spectator through a type of self-reflexivity. To illustrate better how we might approach an analysis of a film (or film sequence) in terms of these ideas on phantasy and the gaze, a specific example might help.

One of the issues that becomes foregrounded in such an approach is that of identification. Clearly there is a difference between the sort of identification that takes place in daydreams (which Freud argued is always a first person subject position) and primal phantasy (which Freud saw as having no point of subjectification), and the act of watching a film. The identification processes might sometimes converge (a film might correspond to some primal phantasy; a film might correspond to, or provide material for, a daydream, etc.); however we must guard against taking such identifications too literally. Many of Hitchcock's films, for example, seem to take such literal convergences as their narrative premise; one of the effects is that quality of the thrill so compulsive in these films, but it does produce some curious inflections of these concepts. In *Psycho* (1960), for example, we are presented with a playing out of Norman Bates's phantasies at a number of levels. There are the second order phantasies based in voyeurism (the shower scene), daydreams (the recounting of wishes and desires to Marion), and the playing out of such desires, such as the bizarre decorations and designs of the parlour room (what Freud would term *Wunsch-phantasie* or wish-phantasy). The primal phantasy is Mother, and the continued manifestation of her through Norman's belief that she is still alive (through a transposition of mother to son) and an active part of his life. The quasi-psychoanalytic explanation of Norman's actions (revenge on the mother and father, but keeping the mother 'alive') at the end of the film is quite in keeping with the (broad) Freudian idea that the structure of this primal phantasy mirrors its manifestation. Indeed, the acts of Norman even parallel the primal phantasy as part of the primal scene,[12] as it is Norman's Oedipal desires (and his discovery of his mother's sexual acts) which brings him to kill first her, and then the others. Even if Norman is unaware of the sexual transgressions of Marion (a sexual relationship outside of marriage) the spectator is capable of providing this link for him and themselves.

Psycho constantly forces a type of identification through the viewer's gaze with these different levels of phantasy. From the literal offering (compulsion) of the voyeur to a more abstract rendition of the primal scene, the film plays out phantasy and identification. There are even recurring motifs of these fantasies; the primal scene, for example, occurs (extra-diegetically) for Norman with his mother, and so is re-presented to the viewer as a motivation for Norman's subsequent acts. But this is paralleled for the viewer in the opening scene of Marion and Sam. Before the viewer has even encountered Norman, he/she mirrors Norman's act of voyeurism and the encounter with the primal scene. Such a reading means that the levels of identification shift dramatically. In the first instance this opening scene becomes a secondary phantasy, providing an erotic daydream sequence; however it also operates as part of the primal phantasy of the film – the dark punishment of illicit desires by the son against the parents. Such a reading also helps us negotiate the difficult terrain of subjective positions. In the first manifestation there is a clear point of subjectification (the spectator is positioned in terms of a masculine point of view/phantasy – just as happens with the shower scene), whereas in the second manifestation of this material (that is, the primal scene itself) things are more diffused through the actions and sequences of the film so that there is never any clearly marked point of subjectification. (This is also part of the disquiet of the killing of Marion a third of the way through the narrative.)

One of the questions that such a reading raises is that of the spectator's own primal phantasies and their relationship to a film. Is such an approach to film arguing that the text itself manifests primal phantasies? Does *Psycho* offer a textual representation of the primal scene, and if so how does this operate in terms of the psychic processes of the viewer/subject? These may well prove to be unanswerable questions, but the issues they raise are as important as any answers posited. It is significant, for example, that Freud's ideas on phantasy relate to a theory of hallucination. As Laplanche and Pontalis put it: 'The origin of phantasy would lie in the hallucinatory satisfaction of desire; in the absence of a real object, the infant reproduces the *experience* of the original satisfaction in a hallucinated form' (Laplanche and Pontalis 1986: 24). If we were to replace 'infant' with 'film spectator', then hallucinatory processes are films themselves, and the act of watching a film becomes part of this important acting out of desires for their satisfaction. It is important to recognise that this interpretation of the operation of the gaze is not simply about the insertion of the viewer into the represented world order (the filmic phantasy), even though this may form part of the overall process. Just as Metz proposes forms of identification outside of camera and character alignment as central to understanding the cinematic signifier, the spectator's relationship to phantasy may be a part of that phantasy, or his/her gaze may form part of the structure of the phantasy. Similarly, the levels of operation for the gaze in the phantasies presented may be at the level of secondary (akin to daydreams) or primary (at the level of the unconscious) processes. In the case of the latter, the idea of identification may never be realised by the spectator of the film.

Another example, one no less convoluted in its structure or phantasy, is to be found in *The Last Seduction* (Dahl 1993). The 'original satisfaction' in this case is power, or, more specifically, the capacity to break social rules and morality and still remain free from punishment. The phantasies of sexual freedom (without guilt), financial gain, power and control over others, entwine to form the idea of the 'real object' which is necessarily always absent. The fact that in this film it is a woman who enjoys the playing out of such phantasies is significant not only for the analysis of the processes of identification, but also in the challenge to the conventions to film *noir*.

The *Punctum*

In his book *Camera Lucida* (1984), Barthes's main point of discussion is photography; and even though he begins by saying that for him the photograph and cinema are inseparable yet positioned as opposites, we can draw out a number of ideas to discuss further the idea of the gaze and the active/passive pleasures involved. That said, it is important to recognise that Barthes's relationship to cinema is far from an easy one, and he seems much more comfortable in this book with the stillness of photography than the motion of film.[13] A key idea in *Camera Lucida* worth considering in terms of the issues at hand is that of the *studium* and *punctum*.

Barthes employs these two terms in much the same way as he does in distinguishing texts of pleasure and texts of *jouissance*, and issues of the readerly and writerly;[14] that is, an attempt to negotiate the terrain between active and passive reading, and the relationship between reader (for us here, the spectator) and text. One particular problem or idiosyncrasy with Barthes's discussion of the *studium* and the *punctum* is that it is heavily invested with personal tastes and details. We need to pick carefully around these relative indulgences to glean the wider implications of Barthes's ideas. Often Barthes (especially in his later works) is a theorist trapped in his own fascinations, but there is still much on offer here, including these important ideas of the *studium* and *punctum*. The *studium* is that part of the image that the photograph brings to us, the spectator. It is the more-or-less closed-off aspects of the image, the culturally saturated parts. As Barthes puts it: 'The *studium* is that very wide field of unconcerned desire, of various interest, of inconsequential taste: *I like/I don't like*. The *studium* is of the order of *liking*, not of *loving*; it mobilizes a half desire, a demi-volition . . .' (Barthes 1984: 27). It is also tied in to the intentionality of the photographer, and has a sense of closure (both textually and in its cultural readings and interpretations) attached to it.

It is the *punctum* that is of far greater interest to Barthes, for this is the concept he sees as being invested with much creative force, dynamic, and interaction between reader and text. If the *studium* drags the viewing process towards a shared understanding and a certain type of desire for a fixed meaning, the *punctum* represents those moments of looking that disrupt both the image (as it has been established) and the spectator. Barthes describes the image as being 'speckled with these sensitive points' and that these are the disturbing of the *studium* as well as the viewer (Barthes 1984: 27). The *punctum* is a specific detail, a moment in the image, as opposed to the *studium* which stretches across the entire image. This detail is that which arrests our gaze, makes us re-evaluate the image and our relationship to it. It is also the element in the relationship between image and spectator that forces a *beyondness* to the image. The *punctum* is invested with a dynamic which makes connections (new and old) between the image and other images, and the image and the spectator.

Before we proceed there is a point that needs to be taken up regarding the idea of a *punctum* of film. Barthes very specifically argues that it is not possible for the moving image to have a *punctum*, but it does have, comparatively, a blind field (Barthes 1984: 55–7) – which is that dimension which goes beyond the screen, a futherness to any image appearing. What we wish to argue here is that on the one hand Barthes is correct to distinguish between the photograph and the film in terms of the operation of a *punctum* and this blind field; however it is not realistic to dismiss entirely the *punctum* from film. This is because all images (photographs, paintings, scenery, films, etc.) must have this same operation of *studium* and *punctum*, even if it differs in how it is performed according to the properties of the medium. Furthermore, even if the 'pure' form of film (its eidetic notion) is its moving image and the flows of motion (from the fluid to staccato), an integral part of the reading of a film (that is, watching, recalling, speaking about, experiencing it, as well as interpreting it) involves both moving and still images. There are moments in a film that we experience as stills, just as there are moments dominated by movement (for example, the camera movements in *Raising Arizona* (Coen Bros. 1987) or *Miller's Crossing* (Coen Bros. 1990)); or the movement on the screen itself such as the masses of the armies in *Ran* (Kurosawa 1985) or the sweep of figures across a seemingly impossibly long and wide plain at the end of *They Died With Their Boots On* (Walsh 1941); or colour, such as its symbolic use in *Three Colours: Red* (Kieslowski 1994) or *Marnie* (Hitchcock 1964); or sound, such as the sound of the breeze through the bushes in *Blow Up* (Antonioni 1966) or the mixture of Ripley's straining breath and ruptured machinery in the closing sequences of *Alien* (Scott 1979). The shower scene in *Psycho*, to return to an earlier example, is a scene dominated by movement and sound. It makes sense to refer to this in terms of the blind field (which also contributes to the terror of the scene) and lacking a *punctum*; however there are scenes in, for example, *Lawrence of Arabia* (Lean 1962) or *La Belle Noiseuse* (Rivette 1991) that operate precisely in terms of Barthes's ideas of the *punctum*. Such scenes (the panoramic sweep of the desert in *Lawrence of Arabia*, the contorted and naked body of Marianne in *La Belle Noiseuse*) may not function in the same way as a still photograph, but we can still argue that the idea of the *punctum* operates, both on the screen and in our later memories and visualisations of the film. Barthes may resist this, arguing that slow, careful time is required to catch the *punctum*, but this would seem to miss a fundamental aspect of reading a film.

The significant thing about the *punctum* is that it works to destabilise what would otherwise be seen as a presented image, a whole and settled configuration. As with other legacies of Barthes's theories, how this disruption takes place, and where the elements themselves are derived from (the text, the reader/spectator, the act of reading, the historical moment, the cultural contexts, etc.), is left largely open. That the phenomenon can take place, and that we, as spectators, should actively contribute to it, is the defining point. There is a scene in *Manon des sources* (Berri 1986) where Ugolin spies on Manon as she dances naked in the hills, playing a harmonica. The *studium* of this image feeds into a whole range of backdrops: there is the very painterly composition of the shot, echoing a series of paintings from the late Renaissance to the Neoclassical (especially in that theme of Susanna caught bathing, and the interaction of nature and humanity in some of Poussin's work); there is, similarly, a *studium* of filmic scenes (the scene in *Sirens* (Duigan 1994) is an example of an ironic construction of this theme as the women are discovered by a blindman, and also has the inevitable self-referential status to painting given that it is a film about a painter); there is also the *studium* of the voyeur, and the construction of a phallocentric gaze. The *punctum* here (or at least one possibility of this) is the moment when the camera reflects back into Ugolin's eyes, and this punctures the eroticised image with a far more powerful emotion of madness. For this is the scene that leads to Manon's revenge through Ugolin's mad love. Such a *punctum* undercuts the Neoclassical contrivances, the intertextual connections, and perhaps even the phallocentric voyeurism.

The *punctum* operates as a point which causes an often radical reappraisal of the image. A principle of Eisensteinian montage is based on a similar idea. An image alters in itself through its juxtapositioning with another image (or images). Such a *punctum* sounds as if it must be of a different order from that devised by Barthes. This is a point outside of the image, but yet is still a part of it. However, such a concept (based on the operation of montage) is echoed in Barthes's own definition. Of the *punctum* he states: 'whether or not it is triggered, it is an addition: it is what I add to the photograph and *what is nonetheless already there*' (Barthes 1984: 55). This addition from the reader to what is there can, it is argued here, be derived from the processes of montage, as much as from *mise-en-scène*. This suggests that we might speak of a *punctum* derived from montage, as distinct from one derived from *mise-en-scène*. Similarly, we might distinguish between a *punctum* as it impacts on the gaze during the scene, or one which is experienced in a recalling of the image. What all of these share is this construction of the gaze, and the interaction between spectator and film.

The four issues through which the gaze has been tackled here – masochism, identification, phantasy and the *punctum* – are ultimately reflections on how some of the debates and issues of the gaze have been dealt with in film theory. These include the relationship of the subject to the image, the politics of gender and feminist readings of the image, the attempts to deliver a psychoanalytic model of film analysis, and the studies of how the spectator and image interact. These constitute the broad scope of the theorising of the gaze. They provide an inmixing of psychoanalysis, feminism, phenomenology, reception theory, semiotics, and, more recently, gender theory. What is curious to note is that even a cursory review of the literature of these debates reveals an explosion of material up until the mid-1980s, and then a sharp turn towards new and developing ideas. Why this might have taken place is open to speculation, but one large intervention that took place is the translation of a number of Lacan's seminars, and it is to some of these ideas that we shall now turn to in the following chapter.

2

Dangerous Supplements and the Envy of the Gaze

The theorising of the relationship between film and the spectator has become increasingly more complex in recent years. This has partly to do with the development of certain theoretical approaches which emphasise the role of the spectator as an active agent in the construction of the text, as well as a development of those theories that focus on positions of subjectivity and intersubjective processes. This has developed out of a complex set of theories that have radically rethought the whole idea of what constitutes subjectivity. It is these ideas on the subject that will inform much of the ensuing discussion. To work through some of these developments this chapter will consider two distinct perspectives: some of the key models of the gaze developed by Lacan, and a number of ideas from Derrida's works of deconstruction. We have already encountered aspects of the first of these in the previous chapter. However, there are a number of very significant ideas and models which, for various reasons, have not been nearly as extensively developed in the area of film studies. Similarly, Derrida's theories have been much less systematically examined and applied to film, but there are a number of ideas that offer a radical rethinking of how we might approach film itself.

The first half of this chapter will explore in more detail some of the key concepts from Lacanian psychoanalysis and how it has problematised the whole issue of the subject. This will include examining how Lacan links the scopic drive to the formation and destabilising of a certain type of subject position. This in turn will allow us to consider how the film spectator occupies a particular type of subject position, as well as some of the broader issues of subjectivity in these contexts. The second half of the chapter will look at some ideas from Derrida, in particular how we might utilise his notion of the supplement to better understand the operation of the spectator in film. Clearly these two theoretical sources − psychoanalysis and philosophy − are far from unified in their approach to such issues. What is of primary interest here, however, is interpreting the differences of the subject in this capacity of spectating, and how we might reinterpret this essential aspect of film studies.

Lacan's idea of the mirror stage has held a particular fascination for film theory for many reasons. This theory, as was noted in the previous chapter, is directed not simply at how we look and are looked at, but deals with ideas about the formation of the subject, the intervention of culture, and the negotiations of meaning through desire.[1] It is a powerful and significant theory that informs and illustrates a great deal of Lacanian psychoanalysis and its applicability to other disciplines and ideas. It also has a logical connection to film analysis, with its emphasis on the gaze and the scopic drive. There are, however, other parts of Lacan's seminars that contain significant readings and explorations of the theory of the gaze, and it is to these that the first part of this chapter is directed. We can also review some of the key elements of a Lacanian approach to film.

The Imaginary and the Drive

A great deal of the work on Lacan's theories of the gaze, the relationship of the subject to the act of looking and being looked at, and, subsequently, the intervention of psychoanalysis in the study of film, is derived from two interconnected ideas: the Imaginary, and the drive. The first of these relates to Lacan's particular developments of the analysis of the subject and the role of psychoanalysis. The Imaginary forms part of a tripartite system, the other two elements being the Symbolic and the Real (although strictly speaking Lacan initially/historically devised these three as quite separate from one another, and it was only later that they became drawn together). It is worth recapping on these three terms so they are fresh in our minds.

The Symbolic is that realm dominated by the signifier – of language and culturally constructed organisations and meanings. The Symbolic is, in short, the domain in which we operate in and through 'language' (that is, in the broadest sense, systems of signification, including the chains of signification that come to be seen as meaningful). It is also the area where laws are formulated, repressions enforced, and processes encoded in order that we might share communications and operate as part of a social order. The Real is a little more difficult to define, in part because Lacan tends to be quite evasive in his use of the term, and in part because it is such a slippery concept. For convenience we might think of the Real as operating in much the same way as the unconscious. It exists as a beyond to the Symbolic order, an otherness that continually threatens to break into this cultural structure and disrupt the relationships established. It is designated the 'Real' because unlike the other forces at play here (the Symbolic and

the Imaginary) it is, if nothing else, consistently part of the subject's psychic realm and so forms something that might approximate to the 'real'.
The Imaginary is not what it might first appear to be – that is, something
of the imagination – but rather it is that dominated by the image, and,
more importantly, the subject's relationship to the image. The term originates from Lacan's postulations on the *imago* and formations of the subject
through the image.

Another way of thinking about these paradigms in terms of film would
be to align them with certain processes in the cinematic domain. In this
sense the Symbolic would be the large order of systems and structures that
allow film to operate as a communicative process, as a culturally recognisable signifying system, and as a point of negotiation shared by members of
the social order. The Symbolic film order is that which we most readily
recognise, as it plays before our eyes, we talk about it over coffee, and we
choose to see it, etc. Within this is the idea of a film's own Symbolic order,
which functions in much the same way as the larger Symbolic order (even if
it might also be totally oppositional to that order). The Real of film is more
difficult to discern because it necessarily includes a diverse set of phenomena. The theories of Metz and Baudry, for example, as they compare the
film experience to the dream work, lend themselves to an investigation of
the filmic Real. But another way of approaching such a concept would be
to consider film's attempt to represent the unconscious. This might include
a Surrealist work such as Buñuel and Dali's *Un Chien andalou* (1928); or
dream sequences such as in Hitchcock's *Spellbound* (1945); or even films
that operate outside of such generic lines or attempts to parallel a dream,
such as Greenaway's *Drowning by Numbers* (1988) or Lynch's *Lost Highway*
(1987), which have dreamlike qualities to them. In this way the filmic
Real is the attempt to represent the Real of the unconscious. Ultimately,
however, the Real is that which is missing from the Symbolic and Imaginary – it is the impossible. The filmic Real is, perhaps then, the impossible
film yet to be, and never to be, made; or the impossibility of film as it resists
the Symbolic. Because it has certain qualities, some (such as Baudry)
might argue that film has a particular and unique relationship to the representation of the unconscious, or a manifestation of the Real. The Real, it
must be added, even though it is that which is not Symbolic or Imaginary,
emerges out of the Symbolic and the Imaginary, as it needs these two other
realms to be manifested and recognised. The Imaginary is where the relationship between the spectator and the film is played out, and it is to this
that we can now direct our attention.

As we saw with Metz, this type of Lacanian reading of the relationship of
the subject to the image is fundamentally premised on the self-reflexive
turn. The Imaginary operates almost entirely in a context of the subject
viewing the image in terms of the self, and the self viewing the self in terms

of the image. Here we have a very complex set of processes that need to be taken slowly so we might grasp the subtlety of what is being argued by Lacan. The Imaginary is formulated in the mirror stage, as the subject 'discovers', through self-reflexivity, his/her position in the Symbolic world order, and then, consequently, the interplay between individual desires and social constraints. The subject, then, becomes an image for itself, how it positions itself in the world, and how the world (the Symbolic order) positions it. Here we witness one of Lacan's fundamental premises: that the subject's formation of the self, via the image, is an interaction of the gaze from the subject, and the subject being positioned by the gaze of the Other. It is the big 'O' Other, for this is the realm of otherness which is distinct from the subject, and the little 'o' other, which forms what Lacan terms the *objet petit a*^{2} – the objects of desire which manifest the realm of Otherness for the subject. In terms of the discussion at hand, it is the gaze itself that becomes both part of the Other and an object of desire for the subject.

The gaze is seen as a force of power and control, of knowledge and capacity. To possess it is much more than simply having the capacity to see – it is part of the legitimising of the subject to itself and to the Other. To have the gaze is to exist, or, to put it another way, to be recognised by the gaze of the Other is to have a sense of presence. It is not difficult to see why such a scenario might create large ideological problems, and it is one of the counters posited by certain feminist arguments against such a model.[3] Simply put, these readings suggest that the Other is a masculine identity (in a phallocentric social order) and so any legitimating must always be positioned in terms of a winning of the male gaze. (This is, for example, in some ways, Mulvey's key point in her analysis of the pacification of the female look.) What is important to recognise is that Lacan himself sees this as a significant point in the theory of the gaze; in fact, it is this idea – the power of the gaze of the Other to legitimise and formulate the subject – that stimulates much of his argument. Furthermore, he posits that it is not a gender-specific process, and all subjects are caught in this process of the subject's sense of presence being determined by the Other. But it is far too simple a reading of Lacan to argue that this is a prescriptive model he is suggesting. Lacan wants us to think about what happens to the subject in his/her psychical makeup and social world order when this takes place. As Lacan puts it: 'From the moment that this gaze appears, the subject tries to adapt himself to it, he becomes the punctiform object, that point of vanishing being with which the subject confuses his own failure' (Lacan 1986: 83). Three examples from Lacan will help explain this.

Lacan tells the story of when, as a young man, he went fishing with a professional fisherman, Petit Jean. The young Lacan – from a different region, and as an academic, a different world in so many ways – felt out of place and wished for a certain recognition. At one point a sardine-can floats by and Petit Jean asks: ' "You see that can? Do you see it? Well, it doesn't see you!" ' Lacan adds: 'He found this incident highly amusing – I less so' (Lacan 1986: 96). Lacan points out that the reason he found it unamusing is that the gaze of the sardine-can cannot see him because he doesn't belong there, he has no right of existence and his very subjectivity is questioned. Film achieves this sardine-can effect in a number of different ways. Watching a film by Spike Lee, for example, directly questions a white viewer's capacity to be seen by the film. That is, it is not simply that a black audience might identify (in Metz's sense) with the film, and a white audience cannot, but rather that the film itself does not recognise and legitimise a white perspective. The gendering of the gaze as being determined as male and heterosexual – what we might term *phallocularism* – is another example. (The counter to this is the situation when the spectator creates his/her own relationship to the film, which leads to a resistant reading practice.) It is important to note that this gaze of the film is not just a prescribed point from which to view the film. It is part of the interaction between the spectator (and his/her social/Symbolic world order), the filmic world order, and the film itself. In this sense it is an encounter with the Real, or what Lacan describes as the *tuché*, and so constitutes an emergence of the subject out of the Imaginary's relationship to the Symbolic order and the unconscious.

A striking aspect of Lacan's story of the sardine-can is the idea that objects, like people, can have a gaze – a point of light that recognises (or fails/refuses to recognise) the subject. The gaze, in this model, does not just simply come from the subject (the spectator of the film), but rather there is a second order of the gaze which emerges from other things (including people, but also objects, films themselves, etc.). Furthermore, this other gaze is what the subject desires, both to be recognised by that gaze and, ultimately, to possess it. It is an impossible desire to satisfy (which is, after all, a requirement of Lacan's definition of desire) so the subject continually posits and encounters the *objet petit a* of the gaze. Such an interpretation does not necessarily lead to the problematics of the powerful phallocentric gaze as being the only one of a legitimate type. The two counter arguments to this are: firstly, the Symbolic order may well set up the phallocular as the desired one, as well as the one to be desired by, but this status requires analysis – which is what Lacan's methodology allows; secondly, it is necessary to recognise the homogenising processes of the phallocular, and its attendant structures of desire, in order to refuse them. Our second example will help illustrate this.

In a short piece written as a tribute to Marguerite Duras, Lacan sets himself the no small task of interpreting *le ravissement*, which is and isn't quite *ravishing*. The interplay for Lacan is commenced by the very enigma of the word, and its attributes. The story he is dealing with − a short novel by Duras entitled *Le Ravissement de Lol V. Stein* − deals with ravishment, but it constantly raises the question as to who is ravishing and who is being ravished. At one point Lacan admits that part of the process is the ravishing of the reader by Duras and the story. With all these twists and ambiguities of power and powerlessness, Lacan, to describe the subjectivity of Lol (as well as the reader of the text), resorts to what he terms *je me deux* (Lacan 1987: 123), or 'I feel sorrow' as well as, literally, 'I two myself'. This, we shall argue, is also the position that the spectator in film comes to occupy − doubled and ravished by the interplay of gaze and image, subject and desire.

The particular fascination for us with Duras's story, and Lacan's analysis of it, is that it is heavily invested with acts of looking and constructions of the gaze as power and control.[4] Lacan, in his essay on this story, reminds us: 'I teach that vision splits between the image and the gaze, and that the first model for the gaze is the stain, from which is derived the radar that the splitting of the eye offers up to the scopic field' (Lacan 1987: 126). This split between eye and gaze is fundamental to the interpretation of the operation of the gaze as a part of the formations of the subject. It is a split that we shall return to again and again here. The *ravissement* is part of the relationship of the spectator and cinema, for it is not just a single gaze towards an image; or even a multiplicity of gazes towards a diffuse collection of images and movements. It is the subject's gaze split through (as well as splitting) the encounter with the image, as it meets the gaze emerging from the film. This is due to many factors, but primary amongst these is the idea of a Symbolic gaze which mediates the subject's own gaze from the Imaginary and the Real. What we see, and how we see it, is determined in the Symbolic by this splitting of the gaze. But there are also forces that emerge from the gaze of the subject which resist and offer counter perspectives to this. Another point from Lacan on this, and then we can resume the analysis of the gaze.

Lacan takes up the theme of anamorphosis at a number of different points in his seminars, but he does have a common aim in all these discussions. For him anamorphosis represents the self-reflexive moment of the gaze − the moment when we become aware of our own gaze, the gaze of the Other on us, and the effects of this interplay. As Lacan puts it: 'The gaze I encounter . . . is, not a seen gaze, but a gaze imagined by me in the field of the Other' (Lacan 1986: 84). His example of anamorphosis is a well-known one − the mysterious floating skull at the feet of the two men in Holbein's painting *The Ambassadors*. But the point Lacan makes from this is more unusual. For him anamorphosis is the gaze revealed 'in its pulsatile, dazzling and spread out function' (Lacan 1986: 89). The moment of anamorphosis is the moment when this self-reflexive revelation of the

function and operation of the gaze takes place. Just as Lol V. Stein replicates the act of looking, so too does anamorphosis present us with the gaze
as it both hides and reveals.

What begins to emerge from a study of Lacan's seminars on the gaze and
subjectivity is that there is an interaction between different sets of gazes;
and that there is a whole range of distinct, competing orders of the gaze.
He speaks, for example, of *invidia* (the envy of the gaze) and *dompte-regard*
(a laying down of the gaze) (Lacan 1986: 105–19), which are forces that
attempt to control and contain the gaze. Once more, it must be reiterated
that this is not just a pacification of the gaze, but also part of the construction of subjection and subjectivity. As such, *invidia* is not simply envy or
jealousy but the subject's realisation of wholeness in the other who is
being watched. This, in cinematic terms, can operate on at least two
levels: the spectator of the film has an envy of the image (and so experiences
desire for the image); or the film itself represents a character that has this
invidia. In the previous chapter we saw how, in *Manon des sources*, Ugolin's
mental state became unhinged when he gazed upon the dancing Manon.
But this scene, read in terms of *invidia* and *dompte-regard*, illustrates the over-
coming of the gaze and what happens to subjectivity. From this moment
on, Ugolin's social and personal position changes dramatically. Driven
by guilt, love, and desire he becomes a non-subject in the eyes of his uncle
and, more significantly, himself as well as the village. His once active and
all-powerful gaze has been subjected to the 'gaze' from Manon so that it is
disempowered – that is, laid down. Curiously, this act of voyeurism, so
often seen as a position of power (albeit an insidious and ineffectual one),
becomes the very act which disempowers.[5] This same sort of effect is a
recurring motif in film, and examples include: *Psycho* (Norman's guilt
after spying on Marion); *Rear Window* (Hitchcock 1954) (Jeff's guilt at
spying at the people in the opposite apartment); *Blue Velvet* (Lynch 1986)
(the guilt manifested from what amounts to the primal scene when Jeffery
watches Frank and Dorothy). It is perhaps no coincidence that the vast
majority of examples are of men looking. This is, in part, a consequence of
a certain type of representation of scopophilia, but also a castration fear
played out through the challenge to the male gaze.

In summary, the idea of the gaze and its relationship to the subject operates at a number of levels: it has a positioning effect, in that it prescribes a
certain Symbolic site to view the image, as well as developing, through the
Imaginary, the subject's sense of the self in relation to the Other and his/
her desires; it has a legitimising effect, in that it recognises certain viewing
types (the idea that the male, heterosexual, white gaze position – phallocularism – is the most dominant in Western cinema, for example); it has
a desiring effect, as systems of desire are positioned to catch, evoke and
stimulate the gaze; it is an interplay of at least two gazing orders – the

subject's own gaze, and that which comes from the Other (the sardine-can, the film, the other person, etc.); it is sometimes locked in a self-reflexive moment of the gaze catching the gaze in a reflection – this is one of cinema's primary functions. It is also a process of interaction, with different gaze systems vying for control. The subject is constantly being subjected to gazes which challenge his/her ways of seeing (the *dompte-regard* effect), and there are a multiplicity of gazes that are offered and denied (the *invidia*). To understand more fully how these actions work we can now consider some of Lacan's major models of the gaze, and in doing so we can examine the two orders of these theories to film studies: the representation of the gaze in film, and the analysis of the act of watching a film.

The Schema of the Inverted Bouquet

The schema of the inverted bouquet recurs, in various guises, throughout Lacan's works, but one of the most sustained discussions is to be found in *Seminar 1: Freud's Papers on Technique*. It is significant that Lacan commences his entire series of seminars with this model of optics, and it is equally significant that this model is Lacan's attempt to engage with the interrelationship between the Imaginary, the Symbolic and the Real. In keeping with the aims of the discussions and analysis here, we shall not be overly concerned with Lacan's psychoanalytic intrigues and meanderings, but instead look to the relevancy of these ideas for the study of film.

Lacan's build-up to the inverted bouquet schema involves a discussion on the subject's relationship to the image, and particularly on the interplay between the objective and the subjective. Lacan argues that in the operation of the gaze, 'subjectivity is implicated at every moment' (Lacan 1988a: 77) because the relationship between objectivity and subjectivity is fluid when we look at something. Lacan's real point here is not an attempt to classify the status of things in terms of their objectivity or otherwise, but the insertion of the subject in the scopic drive. In short, we cannot help but position ourselves (or find ourselves positioned) in the act of the gaze. Once this point has been established, Lacan presents the first part of the inverted bouquet (Lacan 1988a: 78).

What this diagram represents, at least initially, is the curious phenomenon of the spherical mirror. A vase is placed on top of a frame, a bouquet of flowers underneath it, and a spherical mirror is placed near it. The optical trick – the creation of a virtual reality – takes place when the subject looks at the mirror from a certain angle. There appears to be a bouquet of flowers in a vase, and the status of what is real and what is imagined is blurred through the gaze of the subject. Lacan invests this simple experiment with tremendous metaphorical effect; for him it illustrates 'the

original adventure through which man, for the first time, has the experience of seeing himself, on reflecting on himself and conceiving of himself as
other than he is – an essential dimension of the human, which entirely
structures his fantasy life' (Lacan 1988a: 79). Furthermore, it is precisely
the gaze – sight – which Lacan insists on as the fundamental component
of this development, in both its psychic and cultural dimensions.

How might we utilise this part of the model in the analysis of film? It is
certainly a rich model, and one Lacan exploits to full effect, so the implications for the study of film are wide and diverse. At one level the most apparent application of these ideas is the relationship of the film to reality and the
formation of the film signifier. This has been a recurring theme for film studies[6] and Lacan's model offers a different perspective on some of these
issues. It is the merging of the flowers and the vase to compose a complete
image, constituted of elements from what are essentially two different
planes of existence. This can also be seen as how the film signifier operates.
It combines elements from different planes of existence to form a signifier
which exists in, and yet outside of, the world order of objects, subjects,
and histories. Lacan's aim is to map out the development of the self-reflexive subject, and the relationships between body and mind. For him, the
image of the body is represented by the imaginary vase (Lacan 1988a: 79).
For our concerns, that which exists prior to the film forms the missing, imagined elements of what we watch in the film; and what we experience, that
which constitutes the two parts into a complete image, is the film signifier –
something which is there but not there.

Lacan's point about the inverted bouquet experiment goes even further,
just as the inflection and application of the model given here would seem
useful, if somewhat limited, if this was all there was to it. Lacan goes on
to discuss the significance of the eye to the vase of flowers and the mirror.
He states that in order for this optical illusion to work the eye has to be
positioned at a very precise point, and yet this is an eye that roves about.
This eye, in short, represents the subject. This is the key to Lacan's
model – that is, the formation, and relational contexts, of the unconscious
to the social order, and, through such a set of issues, how reality is formulated and maintained in and by the subject, and the relationship of this to
the body. As Lacan puts it: 'in the relation of the Imaginary and the Real,
and in the constitution of the world such as results from it, everything
depends on the position of the subject. And the position of the subject . . .
is essentially characterised by its place in the Symbolic world' (Lacan
1988a: 80). Here, then, we find the continuing negotiations between the
film, and its signifying practices, and the spectator as he/she moves in and
out of the positioned viewing site. However, this model illustrates something which has even greater application to the study of film when Lacan
adds a second mirror (see Lacan 1988a: 124).

This is how Lacan describes the set-up of his experiment: 'if one put a mirror in the middle of the room, while I turn my back on the concave mirror, I would see the image of the vase as clearly as if I were at the end of the room, even though I wouldn't see it in a direct manner. What am I going to see in the mirror? Firstly, my own face, there where it isn't. Secondly, at a point symmetrical to the point where the real image is, I am going to see this real image appear as a virtual image' (Lacan 1988a: 125). This schema illustrates the subject's relationship to its fascination with the self as it is determined by the gaze of the Other, which necessarily includes desire, and the continuing question of the lack of wholeness of the self. For our concerns here, however, it is when Lacan adds an extra dimension that the model has a number of points in the relationship of the spectator to the cinema.

Here Lacan has added what he calls the virtual subject (VS), which is the image that confronts us as we negotiate the fragmented nature of our subjectivity in the world.[7] This virtual subject becomes a representation of the subject, for the subject. As Lacan puts it: 'The human being only sees his form materialised, whole, the mirage of himself, outside of himself' (Lacan 1988a: 140). Here we have the beginnings of a model to explain the spectator's insertion of him/herself into the cinematic signifier. In doing so there is a creative act through the interplay between the gaze from the subject, the gaze from the film's signifiers, and the projection of this subject as a virtual subject which exists within the film. This virtual subject cannot simply be an identification with a character in the film, just as it cannot simply be the projection of the self (as in, say, daydreaming) into the film. This is an entirely different order that exists at another level in the text and from the spectator. It is this because it works at both a conscious and unconscious level, and plays out the acts of desire through the film. To illustrate this better, Figure 2.1 rereads Lacan's model in terms of the spectator, the film and its signifiers. We can rename Lacan's elements to better understand how they explicate the relationships between the spectator and film. The divided elements of the vase and flowers correspond to the raw material of film itself, that is, the objects and actors filmed, lighting, setting, etc. The conventions of cinema (including genre, narrative structures, systems of editing, musical structures, in short all those systems we utilise to make sense of the film, and the film uses to render itself as recognisable) are represented by the concave mirror. This is the point where the raw material is drawn together and fashioned into 'narrative', 'documentary', 'comedy', etc. It is also where conventions of systems such as horror or the erotics of the image are formulated; which means less the actual quality of such things, and more the cultural and textual conventions that allow them to be recognised. It suits our rereading that this concave mirror exists 'prior' to the subject, as these are the focal

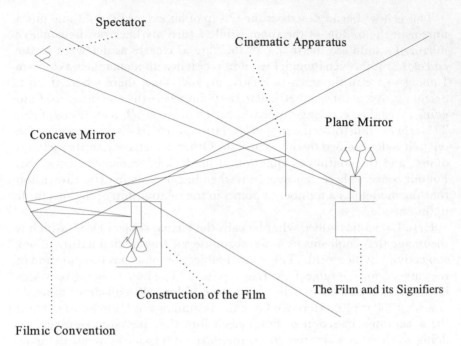

Spectator

Cinematic Apparatus

Plane Mirror

Concave Mirror

Construction of the Film

The Film and its Signifiers

Filmic Convention

Figure 2.1

points which allow a reading to take place, and the spectator may or may not be aware of the action of this mirror in bringing elements together and projecting them out as a film. The spectator of the film is represented by the eye, and is thus positioned close to, but quite separated from, the elements of the raw material. In Lacan's model he points out that the subject is close to the 'real image' but sees it as a virtual one, which is parallel to what is being suggested here. The real image of the objects, settings and actors exists on the same ontological plane as the reader (compared to the fictional world), but remains distant from him/her. The film that we watch is formed on the plane mirror, which here represents the cinematic apparatus,[8] and brings the elements of the concave mirror, the spectator, the filmed real objects, and the processes of ideology (as part of the cinematic apparatus) together. And beyond all this is the virtual subject, which represents the spectator's relationship to this mirage of completeness.

Furthermore, this relationship between the composed image (the cinematic signifier, the film itself, the bouquet of flowers in a vase) and the spectator, as formulated in the virtual subject, is a formation premised on a merging of elements from the subject's own sense of self (the Imaginary) and the drives and desires of the subject's unconscious (the Real). Lacan represents this particular aspect in the psychic apparatus by changing the plane mirror into a pane of glass (Lacan 1988a: 141). For our model of the cinema, such a change works equally well, for the pane of glass reflects the image for the spectator's view, allows the gaze to go beyond it to observe a further object (or have a sense of 'depth' about the object – its history beyond the text's narrative, etc.), and allows a glimpse of the spectator watching him/herself in the act of gazing. The motivating processes in this schema are primarily twofold: there is the seductive process of self-reflection – that is, when we engage in this act of looking we are inevitably drawn into a sense of the self watching the self; there are also the forces of desire. If desire is both inescapable and beyond satisfaction, this act of constructing the virtual subject, 'inside' a domain of complete and whole objects, presents a playing out of a mirage of satisfied desires. This is not simply a model of people watching films and having their desires acted out for them. Rather, it is an explication of desire itself, the formation of a whole different sense of the self, and cinema's role in these processes.

Cinematic Excess and the *Différance* of Cinema

So far we have been primarily concerned with ideas that deal with the spectator's relationship to the film in order to better understand what happens when we watch a film, and offer some ideas about why the cinematic image is so compelling. The discussion will now turn to the idea that within these processes there is always a beyond to the experience of the film itself and the spectating act. In one sense this beyondness has already been introduced through the figure of the virtual subject, and this can be brought to bear later on. It has also been touched on in terms of the filmic Real, that is, the impossibility of a systemics of a filmic order. For the moment the central focus will be on what we will term cinematic excess, and to discuss this we will turn to some ideas from Derrida, commencing with *différance* and the supplement.

Although we need not concern ourselves with too many details here, it is important to recognise a general strategy of Derrida's deconstructionalist approach. Derrida, the philosopher, is interested in taking apart the underlying assumptions and concepts of Western thought. He sets himself the complex task of unravelling what it is we do when we think about things, knowing that so much of how we think (solve problems, recognise enigmas, produce answers, take mental short cuts, etc.) is already in existence for us. It is a project that reaches back some time, most clearly to Nietzsche and then through phenomenology to what is now loosely called deconstruction. One set of issues that Derrida deals with (in different forms, but with recurring motifs) is the idea of wholeness and completeness. In doing so, Derrida challenges some of the key ideas of Western

thought – ideas such as the centrality of presence over absence, and formations of notions such as 'Truth', 'Meaning', 'Logos', etc. To deconstruct
these he devises analysis based on the denied – absence, the supplement,
and excess.

One of these strategies is Derrida's neologism *différance*, which refers to
the idea that the construction of meaning is something that is not fixed and
finite, but rather an action of continual deferral and difference. Meanings,
he argues, are never really arrived at, but are premised on a multiplicity
of possible meanings (the act of difference) and non-arrival (the act
of deferral). As we watch a film, *différance* operates at a number of levels.
We continually propose possibilities of actions, sequences, and meanings,
abandoning some and creating others as the narrative progresses. We also
'arrive' at smaller, more fragile, meanings, whilst deferring others so that
there is an interplay between the actual and the possible. All of this, in
itself, is akin to what we have already witnessed in terms of the spectator's
actions of constructing (and co-constructing) the film itself. Where something like *différance* is distinct is that the process fundamentally undercuts
the larger orders of 'Meaning' and acts of interpretation, so that they
become almost impossible to determine with confidence, except in a kind
of socially acceptable act. In this sense, to speak of *différance* is to speak of a
problematising of the cornerstones of Western thought. Of particular significance, especially within this context of film, is the investment Derrida
makes in terms of space and time.

Différance is conceptually based in issues of spatiality and temporality.
Consider this description from Derrida: '*Différance* is what makes the
movement of signification possible only if each element that is said to be
"present", appearing on the stage of presence, is related to something
other than itself but retains the mark of a past element and already lets
itself be hollowed out by the mark of its relation to a future element' (Derrida 1973: 142). This notion of the temporal is important to *différance*
because it signals the dynamic nature of formulating meanings and interpretations. As Derrida indicates in the above statement, signification can
only take place if there is a sense of presence, connected to what has already
gone before and the almost limitless possibilities of what may follow.

These limitless possibilities are, of course, limited in a number of ways.
If they were not, the act of watching a film, before even making sense of it,
would be an impossibility. Genre is one example of how limitations are
applied to the act of *différance*. Our knowledge of the conventions of a generic form allows us to make certain decisions about the deferred possibilities, and to limit the paradigmatic range. The demise of Cody Jarrett in
Raoul Walsh's *White Heat* (1949) is pretty much a predetermined element
of the film. Audiences had learnt to expect the legal (and moral) punishment of the gangster, so his death in the final scene operates quite within a

deferred moment that has been expected. However, where we might see aspects of *différance* here is the way in which he dies, and the undercutting of the morality of such a death. Cody's death is framed triumphantly, an expression of escape and victory – even if it is uttered from a character presented as criminally insane. Compare the deaths in two gangster films made with a more reflexive eye, and this idea of *différance* becomes even more evident. In Arthur Penn's *Bonnie and Clyde* (1967) the portrayal of the death of the two characters is more graphic in terms of violence, yet more sympathetic than the long-distance shot of Cody Jarrett blowing up. This sympathetic view is even more clearly demonstrated in Coppola's *The Godfather* (1972), when Don Corleone actually dies in the idyllic surrounds of a sunlit garden, playing with his grandson. There is no shower of bullets or purgatorial fires, simply age and 'natural causes', so he escapes any moral retribution or legal capture.

In all three films there is an observance of the conventions of the gangster genre which insist on the death of the criminals, but the spectator must still defer this death scene, because in each case there is difference – and a difference that alters the whole moral, emotive and diegetic calibre of the scene. In each case, the representation of the death of the gangster provides *différance* through and against the generic conventions. An example of this as it orders an entire film is the Coen Brothers' *Miller's Crossing* (1990). The conventions of the gangster film are continually foregrounded in this film, reminding the spectator that they are watching a gangster film about gangster films. The very opening scene declares this, as Johnny Caspar delivers his speech on the ethical dilemmas being posed by territorial infringements and sporadic violence. Gangster films always have this sense of the ethics of violence and pay-back, but rarely is it articulated so directly – and straight at the camera. Vendettas, revenge, violence against violence, are a key part of the code of such films, driving the narrative and providing motivation for characters' actions. But we do not expect an opening speech on precisely this issue. From this point on, the death of the gangster, and in particular Tom, becomes a point of *différance*. Tom's death is always possible, with the strange metaphor of Miller's Crossing standing in for that moment of violence. It is strange because gangster films are, almost by necessity, urban films, with urban violence (drive-by shootings, murderous back alleyways, crumbling buildings, etc.). True to this form, all the violence in *Miller's Crossing* takes place in an urban setting. Yet it is the sepia-infused rustic scene with the profusion of trees (with considerable pans and cuts to the tops of them) and winding paths covered in leaves that offers the greatest threat to Tom. It is here that he seems destined to meet the violent fate of the gangster.

But the film also undercuts precisely this impending threat by deferring many of the gangster traits of Tom. Caspar's opening speech of ethics is directed, in many ways, at himself, but it is really a summation of Tom's position. He is the gangster without a gun (for most of the time), whose status seems invested more in his hat than any weapon. And he is continually cast as the voice against violence. He is certainly not an upholder of the social order of law, but he does have a clear sense of morality and ethics. He becomes an embodiment of *différance* of all the conventions of gangster films, and yet he is continually positioned within a profusion of them. The dress, actions, speech, and events of the film declare 'gangsterness', only its main character defers and differs them. This *différance* makes sense if we think of it in terms of Derrida's point on the movement of signification. The *idea* of Tom's death (even though it never eventuates) originates prior to his existence because it is embedded in the codes of the gangster genre, and thus it retains the mark of past elements (that is, the paradigm of gangster films). Its possibility is 'hollowed out by the mark of its relation to a future element', that is, Tom's violent death is constantly deferred, but never diminished as a possible (perhaps probable) event. And all of this takes place in the relationship of the spectator to the film, as he/she constructs signification and interpretation through deferring the meanings and producing different ones.

Dangerous Supplements and Cinema

Another way of looking at this process is through Derrida's idea of the supplement. For Derrida, the concept of the supplement, the very idea of supplementarity, suffers badly in the hands of the philosophers of the Enlightenment. From their perspective (Rousseau is one of Derrida's prime examples), that which is supplementary is seen as marginal, an addition to the centre or origin; it is something that is of lesser significance. It is what Rousseau calls the dangerous supplement, describing it as that which 'adds itself from the outside as evil and lack to happy and innocent plenitude' (Rousseau in Derrida 1976: 215), which is why it is so dangerous. The supplement, in such an interpretation, contaminates the whole and complete world order, bringing to it excess and imbalance. It is premised on the conviction that there can exist completion and wholeness. Derrida reinterprets the status of the supplement (his prime example in his book, *Of Grammatology*, is writing as the supplement to speech), and in doing so challenges many of the constructs of Western metaphysics, such as truth, centre, knowledge – in short, the ways in which we think, and the systems which are developed to produce such thoughts.

 For Derrida, there can be no origin to which supplements are attached, because everything is a supplement to another supplement. The idea of a centre is a privileging construction, just as the supplement is defined as other and lack. This is part of the dynamics of generating meaning, of representational systems, of categorising and ordering. To quote from Derrida's *Writing and Difference*: 'One could say ... that this movement of play, permitted by the lack or absence of a centre or origin, is the movement of supplementarity. One cannot determine the centre and exhaust totalisation because the sign which replaces the centre, which supplements it, takes the centre's place in its absence – this sign is added, occurs as a surplus, as a supplement' (Derrida 1978: 289). This is what we might call the chain of supplementarity, or the unending roll of references and connections to other supplements, none ever claiming or holding the status of centre or origin. As Derrida puts it: 'The supplement is always the supplement of a supplement. One wishes to go back from the supplement to the source: one must recognise that there is a supplement at the source' (Derrida 1976: 304). In terms of theoretical models, this idea has been expressed (in various guises) in areas such as postcolonialism (the denial of the colonial power as a centre or origin of the production of the colonised culture) and feminism (woman as the supplement to the originary male) to deconstruct the fundamental paradigms of thought and knowledge.

One of Derrida's key points is that the positioning of the supplement, as addition and as lesser than the centre or origin, means that anything defined as such will carry with it such supposed qualities. So, it is the investment of presence over absence, of the originary over that which follows. Our concern here is not the status of cinema as such (which has had a certain attribute of the supplement placed on it), but how we might employ this idea of the supplement in the analysis of film itself. We can begin by teasing out a few of the key ideas from Derrida's investigations, focusing on two permutations: the representation of supplementarity (that is, the supplement as theme); and the ways in which the supplement might be figured as a critical concept in film studies.

Representing the Supplement

To understand how the representation of the supplement can be seen to be operating in film we can select a few of the key ideas on what constitutes this supplementary status. In doing so it will be possible to examine how film engages in different ways of representing the supplementary element, and how this quality of the supplement is created, and possibly sustained. These key ideas will include: the notion of the natural (and evil); the excess of the supplementary agent and its disruptive qualities; the function of the substitution; and the questioning of the origin. We will also be concerned with the ways in which some cinema has actually celebrated the supplement over the origin, and how this has impacted on the development of cinematic styles as well as content. To illustrate these ideas we will take one of the foundational models of the supplement in phallocentric culture, that of woman, and in particular the form of the vampire. This example ties in particularly well with the idea of the supplement because the so-called centre of such supplements operates both culturally (the phallocentric, morally defined 'good', the balance of society, the natural) and textually (the vampire film is a well-established form with quite clearly defined conventions). Rather than attempt a history of this representation (a project beyond the direct concerns here), we will be more interested in examining the construction and alteration of the female vampire as supplement through a number of film examples.

One of the defining qualities of the supplement is its capacity to corrupt what has been interpreted to be a site of wholeness and order, and in doing so it is seen as a direct challenge to perceived notions of the authentic. To refer once more to Derrida's citations of Rousseau in *Of Grammatology*: 'In it [the supplement] everything is brought together ... regression toward an evil that is not natural and that adheres to the power of substitution' (Derrida 1976: 147). Derrida's (philosophically orientated) point is that this is precisely how Western metaphysics works in sustaining ideas on, say, truth, when they are really just constructions. (This can be seen as an indirect reference to Nietzsche's famous dictum that truth is a metaphor that has forgotten its status.) In terms of the female vampire there is a double supplement, both of which inflect it towards this sense of an unnatural evil. There is the woman as supplement to man, and the vampire as supplement to humanity. A third supplement, derived in part from these two is the lesbian vampire, which acts as a supplement to heterosexuality.[9] So the female has it all in terms of a supplementary positioning; she is denied the centres and originary functions of masculinity, morality and 'normal' sexuality. Of course this is precisely what gives such a figure this powerful, seductive and compelling representation. In much the same way as the *femme fatale* of *film noir* is both supplement through, and site of, dangerous desire, the lesbian vampire is both abject and alluring – an absence and a presence at the same point in time. These representations of women are constructions of the phallocentric order that excludes them as supplements, and yet continually returns to them. They are also logical extensions of the ways in which phallocentrism constructs women overall – the feminine is the supplement to the masculine in the patriarchal order.[10]

It is interesting to note that this theme of the lesbian vampire and the lure of the supplement fits into the larger representation of lesbianism as part of a culturally acknowledged phallocentric fantasy. It does raise the question as to why such seemingly (male) excluding scenarios are positioned as recurring (and almost universal) masculine fantasies. There are many possible answers but the one that is to be posed here is that this representation of lesbianism as male fantasy operates as a hegemonic process.

By drawing what would appear to be a threatening scene (women's pleasure as a beyond to the masculine; the lack of the male figure; the satisfaction and unity of the lesbian couple in their sexuality, the threat of
castration through the lack of the phallus, etc.) into the controlling order
of masculine sexuality, there is a hegemonic disempowering of lesbianism
as a challenge to masculine centrality. Such an interpretation means that
rather than attempting to deny or exclude lesbianism, phallocentrism
instead locates it within its controlling domain, designating it as part of
the 'acceptable' male sexual fantasies. In this sense it can be accommo-
dated into the phallocularism rather than resisting it. Interestingly, the
same process does not appear to have operated in the same fashion with
male homosexuality, where for a long time repression through absence
or linking it to mental disorder has dominated representations. Lesbianism, however, operates as a supplement even within this sense of male
sexual fantasies.

Our first example of this representation of the supplement is one where
there is a clear sense of the unnatural evil and the power of substitution.
It is drawn from that period in film history that witnessed the production of
a large number of horror films by the Hammer studios in the late 1960s into
the 1970s. On the surface these were horror films, but their mixture of sex
and nudity with horror themes were thinly disguised attempts to circum-
vent the repressive censorship laws and codes of the time. There is still the
strong moral code running through these films, with all transgressions,
especially the sexual, being punished and a return to the phallocentric
social order. The recurring representation of women in these films ties
in with the long tradition of hysteria, borrowing extensively from late
nineteenth-century thought. Witchcraft (in this case the figure of the witch
is transposed onto the vampire) and hysteria ran parallel, with women
being seen as especially vulnerable to seduction towards evil. It is noteworthy that the social interpretation of an association between witchcraft
and mental illness occurs at the same time Rousseau is theorising the dangers of the supplement.

A cycle of films made in the mid to late 1970s, based on the short story
'Camilla' by Sheridan Le Fanu, consistently presented the lesbian vampire
as powerful, passionate, and quite irresistible. Given that these films were
never particularly underground (they were popular, mainstream films,
even if the audience tended to be almost subcultural) or revolutionary in
their sexual politics, the question arises as to how we might read this figure
in terms of the supplement. One the one hand these representations are part
of a general phallocentric fantasy of lesbian eroticism. It is perhaps not
enough to attribute to the lesbian vampire figure the qualities of the forbidden, or a projected male intervention, to explain this recurring phenomenon. What is needed is an examination of how such a supplement works

for and against the phallocularism of such mainstream films, which will also allow us to consider how effective the hegemonic processes actually are.

Mircalla/Camilla, the female vampire in *The Vampire Lovers* (Roy Ward Baker 1971), represents the supplement in a number of ways. She is immediately positioned as an outsider who comes into the girls' school. Her sexual encounter with Laura Spielsdorf, her roommate, is presented variously as forbidden (the scene where the two are caught semi-naked by the teacher prompts a quick cover-up and awkward glances), sensual (the kiss in the lake), and ultimately destructive. In such terms the existence of Mircalla would seem to be the evil and dangerous supplement that disrupts the lives of the women and the social order of the school. However, the parallel romantic couple, Roger Morton and the school teacher, which is presented as a sustainable relationship, is one of restraint and repression. Where the supplementary desires of Mircalla are allowed freedom (with consequences of death), the heterosexual couple is bound to censorship. At one point the teacher almost succumbs to the advances of Mircalla but, as is so often the case in these films, the masculine intervention prevents this. This is the lesbian vampire as dangerous supplement to the masculine world order, the 'always open possibility of a catastrophic regression and the annulment of progress' (Derrida 1976: 298), with both 'regression' and 'progress' being very much determined through the phallocentric domain. Even in those films where the masculine intervention seems to be ineffectual in preventing the dangerous supplement, we still find certain prohibitions and curtailment. There are films that appear to escape this, although there is usually a scene of punishment for the supplementary (vampiric) force. *Daughters of Darkness* (Kumel 1971), for example, retains the death of the lesbian vampires, but closes with a metaphoric reincarnation of one of them in the body of another woman. Whether this amounts to transgression, or simply a cycle of supplement and punishment, raises another set of issues.

Derrida's desire to recoup the supplement, or at least to read it beyond the constrictions of the dominant interpretations, leads him at one point to argue that all that the Enlightenment attributes to the supplement is also what gives it its power. This is the supplement's capacity to resist and invert. It is the quality of the supplement to be an excess and an outside to the social order. As Derrida says: 'Thus supplementarity makes possible all that constitutes the property of man: speech, society, passion ... supplementarity, which is nothing, neither a presence nor an absence, is neither a substance nor an essence of man. It is precisely the play of presence and absence, the opening of this play that no metaphysical or ontological concept can comprehend' (Derrida 1976: 244). This is equally applicable to the lesbian vampire, for she is beyond the systems of rational thought constructed within the social (religious/metaphysical) world order. There is little difference in whether or not such figures are ultimately punished (as in *The Vampire Lovers*) or whether they appear to escape (as in *Daughters of Darkness* or *Blood and Roses* (Vadim 1960)), their presence continually acts as a type of representation of the dangerous supplement, allowing both interpretations to take place.

The Filmic Supplement

In this section we will be concerned with the idea of the filmic supplement, that is, some of the ways in which film constructs a particular type of supplement unique to itself, and how various aspects of film utilise these supplementary values and structures. This is the idea that, rather than just representing the supplement (as dangerous or otherwise), film actually incorporates it into its own textual formations and operations. Clearly the documentation of the whole of cinematic supplementarity is too large a project to detail here, so a few examples will serve to illustrate how such an idea might be approached.

For a considerable part of the early years of film and its theories, montage and *mise-en-scène* were positioned as antithetical both in terms of the construction of film and the overall effect on (and relationship to) the spectator. The domination of early film theory by Arnheim (for expressionism) and Kracauer (for realism[11]) fed this division; as did cinematic practices by people such as Griffith and Eisenstein (privileging montage) and Welles (privileging *mise-en-scène*, especially in, for example, *Citizen Kane* (1941)). Basically this was a theorising, and practice, based on constructing realism to have an effect on the viewer. Depending on which theory and practice one subscribed to, the realism of the film (its construction as well as its mental/emotive effects) was better served by montage or *mise-en-scène*; and any intervention by the other was seen as a dismantling of the desired synthesis.

So, following on from this tradition, something like Bazin's theories illustrate how montage has been positioned as a type of supplement to *mise-en-scène* in the production of realism. Taking our lead once more from Derrida we witness a similarity in how the issues of verisimilitude and imitation are defined in the discourse of the supplement. Derrida deconstructs Rousseau's denouncement of mimesis and art as supplements to reality/realism, premised as they are on a sense of the authentic and immediate. Bazin's insistence on the realism of film, and in particular the spatial properties, means that so much of his theory has nowhere to go. When he declares, for example, that cinema's realism is 'not certainly the realism of subject matter or realism of expression, but the realism of space' (Bazin 1967: 112) then it follows that so much must be invested in a theory of *mise-en-scène*. Thus montage becomes a supplement to depth of field in Bazin's theories because of this investment in realism.

It was Godard who can be seen to have developed a way out of this sense of montage as supplement to *mise-en-scène*. In his theoretical writings (see, for example, his essay '*Montage, mon beau souci*' in Hillier 1986), and throughout many of his films, Godard demonstrated a type of deconstruction of the impasse that had existed in this realist/expressionist–montage/*mise-en-scène* debate. Godard worked in terms of montage and *mise-en-scène* operating together, so that neither could be attributed as supplement of the other. There are many examples of this in Godard's work, but one of the most interesting (and self-reflexive) is *Passion* (1982). Here Godard plays with a theorising of composition through the devising of elaborate reconstructions of famous paintings. This becomes a treatise on the difficulties of a stable *mise-en-scène* as elements keep breaking up within the scene itself. At one point in the attempt to replicate Delacroix's *Crusader's Entry Into Constantinople*, two women constantly run about the set, resisting composure and stillness. They become dangerous supplements to the very act of cinematic *mise-en-scène*. This is something we see again in Godard's short film 'Armide' (included in *Aria* (1987)), with the fluid movement of the two women around the sharply composed figures of the weight-lifters.

The contrast to this deconstruction of *mise-en-scène* (which is not its negation of course) in *Passion*, are the typically Godardian jump-cuts that emphasise – and equally deconstruct – montage. This scene of the Delacroix painting does, at the final moments, reinvest a power to *mise-en-scène* with a formation of the image almost without cuts and pushing depth as an integral part of the cinematic apparatus (the lowering of the women on the platform into the frame is particularly noteworthy for this). This comes after there seems to have been a type of supplementarity attached to *mise-en-scène* composition as part of the narrative processes. Immediately following this scene, however, is a jump-cut to a closeup of a car headlight, and then into a factory. The contrast is as sharp and disruptive as the two women are to the breakdown of the *mise-en-scène*. Each function as dangerous supplements, but both are rich, and work, in Derrida's terms, outside of presence and absence.

We have gone a long way from the starting point of this chapter – that of the relationship of the viewer to the image – yet so much of the material discussed in this second half is invested in a similar set of issues. After all, from the early theorists, through Bazin and then on to the New Wave, the issues of the realism of the image, the processes of montage and *mise-en-scène*, and the synthesis of ideas we find in the works of people such as Godard, all revolve around the fundamental relationship of image and spectator. Bazin's assertion, for example, on the realism of space has strong connections to Brecht's ideas on realism as an ideological construct;

this, in turn, is about the spectator's relationship to the 'realisms' of the image, and how they operate. If we were to extend the discussion of the supplement even further, it would be possible to argue that the film and the spectator operate in a Derridean sense of the supplement, each positioning the other as a supplement to itself. Seen in this way, the act of watching a film is very much about how we formulate relationships of meaning and subjectivity. This is an idea that will be continued in the following chapter on discourse.

3

The Shattering Pluralism:
Film and Its Discourses

When we ask the question 'What is cinema?', one initial response is that it is the experience of watching a film. But even so simple a response evokes a seemingly unending roll of questions. What, for example, is considered part of this experience? (just the watching? or the conversations afterwards? is remembering a film part of the cinematic experience? are the emotional responses to a film part of cinema? is it the entire film, or just parts of it? etc.); what is it to watch? (what are the pluralities of spectatorships involved across audiences, and even within the individual who watches the same film more than once?); does watching a film mean something different from watching other things, and if so what are the differences and how are they formed? How much a part of cinema are cultural contexts? or individual histories? or the force of the images? And each of these such questions elicits even more questions. In part, just recognising such issues formulates cinema itself. The capacity of film, and its theories, to actually provoke a questioning of what it does, and how it does this, and how we recognise it, all forms part of the cinematic experience. The aim in positing, and considering, such questions is not necessarily to resolve them, or even to move towards a sort of eidetic reduction of cinema (to grasp 'cinemaness' as the phenomenologists might say), but we do gain a great deal in foregrounding them. Part of the aim of this chapter, and the following one, is to consider what cinema is (and what it does, and what we do to it) by working through some ideas on discourse. By this is meant that we can consider cinema through its discourses, and how ideas on discourse can be applied to cinema.

We will be primarily concerned with two configurations of discourse in this chapter. The first is that of how semiotics attempts to analyse filmic discourse through an interaction between structures, systems, and cultural contexts. This follows a strong textual tradition found in semiotic studies. The second reading of discourse will be derived from some of the ideas of Michel Foucault, in particular the relationship between power and discourse, and the constructions of meaning through discourse. These two different approaches to the idea of discourse (the textual/cultural of semiotics and the power/knowledge of Foucault) will allow us to gain a different perspective on how film itself operates as a discursive practice.

Semiotics and Discourse

A great deal of work exists on semiotic approaches to film[1] so we will not be overly concerned with sketching out all the basics of this theory here. It is important to recognise that what this analytic model provides is a way of understanding not simply *what* something means, but *how* meanings are produced, sustained, negotiated and devised. This is one of the major legacies of poststructuralism's contribution to semiotics. By challenging the notion that meaning production is a fixed and potentially finite system, thinkers as diverse as Umberto Eco, Derrida, Julia Kristeva, Barthes, and Lacan reorientated semiotics to become a system of questioning rather than just providing resolution. No longer was there an emphasis on the pursuit of the signified – analysis at the level of constructed meaning – and more deliberation was placed on the production and operation of the signifier, and the dynamics and slippage between the two. It was the pluralism of meaning that defined the direction of the theorising, rather than any sense of closure. The semiotic analysis looked at the ways in which signs function and interact in the unlimited production and play of meanings. Furthermore, in this interpretation of the production of meanings, semiotics attempted to examine the relationship of this to cultural, historical, and readerly contexts.

It is well known that one of the initial conundrums of film semiotics was its attempt to investigate the idea of a film language. Various theorists deliberated on whether or not there was a language; and if there was, how do we recognise it and read it; and how does it compare to other languages. We only have to have a casual glance at any of Metz's earlier works to see how complex such questions are, and how much they shaped this approach to film studies. What is also of significance in these terms is that many of the other key developments in film theory were tackling the same sorts of questions, but with different inflections. Psychoanalysis was, in itself, concerned with the idea of language and the psychic apparatus (leading to Lacan's famous 'The unconscious is structured like a language'[2]); feminism was examining the relationships between language and gender, as well as developing different signifying practices (such as Hélène Cixous' *écriture feminine* and Luce Irigaray's *parler femme*); deconstruction was tackling logocentrism as a problem of Western thought and systems of meaning, etc. One of the effects of this was that when any of these theoretical paradigms came together, there was often a continuing and sustained examination of the idea of language itself, its constitutive elements as well as its operations and structures.

Metz's desire to construct a theory of film language produced some highly influential ideas and much of the shape of film semiotics is derived from his work. There are, however, a number of questionable propositions in the ideas and often it is at these points of theoretical discomfort that we find a need for further elaboration and/or the intervention of different perspectives. This is especially the case for our concerns with filmic discourse. For example, one of his qualifications regarding the existence of a cinematic language system is that cinema lacks true communication (as distinct from its signifying practices). In some ways this is a logical enough idea – Metz argues that film cannot communicate (like speech) because it is invested in expression rather than communication. This idea becomes more problematic, however, when we consider ideas from other semiotic perspectives (such as Eco and Barthes), which have a greater emphasis on the role of the reader. From these other critical positions it is more difficult to argue the line that 'one does not respond to a film with another film produced at that instant' (Metz 1976: 584) because, in some ways, this is often what takes place. The activity of reading/spectating involves intertexual connections (see below) so we are continually responding to a film through a variety of other films. Even the very act of going to the cinema immediately links us to a coded practice of the film form. In such an example we witness how the developments in film semiotics have attributed greater force to the reader's construction of the film (and language) itself. This is, of course, not a failure to recognise the literalness of Metz's idea (film, unlike spoken language, is not an immediate statement–response process), but even this does not negate the idea that films are experienced within contexts of other films.

Another way in which we might tackle this idea of the reading of film, the orders of language, and the signifying practices, is through theories of discourse. This will allow us to continue to work through this idea of the interplay between the spectator and the elements of film in the construction of a cinematic language and discourse. Ultimately we will be concerned with defining discourse through the ideas and themes of Foucault, but for the moment it is worthwhile considering a specific example to see how a general notion of discourse and semiotics might be enfolded. The example is intertextuality, largely because it will allow us to map out certain points of connection and development between semiotics and discourse in both theoretical concerns and film examples.

Intertextuality

There have developed two large orders of 'interpretations' of intertextuality. The first is what we might most readily recognise – an interweaving of texts as they refer to each other, either specifically or through a general sense of connection. The second is a more semiotically driven version, most notably found in the works of Kristeva and, to a lesser extent, Derrida. It is useful to take these two orders separately so that we might consider both their differences and points of similarity. There are a number of ways in which films can construct intertextuality (and this necessarily includes both the text as intertextual source and the spectator's intertextual constructions). The four that we will concentrate on here are derived from a critical sensibility which includes both the traditional sense of texts referring to other texts, as well as Kristeva's innovations and reworkings. These include: (1) structural reference; (2) thematic reference; (3) synecdochic structures; (4) mosaic formations. Even though most of these overlap in one way or another, we will take each of them separately to begin with.

Structural Reference

Films can structurally refer, or be connected, to other films in a number of ways. In one sense genre almost inevitably establishes and relies on a type of structural intertextuality as films observe the conventions of the form. Of course just because a film is located within a specific genre does not necessarily mean that it has some form of intertextuality. There is no real referential sense in *The Man Who Shot Liberty Valance* (Ford 1963) to, for example, *High Noon* (Zinneman 1953), and it would be a difficult line to argue for intertextual connections between the two just because they are both Westerns and deal with certain themes and styles in a particular Hollywood fashion. So how is it possible to argue that Raimi's Western *The Quick and the Dead* (1995) can be seen to have an intertextual reference to *High Noon*? Curiously, intertextuality cannot simply be seen as a straightforward textual strategy, even though this is what it sounds like. One of the factors which allows an intertextual reference to operate is the diachronics of the films. There is a specific place (Hollywood) and time (1940s through to the early 1960s as an indicator of the 'classic' period) when the genre of the Western film was made and formulated. Films made outside of these two factors of place and time (in Italy or Spain, or in the 1980s and 1990s) are almost necessarily positioned as operating intertextually – whether the films openly display this reference or not. The force of the established ideas (and ideality) of the Western make it difficult not to see some form of connection. A 'spaghetti' Western is structurally (and thematically) intertextual because it is clearly not a product of the Hollywood system. Similarly, *The Quick and the Dead*, like so many post-1960s Westerns (such as *Unforgiven* (Eastwood 1992), *The Missouri Breaks* (Penn 1976), *Bad Girls* (Kaplin 1994)) seem to be referring to the Western through a system of intertextuality, rather than being one. One of the best examples of this form of intertextuality which produces a Western which exceeds the textual form itself is Sergio Leone's *Once Upon a Time in the West* (1968); this is a hyper-Western as it continually asserts the genre over the film itself. All of these films, including Leone's, rely on the intertextual not simply because they swap between adhering to the structures of the Western and breaking or usurping them (such as, in the example of *The Quick and the Dead*, with the main gunfighter being a woman), but because the core structures which constitute the Western film have already been laid down as a textual form. In this sense these other films become meta-Westerns, as distinct from the classic Western or even Bazin's notion of the sur-Western (films which go beyond their generic sensibilities – Bazin's example is *Shane* (Stevens 1953)).

So, for example, the gunfight in the middle of the town is so textually established that in a film such as *The Quick and the Dead* it becomes almost impossible for the spectator not to make a general reference to all Westerns, and perhaps even something specific like *High Noon*. This is the operation of a filmic language, through the reading competence of the spectator and the film's constitutive elements, in the production of a discourse. Characters are shot without blood, time is continually foregrounded, there is a clear delineation between gunfighter and townspeople, etc. All of these operate *in potentia* to form an intertextual system. The parodic elements (in a postmodern sense) in *The Quick and the Dead* such as bullet holes appearing as clear tunnels through both the bodies and shadows, and the dreamlike movement of the camera, serve as reminders of the distance that is covered by such intertextuality. *Unforgiven* does this in a different way, with the characters openly discussing the mythos of the gunfight, and its position as an event of the past. In this way *Unforgiven* makes an intertextual reference both to a part of its own extra diegetic history, and to the Classic Hollywood texts such as *High Noon*. In doing so it also foregrounds a particular sub-textual theme of the Western, that of the morality and ethical coda. (A further, different type of intertextual relationship, this time between *Unforgiven* and *The Quick and the Dead*, is that the same actor – Gene Hackman – plays virtually the same character in both films.) In this way *The Wild Bunch* (Peckinpah 1969) anticipates the meta-Western of these later films, self-reflexive in its tone, yet participating in the genre enough to be included in it. The characters here, as with William Munny in *Unforgiven*, do not so much lament the passing of the 'old ways', but self-reflexively acknowledge their anachronistic positions and actions.

Thematic Reference

Structural intertextuality is often closely tied to thematic references – that is, when films refer to other films at the level of narrative themes and events. This can take place in any number of different ways, but some of the more common ones include paralleling the action (or sequences) from another film; positioning elements from other films within new contexts; recreating plots or sections of plots. Brian De Palma does this almost methodically by 'remaking' scenes, sequences and styles from Hitchcock films. The stabbing scene in *Sisters* (1972), for example, is unavoidably and forcefully an intertextual reference to the shower scene in *Psycho* for those who have seen the Hitchcock film, or at least know about the specific scene itself. This sort of intertextual reference works at both a thematic and structural level.

Intertextuality does not necessarily have to be from one film to another, as it can also involve references to cultural, historical, and artistic events. If, for example, we accept that the rise of feminism as part of a social and political order has a certain textuality about it, then the spate of women's revenge against rape films that were made in the 1970s can be seen as a type of thematic intertextual reference by films to particular social changes. Another variation on this would be films which derive their narrative material from actual events. Malik's *Badlands* (1973), for example, is based on quite specific people (Charles Starkweather and Caril Ann Fugate), times (1958), and events (their killing spree and eventual capture), but its narrative does not rely on an intertextual knowledge of this. This interpretation of intertextuality is possible if we adopt the semiotic notion that cultural events are also textual systems. This doesn't resolve all the analytic difficulties of combining what are commonly seen as 'texts' (such as a specific film or set of films) with the socio-historical events which take place in the world. However, such a semiotic approach does allow us to formulate a sense of the intertextual across textual orders. This is an important issue in this different formulation of the intertextual.

A similar idea could be developed in terms of the filmic representations of Afro-Americans with the appearance of films such as *Shaft* (Parks Sn. 1971). The character of Julius (Samuel L Jackson) in *Pulp Fiction* (Tarantino 1994) demonstrates a further intertextual level, operating as part of the structural referencing. In this case we witness at least three levels of intertextuality, but each one operating in a different referential manner: Julius's dress, speech and mannerisms refer to the representation of Afro-Americans in the films of the 1970s, which in turn have an intertextual reference to the changing cultural order (as opposed to the representation of Marcellus, who is very much a post-1970s representation). The fact that these representations (the three orders being: the representation of blacks in the 1970s; the representations of blacks in the 1990s; the representations of both these representations – that is, as found in *Pulp Fiction*) are so different, combining (and juxtaposing) one cultural attitude with another, produces a postmodern hybridity that can be neither nostalgia nor parody, but has a sense of both. This, then, forms the third level of intertextuality, spanning the structural and thematic to produce a sign caught up in its own sense of intertextuality for precisely this point of self-reflection. Furthermore, it is this self-reflexive turn which feeds into the intertextuality of texts and cultural event. What makes such formations interesting is their positionality, for they can be located neither simply in the text nor the socio-historical event, but rather must exist in a realm independent of the two. The textual reference cannot be part of the cultural events, nor can those events be defined as strictly part of the textual order. Instead they liquefy the status and relationships of events and representations of history and culture.

Synecdochic Structures

One of the effects of intertextuality is that it does not simply make a point of reference, but it necessarily brings elements of both sources together. All forms of intertextuality rely on the capacity of the spectator to recognise the references and make the connections. This does not mean that if the reading competence is absent then the *meaning* of the film (or that part of the film) is lost or misread, but rather that different meanings are produced depending on the sense of the intertextual reference. This action of conflation is mirrored in what we might call synecdochic structures, and such a reading allows us to consider how these complexities might be positioned as part of an intertextual process. In the operation of synecdoche, the intertextual is formed through the part of one film relating to a much larger order, including another film in its entirety, or a filmic form. As distinct from the two formations of intertextuality listed above, the synecdochic tends to operate at a level less invested in the strictly textual and more in the associative. By this is meant that with either a thematic or structural intertextual reference the spectator may well pick up actual comparable points between a number of films, but with intertextuality formed through synecdoche there is a positioning of the part (either literally a part of a film, or, more broadly the film itself) standing in for the whole. Hitchcock's brief appearance in *North by Northwest* (1959) operates as a synecdochic formed intertextual reference for all of Hitchcock's films. In such an example there is a double inflection: Hitchcock as a synecdoche for his oeuvre; Hitchcock's appearance as a synecdoche for all of his appearances in his films (which operates, for example, as corporeal signature in much the same way as an author might sign his/her book, or a painter signs their name on the canvas). But the distinguishing feature is that there is no reference to a specific film through this appearance of the director.

Mosaic Formations

There is a certain type of intertextuality which is formulated not through a system of referential processes, as we find in the above examples, but an mixing of components of films and their contingent elements. This mixing operates intratextually, rather than within the intertextual or extratextual. This might sound a little paradoxical, after all to argue for an intratextual system actually being intertextual would seem to go against the spirit of textual relations. However what is being posited here is that in fact there are certain texts which have elements which by their very inward-looking status force/encourage the formations of intertextual discourses. One of the more common motivating factors for this type of reading strategy is a deeply problematising narrative structure. *Un Chien andalou* and *Last Year at Marienbad* (Resnais 1961) are examples of this, where the spectator might struggle to make narrative sense of the wandering images or disjunctions of time. In efforts to render sense to the films, the spectator may go beyond the text itself and look to other, similar films, the context of the artistic movements (and so refer to other films from those movements), other films by the directors, etc. In doing so the intratextual becomes intertextual.

One of the effects of such a system is the sense of disparate parts linked together in structures of a mosaic. The differences are dissolved in the attempts to secure an interpretation, or just access into the film. In some ways this is akin to what Eco (1979) calls extra coding. When confronted by a totally new or different object, sign, event, etc., Eco suggests we have two alternatives in our attempt to make sense of the new: to bring this sign into an established code system; or to devise a totally new code system to accommodate and interpret it. The intertextual mosaic draws on both these strategies, using the known to explain the unknown, and developing new techniques of interpretation from this. *Last Year at Marienbad* resists interpretation through the established codes of narrative structure – although we can gain some meaning through these; so we also need to explore the idea of a cinema which deconstructs space and time, and is not necessarily a reflection of a character's madness.

Within these terms (and including the points listed above) it is important to recognise the intertextual systems as they are positioned through the phenomena of the remake. Do we, for example, consider *Twelve Monkeys* (Gilliam 1996) an intertextual reference to Chris Marker's *La Jetée* (1963)? Or is it necessary to distinguish between the production of another version of a film and an intertextual reference between films? What such

questions reinforce is the idea that the spectator is fundamental to any connections made. In these terms, one spectator may make certain types of
intertextual references to science fiction films when watching *Twelve Monkeys* (the similarity between this and other time travel films for example),
whilst another might make the connections between it and the Marker
film. Significant for the discussion here is how we compare these two processes, for this is an issue beyond textual references, and involves the idea of
filmic discourse and its operations.

The Shattering Pluralism of Film

Kristeva's ideas on the intertextual are quite distinct from the more
common use of the term – in fact she specifically states that for her intertextuality is not this sense of the reference of one text to another. Kristeva
offers the terms 'dialogism' and 'transposition' as alternatives to intertextuality to get around this problem. Both terms are derived from the works
of Mikhail Bakhtin, and although he was primarily concerned with the
novel, there is much in his work, and Kristeva's use of it, which can be fruit-
fully applied to cinema. In doing so we can move towards a further understanding of how filmic discourse works. To commence it is useful to
consider Kristeva's definition of the term:

> The term *inter-textuality* denotes this transposition of one (or several) sign systems into
> another; but since this term has often been understood in the banal sense of 'study of
> sources,' we prefer the term *transposition* because it specifies that the new passage from
> one signifying system to another demands a new articulation of the thetic . . . If one
> grants that every signifying practice is a field of transpositions of various signifying
> systems (an inter-textuality), one then understands that its 'place' of enunciation
> and its denoted 'object' are never single, complete, and identical to themselves, but
> always plural, shattered, capable of being tabulated. (Kristeva 1984b: 59–60)

This is a rich set of ideas, and there is much to be teased out for an analysis
of cinematic transposition. Kristeva requires us to abandon the simple
reading of intertextuality (where one of the principal aims is to track
down reference points from one text to another or others), and instead to
consider how textuality itself is necessarily heterogeneous and plural.
To relate these ideas directly to film studies, if the 'signifying practices'
Kristeva speaks of is replaced by 'cinema' then we need to examine what
would constitute the 'field of transpositions', as well as the shattering pluralism of film itself. This will also lead us to consider the idea of an articulation of the cinematic thetic. What we find continually emphasised here is

that there is no single, homogeneous object called 'film' or even 'a film'. It is in what Kristeva calls the demands of the new articulation that we find the definitional aspects of film's intertextuality. Or, in short, film is not formulated in the composition on the screen, but the forceful moments of the act of watching a film, which in turn shifts where the images, sounds, and so on, are placed and how these 'objects' are read. This will be made clearer if we consider some of the other points that Kristeva is dealing with.

To begin then, and to shift the emphasis directly onto our concerns here, what is meant by film's field of transpositions? It is important to recall that these ideas are generated by a Kristeva emerging out of a conflation of linguistic theory, semiotics, and Freudian psychoanalysis, and this in turn had led her to consider things beyond the 'surface', an examination of the disruptions and flows of what she describes as the 'poetic' over the Symbolic.[3] This means that these fields of transpositions are more often formed at a level beyond the referential (that is, a beyond to a film's reference to another or others, and even to its own *cinemaness*); they are, as it were, an inherent aspect of film's signifying practices. This means, at the most simple level, that every film operates within a field of transpositions which include 'cinema', but also 'culture', 'history', 'ideology', 'power', etc. It is not that a film refers to these, but rather that this continuous unrolling of transpositions actually constitutes that which we call 'cinema'. It is significant that Kristeva argues that transposition is 'the signifying process' ability to pass from one sign system to another, to exchange and permutate them' (Kristeva 1984b: 60). So films exchange and permutate each other, and they exchange with, and permutate/are permutated with, other sign systems. They also perform this process through the act of spectating, which includes the sorts of actions and systems discussed earlier. This is a line of thought which necessarily runs counter to some of the points proposed in Metz's view of cinema and its language systems.

Herein lies the shattering pluralism of film. It cannot be contained within its signifying practices and processes because film is one of the most highly transpositional of all textual systems. There are a number of reasons for this, including:

- Film's compositional nature to what, and how, it represents (including its relationship to reality; its representational systems; its relationship to realism; its parallels with dreams[4]) means that the raw material of film, as well the act of watching a film, will always contain aspects of a transposition between the represented world order, the spectator's world order, and the created world order of the film itself (this is also part of the reason why there is such an extensive debate about realism in the history of film theory);

- Film's immense textual range (such as genre, cultural styles, film history) means that what is included is necessarily large. If one considers
  that a documentary by Flaherty (*Nanook of the North* 1922), a surrealist
  film by Buñuel (*Simon of the Desert* 1965), a social commentary film by
  Mike Leigh (*Naked* 1993), and a Hollywood studio film by Cameron
  (*Titanic* 1997) are all part of the signifying practices of cinema, then
  the acts of transposition at both form and content levels are complex
  and ongoing;
- Film draws readily and smoothly from other sign systems. Literature,
  painting, drama, music are obvious examples, but we should not overlook the relationships between, for example, film and historical discourse, film and politics, the representation of cultural identity in film.

Such a list can easily be extended, but what is clear from even such a limited set of examples is that the transpositional aspects of film are much
more than consequential, and actually are formative of that which is
deemed film's signifying systems and practices. In this sense it can be
argued that this transpositional aspect is an essential part of the filmic discourse. We have moved from the position that intertextuality is evident in
certain films (for different reasons) to the idea that this inflected sense of
intertextuality as transposition is constitutive of filmic discourse.

One final term from Kristeva needs to be noted before we can examine
how such ideas might operate in a specific film example. Kristeva coins the
term 'thetic' to analyse the threshold of language, and designate a line of
demarcation between what she calls the *sémiotique* and the Symbolic. Once
more, even though her concerns are more directly related to language
(its acquisition and utilisation) there is much here that is important for
the analysis of film. Some key questions include: is there a filmic *sémiotique*
which operates as a disruptive process to the filmic Symbolic? what constitutes film's thetic boundaries? does film, in its transpositional processes,
problematise the thetic order of other signifying systems?[5] Perhaps the
best way to consider such questions is one by one, drawing on examples
as we go.

Is There a Filmic Sémiotique?

The *sémiotique* is part of a wider set of issues related to the subject's formation, and the relationship of the subject to language. For Kristeva there is a
constant interplay in the development of the subject (what she describes
as the subject-in-process) between the social order of the Symbolic, and
the drives (from, for example, the unconscious) of the *sémiotique*. In these
terms, that which originates from the *sémiotique* is disruptive, anarchic,
possibly antisocial, and a continual challenge to the Symbolic order.

Depending on your perspective, it can be seen as a creative, fecund intervention, or a threat to the (social) order of language and the subject; more often than not it is both of these. Interestingly, this division has produced a sort of political reinterpretation of the concepts, with some perspectives (for example certain branches of feminism) seeing the *sémiotique* as a celebratory and potentially revolutionary 'space' to develop a new system of language, whilst others have seen it as a chaotic and socially disruptive set of processes.

There is certainly an organised and recognisable system in film (its Symbolic discourse order) which dictates how things are represented, how meanings are constituted, how film operates as a 'language', how film fits into a social order of things, etc. But does there exist a filmic *sémiotique* which would challenge and disrupt such an order (as well as social orders), and if so what are its functions? To simplify matters we can treat such a question at a formal level and at the level of representing such a *sémiotique*. We shall begin with the second, for it is there that some of the fundamentals can be most readily recognised. It is noteworthy that it is precisely the combination of the two (formal features and representation) that illustrates the idea of transposition, for each of the aspects necessarily impacts on the other, and that more often than not we encounter both formal and thematic aspects of the *sémiotique* in the same text.

One of the recurring defining qualities of the *sémiotique* that we find in Kristeva's writings is its fluidity. She constantly emphasises the flows, effusions, rush and inundations that mark the effects and nature of this powerful process. The *sémiotique* is that which resists the fixing qualities of the signifying orders, and as such it is part of the disruptive qualities of the drives rather than the establishing of meanings. As Kristeva puts it: 'We shall distinguish the *sémiotique* (drives and their articulations) from the realm of signification, which is always that of a proposition or judgement, in other words, a realm of positions' (Kristeva 1984b: 43). To dangerously oversimplify, the *sémiotique* is part of the sliding drives of the unconscious, as distinct from the positioning actions of the Symbolic, which attempts to render signs in terms of the practices of the accepted social language structures. Film can be seen to be operating at a number of different levels in this context. It could be argued that film itself operates as part of the *sémiotique*, posing difference in terms of the other textual forms because it is largely an invention of the twentieth century. Another approach would be to consider what certain films portray as part of a *sémiotique* process. This would be the subject-matter of the films themselves (Pasolini's *Salo* (1975) is an example of this) as well as how these films are resisted by the social order. The representation of the forbidden or repressed is part of cinema's discourse, and in this it has the potential to produce a *sémiotique* disruption. Or we could consider the filmic *sémiotique* as the differences produced in the materiality of film – how, for example, the body represented on the screen becomes more than a body.[6] We will discuss one further point on defining the relationship between the *sémiotique* and the Symbolic before we attempt to apply these concepts to some examples.

The interplay of the *sémiotique* and the Symbolic takes place in and through the formation of the subject. This is Kristeva drawing on psychoanalytic theory (especially Lacan) to examine both how the subject is formed, and the relationship of this subject to language systems (in the broadest possible sense – even if Kristeva's emphasis at the time of writing *Revolution in Poetic Language* was very much with written and spoken language). The *sémiotique* exists prior to the subject's entry into the Symbolic world order of language and relationships. For our concerns here, the subject can be located in at least three different, but related, sites: the filmic spectator; the characters in the film; the fusions and interlockings of spectator and character in the formation of an 'identificatory' site. This third site necessarily exists neither in the text nor the act of spectating, but in a liminal zone constructed out of the act of watching a film and the larger order of film watching practices. (This has connections to the idea of the envy of the gaze that was examined in the earlier chapters.) Here we witness further possibilities in film studies, for Kristeva's idea that transposition demands another level of articulation is especially relevant to how we might come to understand the operation of the cinematic apparatus. It is the interplay between these three sites which formulates relational contexts of the Symbolic and *sémiotique*, and, in turn, the subject as film spectator.

One way we might utilise such concepts in the analysis of film is to consider the ways in which film constructs and utilises the *sémiotique* in terms of the disruption of the filmic Symbolic. An example of this would be the initial use of the jump-cut by the French New Wave. (I say initial here because the jump-cut device follows the way of many manifestations of the *sémiotique* by being drawn into, and even 'normalised' by, the Symbolic order.) Godard's *A bout de souffle* contains many examples, but a striking one is in the apartment scene when Michel Poiccard leans over to kiss Patricia Franchini. There are a number of quick, disjunctive cuts prior to the kiss, and then a visual and aural jump-cut to a travelogue-type aerial view of Paris. All of the established conventions of romance are dramatically usurped by the technique, and the swirling camera above Paris alienates the usual romantic connotations of the city, rather than confirming or concentrating them. This has the effect of undercutting the usual conventions of shots of Paris standing, metaphorically, for love and romance. It deconstructs the line between Rick and Ilsa in *Casablanca* (Curtiz 1943) that 'We will always have Paris'! In this example from *A bout de souffle* the filmic Symbolic operates within the conventions of the romance genre, as well as the narrative structures of film. The *sémiotique* functions of the jump-cut perform at both structural (that is, narrative) and thematic levels to disrupt them.

Another example of a technical process functioning as the *sémiotique* is the depth of field perspective in *Citizen Kane*. Here the invention of a camera lens that enabled focus to be held much further 'into' the scene allowed different sorts of relationships to be formed within the screen. This may seem less disruptive that the jarring effects of the jump-cut, but we should not lose sight of the profound impact that such a change in depth of field had on narrative discourses. Representations of relations between characters (including power, love, hate, and mistrust), temporal shifts and spatial enormity, and characters' states of being (such as loneliness and mistrust) are all conveyed through this device. Included in all this is the irony of a narrative that sweeps across power structures of the world, only to return to a single tightly shot focus on Rosebud. What gives *Citizen Kane* much of its uncanny feeling is the operation of what, for its time, were excessive depths of field constructions, which perform as a type of filmic *sémiotique*.

Another possibility is to examine how potential, as well as actual, reading sites are formed (in those sites mentioned above) through the interplay of the *sémiotique* and the Symbolic. Part of the complexity of this issue is the dynamics between the spectating sites posited by the film itself, the relationship of these sites to the film's Symbolic order, and the further relationships of this interplay in terms of the spectator's own Symbolic and *sémiotique* positionalities. Some films openly contort these relationships, and a specific example can be used to illustrate this. Wes Craven continually draws on the established codes of the horror film to foreground them, not always in terms of parody, but rather to reassert the function of horror − to deliberate on horrality and its operation in watching these films. Films such as *Nightmare on Elm Street* (1984), *Scream* (1996), and its sequel *Scream 2* (1998), function precisely on acknowledging the horror genre (that is, a specified Symbolic order of film), openly stating its operations (deconstructing it through a *sémiotique* disruption of those conventions) in order to intensify the horror (a second-level *sémiotique* which attempts to discard the formula of the genre in order to create a greater level of terror). This formal redefining of the Symbolic and *sémiotique* orders of a specific film genre is extended into the social Symbolic through a similar process. The strict morality of the horror genre in the 1980s and 1990s (the punishment of middle-class suburban teenagers for what is represented as sexual openness or transgressions − which has such strong resonance of the morality of the AIDS age) is foregrounded in Craven's films, as well as other examples such as *I Know What You Did Last Summer* (Gillespie 1997) (where we find an open discussion by the characters of the urban myths of sexuality in contemporary horror narratives).

The curious aspect to all this is that the seemingly *sémiotique* elements of these films (the elements of horror, the personification of evil, the socially disruptive forces) are inverted to actually reinforce the Symbolic orders of both film and the cultural climate. It is almost as if one of the most seemingly disruptive aspects of the genre has been relocated into the centre of the Symbolic, rather than at any point in the thetic disruptions. It is the Symbolic order which produces the themes and images of horror, rather than the *sémiotique*. In the horror films of the 1950s and 1960s (such as the vampire films, the Frankenstein films, *Psycho*, *Peeping Tom* (Powell 1960), *The Wickerman* (Hardy 1973)) the site of horror was almost always positioned as socially disruptive, anarchic and morally perverse. The Hollywood reworking of the Frankenstein story illustrates just how pervasive this process was, turning the persecuted figure in Shelley's novel into a social evil. Shelley's original representation of Frankenstein's 'monster' is perhaps much closer to the socially maligned figure of Freddy Kruger than might first appear to be the case. The second wave of horror films invests the terror much more closely in the domain of the social Symbolic (in an American context, at least, the overtly normal and average teenager, located in the most ordinary of suburbs), which in turn leads to the filmic representation of the *sémiotique* (the terror and abject) to be part of this ordinariness. Lynch's *Blue Velvet* positions its whole narrative structure and film style in this recognition of the blandness of the social order, underscoring with a dark menace that which is ultimately revealed to be another inflection of that social order. A significant film in this change is Kubrick's *The Shining* (1980), as it seeks to offer a reading site from the perspective of the mad and possessed Jack. He commits no great 'sin', except for going against the morality of the work ethic, and perhaps for being ordinary. In this reinterpretation of the horror genre, it is the ordinary that defines the potential for transgression. This, in turn, positions the everyday as harbouring the *sémiotique*. In order to understand the interplay between the Symbolic and *sémiotique* more we can turn to this issue of the thetic.

What Constitutes Film's Thetic Boundaries?

This is a difficult question because it taps into one of the unresolved (and perhaps unresolvable) issues of film studies, that of what constitutes a film language. However, we can bypass those difficulties here by considering how something like a thetic boundary can operate in film. The thetic represents both boundary and disruption to the various orders of the Symbolic and *sémiotique*. Importantly, it is not simply a division between the two, for its operation is fundamental to the formation of meanings, or what Kristeva describes as 'the positionality of signification' (Kristeva 1984b: 43). This meaning formation is derived from the positioning of elements within contexts, as well as specifying a position in which they can be interpreted. Significant to our concerns for film, Kristeva specifies that this process is not simply language derived, but depends on the subject's relationship to the image. To sum up then, the thetic has the following attributes: it represents the positioning of subject to object; it demarcates difference between these two; it marks the threshold of language systems (including the cinematic); it presents a certain type of relationship of the subject to the self, via the image; it provides a line of demarcation between the Symbolic and *sémiotique* (as well as containing the moments of the disruption between them); it marks the moment of the subject's entry into the Symbolic.

As we have just noted, there does appear to be a realm of the *sémiotique* necessary to film's operation, so it is reasonable to posit that there is also this thetic boundary in operation. The trick then becomes attempting to define what constitutes it and how it operates in terms of film and the spectator. It is important to recognise that film necessarily has at least two codifications of the thetic: a boundary outside of the textual order (the social/cultural and historical, for example); and a set of thetic boundaries which exist within the films themselves. Not all films challenge one or both of the operations of these boundaries (and in doing so foregrounds them), but they all have them. At one level the thetic marks the spectator's entry into the film, shifting the sorts of spectral and image relationships to the self in terms of a broader set of cultural and textual issues. It also marks the point where the spectator engages in the Symbolic order of the film itself, in turn altering that through interpretation, response, and creation. So the act of spectating necessarily contains within it the acknowledgment and crossing of the thetic into a different world order – one derived from the film, the cinematic apparatus, the Symbolic order, the *sémiotique* and the spectator's own positionality. To engage in this issue further we must now turn to another source and consider the interplay between spectator, film, and discourse.

Cinematic Power/Knowledge

Foucault's ideas on discourse are at once complex and rewarding. His challenge to how we might read the relationships between the subject, social institutions, and power are dependant on his theorising of the operation and functions of discourse. Our concern here is how we might utilise Foucault's sense of how discourses are formulated, operate, and collapse in understanding on the one hand film's discursive practices, and on the other, the relationship of film to other discourses. Once we have considered some of these aspects it will be possible to consider in greater depth the possibilities of these ideas for film studies – something that will be taken up in the ensuing chapter on the body. We can commence this part of the study by considering one of Foucault's key works, *The Archaeology of Knowledge* (1986a), and how the ideas might be translated into the study of filmic discourses.[7]

One of Foucault's primary concerns in *The Archaeology of Knowledge* is no less than the ways in which knowledge is produced, formed, and restricted through discursive practices. As Foucault puts it, his aim is to examine 'that field in which the questions of the human being, consciousness, origin, and the subject emerge, intersect, mingle, and separate off' (Foucault 1986a: 16); and what we shall be concerned with here is film's position within such a scheme. Foucault is attempting to write his own theoretical treatise here – a self-reflexive turn on how to isolate and analyse the very methodologies that are in use. Clearly with a project such as this, without a hint of film studies in it, we are proceeding into territory that will need to be carefully developed. Some of Foucault's ideas will have little or no direct relevance to the concerns here, whilst others should prove fecund and stimulating. The proposal here is to follow Foucault's own developments of the idea of discourse, which will then make it possible to apply these concepts to film.

Foucault begins *The Archaeology of Knowledge* by examining what he terms the unities of discourse – those aspects imposed on a collection of materials/textualities/phenomena that makes them seem somehow united. His examples include the book, the formations of the *oeuvre*, and even large-scale unities such as 'science' and the 'humanities'. Whatever they are, and whatever seems to keep them involved in processes of cohesion, these unities function in a very powerful way. Part of their operation is to link, sort, exclude, and define groupings of knowledge. One of the effects of this is that these unities gain, over time, a sense of truth and knowledge itself. They pass from the status of artificial constructions and subjective positions to becoming ways of thinking about things, and the ways in which cultures produce systems of knowledge.

We have already encountered some of the implications of this notion of discursive unities with film. The very diversity of the filmic form seems to initially suggest that sometimes its unities are premised entirely on a technological and material basis, for how else could such a heterogeneous set of objects be seen as part of the same field? Yet how fruitful and accurate is this? So, for example, how is it possible to demarcate 'film' through its material form when there is a slippage across television, video, DVD, MPEG (perhaps even animation), as well as different film stock (16 mm, 35 mm, 70 mm)? 'Film' may initially appear to be a designation of a textual form derived from its material base, but the experience of film is clearly something much greater than this; and it is this *something more* that constitutes its discursive unities. In order to try to understand what this might be we can turn to other, connected points from Foucault.

Foucault employs the term *statement* to designate the 'elementary units of a discourse' (Foucault 1986a: 80). The division does create some problems for his project (distinguishing exactly what a statement is, what its constitutive elements are, etc., proves to be a huge and perhaps impossible task), but the strategy behind it is for Foucault to work on how discourses produce these statements, and how the statements themselves function in the operation of the unities of the discourse. Foucault, using ideas from his earlier works, gives the example of a discourse of madness (Foucault 1986a: 32–3), asking if all statements referring to, and representing, madness constitute part of the unities of that discourse. Following Foucault, we can ask if a case study by Freud, a schizophrenic walking down the street in front of us, and *Silence of the Lambs* (Demme 1991) are part of the discourse of madness – and if so, how does each of these statements relate to the others in the unities of the discourse? Or, approaching this from a different angle, does a corpus of films treating the same subject in totally different ways (pro- and anti-war films for example) constitute a set of statements that are tied together, even if their ideological basis is in total opposition? These two examples illustrate that the issue of a filmic discourse takes on both the relationship of film to other discourses, and the relationship of discourses within film itself. Either way we still need to tackle the same issues that Foucault foregrounds in order to define and understand the concept of discourse in film.

What is important to recognise in Foucault's analysis here is not that he simply wants a theory of discourse and unities, but more to understand the elements of the production of these. In other words, this is a theorising about how, and possibly why, the formation of discourses takes place, and what relationship this has to the ways in which the cultural, epistemological, political, and textual forces are involved. Foucault suggests four hypotheses in approaching this difficulty of defining statements, their relationships to objects, and their positionality in discourse:

1. 'statements different in form, and dispersed in time, form a group if they refer to one and the same object' (Foucault 1986a: 32).

Foucault rejects this because of the impossibilities of describing the vast range of differences between different statements, and the relative 'weakness' of the unification of the object. That is, it may not be enough to say that the object of the statements unifies them sufficiently. A documentary film of an operation to train medical students and a film by Peckinpah (such as *The Wild Bunch*) or De Palma (such as *Body Double* 1984) may have the same amount of blood, but such filmic statements of the consanguinity do not necessarily form a discursive grouping (even if for the viewer they produce the same squeamish effects). This is not simply about intentionality of form (for example, the didactic against the entertaining), although this can be part of the differences, but involves a far wider sweep of issues. Blood, in these two examples, has a direct attachment to violence (and an aesthetics of violence) in Peckinpah's *The Wild Bunch*, but considerations of either violence or aesthetics are not readily apparent in most medical training films. Similarly, the 'reality' of the blood distinguishes the two films: the medical film has real blood (but which may look fake because of the domination of Hollywood notions of realism) and *The Wild Bunch* has fake blood (but has been presented to look real), but our perception and reading of this status does not necessarily rely on how real or fake the blood actually is.

2. The group of relations between statements is designated by their form and type of connection.

Foucault's example here is how medical science in the nineteenth century became defined 'not so much by its objects or concepts as by a certain *style*, a certain constant manner of statement' (Foucault 1986a: 33). He abandons this idea because a style of discourse is necessarily in a constant state of evolving, so much so that, as Foucault puts it, the discourse disintegrates as soon as it appears (Foucault 1986a: 34). German Expressionist cinema could be considered in a similar way. There are a group of films which are dominated by stylistic features, clearly recognisable and forming quite specific connections. However, as with Foucault's example of nineteenth-century medical discourse, there are a number of factors which formulate this group of relations which may well exist outside of the films themselves, so that the idea of a discourse defined along these lines becomes difficult to argue. Which is not to say, as may first appear, that something like German Expressionist cinema cannot be considered a discourse (or have these Foucauldian unities), but rather that we must find alternatives of defining such a discourse other than through this hypothesis of form and types of connection. German Expressionist cinema was, amongst other things, a conflation of historical factors and moments, a certain economic force in Germany, a positioning within a particular moral code, and a response to particular artistic (largely painting) styles and developments. It would be far too simplistic to argue that German Expressionist cinema was just a style, because as these historical and textual forces and influences altered, so too did the cinema. The discourse of this film movement did disintegrate with the release of one of its first films, *The Cabinet of Dr Caligari* (Wiene 1919), because it was in a constant state of flux, as well as continuously redefining itself. Furthermore, determining discourse in this way is always open to the difficulties of historicism. German Expressionist cinema is more clearly formulated afterwards when paradigms of histories and relations are placed over events.

3. Groups of statements can be formed 'by determining the system of permanent and coherent concepts involved' (Foucault 1986a: 34).

What Foucault is getting at here is the idea that, through constant use and rule defining, certain concepts come to be recognised as continuous in, and therefore formulate, the discourse. Foucault gives, and then undermines, the example of Classical analysis of language. Here, he argues, there seems to be a distinct set of rules and concepts that can be clearly defined and recognised through their continued usage. The problem, Foucault says, is that these are false unities because they cannot account for all variations, and the supposed coherency can only ever operate within a strictly defined perspective (in Foucault's example a historical and linguistic one). The same can be argued in terms of film. The idea that filmic discourse might have permanent and coherent concepts is quickly dismissed if we consider how rapidly it has changed in its relatively short history. Even something as seemingly pervasive as the length of a narrative film varies a considerable amount both in cross-cultural examples and within specific industries, as well as film forms. Hollywood's narrative films tended to get longer in the 1990s, breaking the coherency of the 90-minute film which preceded it.

4. 'a fourth hypothesis to regroup the statements, describe their interconnexion and account for the unitary forms under which they are presented: the identity and persistence of themes' (Foucault 1986a: 35).

Here we have a corresponding idea to that of styles, only motivated this time by the themes of a discourse. Once more Foucault sees the difficulty in this as being the diversity of the themes, the disagreements within the treatment of such themes, and the problems of recognition when a theme still fits into the unities of the discourse, or has altered the discourse itself. Foucault instead argues that it is not in the solidification of themes as unities that such a strategy might rest, but rather in the 'dispersion of the points of choice that the discourse leaves free' (Foucault 1986a: 36). This reveals Foucault's thinking that if we look to the moments between the unities, the gaps in the seemingly coherent groupings, then what appears are the very mechanisms for such formations. This is the case not just of this last type, but of all the four hypotheses, and one that may prove most useful for our concerns on cinematic discourse.

Foucault's tactics for going beyond the sorts of discursive formations that have come to hold a powerful legitimacy in, for example, the production of meanings and interpretive processes, as well as defining the discourses themselves, becomes his concern for many years, and the subject of many of his books. In *The Archaeology of Knowledge* he introduces the idea of the statement, which is the sign transformed into a validated and valorised unit. In other words, discourses privilege certain signs to make them seem more meaningful, more truthful, more substantial of that discourse. A scientific discourse will invest certain signs with the sense of scientific 'truth' or 'fact', thus positioning them as statements (and subsequently of greater significance and importance within the discourse of science). Foucault sees this as the *will to truth*, which in turn becomes what he argues is a relationship inextricably tied to power: 'It's not a matter of emancipating truth from every system of power (which would be chimera, for truth is already power), but of detaching the power of truth from the forms of hegemony, social, economic, and cultural, within which it operates at the present time' (Foucault 1986b: 74–5). Foucault designates those elements which produce these importance-laden statements the enunciative function. (We shall retain this term of enunciation here, even though a more apposite word for the visual could perhaps be coined. The reason for this is that it is the positioning of subjectivities that comes to underlie much of the enunciative function, so there are certain advantages for extending the sense of the term here, rather than offering alternatives.)

There are a number of different ways we might make use of these ideas in terms of addressing the idea of cinematic discourse. Perhaps the most direct approach to take here is to consider the idea of cinematic statements and the sorts of enunciative functions that operate to form them. Put another way, this would be considering that which seems to be cinematic – that which has cinematic 'power' and cinematic 'truth' – and how such designations have come to be attached to these statements. Once we have looked at this it will be possible to consider how the relationship of power/knowledge (as figured by Foucault) functions in the formation and operation of cinema. Once more we shall proceed by mapping out some of the key ideas and then considering them in terms of film.

Foucault commences his defining of the enunciative function with an example of the production of a statement. He argues that by copying down the letters of a typewriter keyboard we produce a statement. This is the statement of 'the letters of the alphabet in an order that makes the typing of them easier, and the statement of a random group of letters' (Foucault 1986a: 88). He sets out to dismiss what might appear to be two possible methods of the enunciative function: reproduction and the intervention of the subject. The first of these relates to the capacity to reproduce the signs to make copies; yet the act of copying (recognising rules, etc.) does not produce statements. The intervention of the subject is also not necessarily part of the enunciative function, for the reproduction of a series of signs by the subject does not necessarily mean that a statement is formed. Instead, Foucault argues, 'a series of signs will become a statement on condition that it possesses "something else" ... a specific relation that concerns itself – and not its cause or its elements' (Foucault 1986a: 89). After detailing all the things that this is not, Foucault produces what hc sees as one of the key concepts: the enunciative function is invested in the subject/text who is given the right to 'speak', the sites from where such statements are produced, and the power relations involved. From this position Foucault moves towards defining discourse and the archaeological method, but before we take up those particular ideas let us consider these points through some cinematic examples.

There are three basic inflections to this idea of the cinematic enunciative function and the statements formed by it:

1. That of certain *external* enunciative functions and statements as they might be applied to cinema. This would be how we might consider the transposition of statements from one discourse into the cinematic discourse, the sorts of effects that these statements have on cinema (and vice versa), the interaction between discourses, and so on.
2. The relationship between cinema and the formation of such statements. This would be to argue that cinema actually produces statements which are positioned outside of itself (that is, have an effect beyond the experience of film) by utilising its enunciative functions.
3. Specific formations of cinematic enunciative functions and statements. This would be the production and operation of signs of cinematic power and truth as they operate within and across films. (A formation we witnessed earlier in a different modality in terms of transposition.)

It is important to note that these three are not mutually exclusive, and it is quite possible, and common, for all three to be in operation at once. This is significant because the whole analysis of the discourse depends on a breaking down of those aspects which might attempt to provide division. Deleuze points out that a literary piece, a proposition from science, an everyday sentence, and the utterance of a schizophrenic are all equally statements (Deleuze 1972: 44–5). Acknowledging this, it is perhaps most useful to consider how we can observe all three in operation at once, as well as seeing them function independently within specific examples.[8] To keep with the Foucauldian theme here the example chosen is Beineix's film of madness and sexuality, *Betty Blue* (1986).

Let us proceed somewhat artificially to begin with and try to transpose some of these ideas from Foucault onto the film, looking, as it were, for

Foucault in the abandoned seaside, the outer reaches of Paris, and the escape into the rustic idylls of the country town. In doing so it may be possible to preserve a certain distance from the themes themselves. On this note, it would be tempting here to dip into Fouacault's *Madness and Civilisation* (1987b) and the *History of Sexuality* volumes, given that so much of that material resonates in the film. However, to avoid too literal a reading of Foucault, and of Betty in *Betty Blue* (that is, the closeness of themes should make us wary of being led away from the critical aspects) we shall continue with certain archaeologies of discourse, leaving the genealogies for later attention.

For all the problems Foucault's methodologies produce in developing the study of discourse – and it is clear that far more uncertainties are raised than answers yielded – one of the more certain aspects is the idea of the enunciative position. This concept of the 'speaking' subject is a recurring theme in poststructuralist work and one we shall return to often. For Foucault it is the subject who produces the discourse, as well as the subject produced by the discourse. This is a potent process to attribute to discourses, their statements and enunciative functions, for it is nothing less than how the subject is positioned within the power structures of meaning, knowledge, truth, and existence. Film, like other narrative systems, develops such enunciative functions within the created world order. This can be as simple an example as the sorts of truth statements linked to the narrating position. The camera itself operates as part of the filmic enunciative function, constantly producing statements about events, histories, ethics, interrelationships – in short, the whole range of discursive practices of narrative – by representing them within the shots. The term 'discursive practice' is used here in the very specific sense developed by Foucault as 'a body of anonymous, historical rules, always determined in the time and space that have defined a given period, and for a given social, economic, geographical, or linguistic [or, in our specific concerns, filmic] area, the conditions of operation of the enunciative function' (Foucault 1986a: 117). Discursive practices, then, determine how things are represented, what is permitted to be represented, and the distinguishing features such as truth and meaning.

Betty represents a sort of Foucauldian resistance to the culturally defined discursive practices (especially of sexuality and rational behaviour), and in doing so the sorts of statements she produces are read as anarchic, socially transgressive, excessive, and, ultimately, insane by those operations of the social order. Betty's enunciations are not simply dismissed by the filmic narrative (which has its own, internal discursive practices), but rather they are offered as having their own sense of the statement. Such statements are presented as bewildering, violent, confused and confusing, yet they are consistent. This quality of consistency (her various obsessions with production – love, sex, Zorg's manuscript, a baby – is one example of this) is not necessarily part of the statement-making process, nor does it provide an explanation for Betty's actions and outbursts (such explanations would be generated out of the discourses and enunciative statements of the social order – such as psychiatry, law, social restraint – she resists), but it does provide a sense of development – a history of the spiral towards madness – which comes to operate as a discursive practice. In other words, we can look not simply to the demonstrations of resistance that Betty operates in for a detailing of this other discursive practice, producing its own enunciative functions and statements, but to the ways in which the conditions of operation are developed and performed. The monotonous painting of the beach houses, for example, is 'meaningful' for Zorg and his employer in part because it fits into the discursive practices of economic exchange and capitalism, yet to Betty it is a futile, unproductive exercise without change and therefore of no significance. It is through her eyes that the spectator is repositioned to see Zorg's passive acceptance as an act of madness, even if her own responses (such as burning the beach house) are seen as just as mad, and more excessive, but in a different way. Betty's discourse and statements of passion alter the way in which the spectator interprets her actions.

This economic exchange is also about power and punishment – both of which Zorg, for most of the film, accepts as inevitable. What is significant is that the discursive practices presented are based not on the issues of the sane against the insane, but on statements of productivity and change. Betty reacts against the Sisyphus-type qualities of this employment; just as she reacts against Zorg's unproduced manuscript, and her own role of mother as producer. This is not about death and stasis however (the comic elements of the funeral and Betty's refusal to sleep in the dead mother's bed undercut that sort of reading), but rather about the meaningfulness of the statements produced by the enunciative functions. The Symbolic world order determines Betty's statements as excessive and therefore mad; yet Betty sees the sorts of meanings offered in the everyday as falsehoods and pointless. It is quite in keeping with Foucault's perspective on the operation of discursive practices and power/knowledge that Betty would suffer so terribly in this inevitable clash of discourses. His *Discipline and Punish* (1987a) (as well as the case study entitled *I, Pierre Rivière, Having Slaughtered My Mother, My Sister, and My Brother*) is full of similar examples of the power of dominant discourses enforced against the subject and the pains caused.

What we observe in such an analysis of *Betty Blue* is not just a type of representation of some of these ideas on Foucault and discourse, but also how they operate within the filmic utterance. As was noted in the previous chapters, the relationship between a film and its spectator is informed by certain relationships; one of the fundamental attributes of many of these relationships is this construction of power/knowledge. This includes the investment of certain cinematic signs and discourses (including sites of spectating) with a sense of power and meaning. These are the statements that the spectator uses to create meanings and understand the film, as well as those attributes that the film uses to construct the spectator and his/her site of interpretation. This interplay (which necessarily includes the formation of the subject as spectator) will be taken up in the following chapter when we consider further the formation and operation of cinematic discourses and their power/knowledge. It is here that we can also observe in more detail the processes of not only the representational fields of cinematic discourse, but also its operation.

4

Flesh into Body into Subject: The Corporeality of the Filmic Discourse

Desultory Bodies

Following on from the previous chapter, our principal concern here will be to map out a particular type of film discourse. This is the discursive practice of the filmic body – which includes the body in film, the transformation of the body through film, and film as a corporeally driven form. In part this will be to explore further some of the critical issues raised by Foucault and Kristeva, but also to extend the idea of a filmic discourse, as illustrated through its treatment of the body, to other theoretical models and debates. The chapter will be divided into three closely related sections: cinematic libidinal economies; the *mise-en-scène* of flesh; the corporeality of filmic discourse. In each section one of the central themes will be how film treats, constructs, displays, manipulates, and invents a pluralism of the body, and how those cinematic bodies pose powerful influences within the cinematic discursive practices. In Foucauldian terms the body becomes a *statement* as it is displayed in film, and filmic statements are transformed through the power of desultory bodies. It is this quality of *desultoriness* that impacts significantly on the discursive practices of cinema, and beyond them.

Before proceeding, a short note may be useful on what is meant by the desultory body of filmic discourse. The active, almost unpredictable connotations of *desultorius*, with its sense of the unconnected, the volatile, and the unstable, are well suited to the body in film. For it is not the consistent, homogeneous or even unified body that appears in film, but the random and the plural. Recall that one of the origins of desultory is from the circus riders (the *desultor*) as their bodies are thrown to earth, leaping from the backs of charging horses. Bodies are thrown and leap from films, not always in control of where they might land, or the positions they might find themselves in, or the contortions forced on them. This is the case not only in the more obvious examples of the body in the thriller, horror film and the sexualised body, but of all cinematic bodies. It could be argued that the discursive practices of cinema are repressive ones in terms of the body; that cinema is the containment and pacification of the body, producing a docile corporeality. This may prove to be the case in many examples, and it is important to consider how filmic discourse does have such a controlling effect on the bodies it constructs. However, we must also look to the disruptive and uncontrolled/uncontrollable aspects of the body as it is presented in film; how the excesses of the body always threaten whatever restrictions from the discursive practices may be placed on it; and how film itself forms such disruptive bodies. Further to this, it is the transpositioning and desultory aspects that move the corporeal from, and into, flesh, the body, and subjectivity formulated through the body. Part of this issue will be to ask what it is that renders the status of flesh, body and subject, and how is flesh turned into a body, and a body into a subject, and vice versa?

Lacanomy and the *Extimaté*

Lacan coined the term *extimaté* to explore the idea of a something which is more than the most intimate, a something so deep within the subject that it seems almost foreign and, consequently, fearful. We can see a certain resonance of Freud's ideas on the *Unheimlich*, that which is both the familiar and the unfamiliar, the homely and the uncanny.[1] The *extimaté* for Lacan is how the unconscious is positioned and perceived – what he once expressed as the 'in you, more than you' sensation.[2] Part of our concerns here will be to consider how film can give the body this extimacy by taking what is deeply intimate (our corporeal identities and qualities as they are formed by ourselves, and the interplay of this sense and the cultural contexts and exchanges) and exposing it as even more closely tied to what we see as part of our subjectivities. In this sense film makes the body more intimate, and yet at the same time has the capacity to render the body as something alien and strange to behold. This is similar to what the Formalists called, in referring to the literary qualities of literature, *ostranenie*, or defamiliarisation. Film is especially good at this because it can defamiliarise the body, giving it qualities that have been unseen and unthought of before, and still construct the body as something we recognise as part of the known. In one sense film is continuing a line, originally found in painting and sculpture, of exposing the body, transforming it as distinct from re-presenting it. However, the differences of motion and narrative mean that the body in film is marked and devised in many different ways, and ultimately constructed along different representational lines.

To take what may seem a quite literal example, Emmanuelle Beart's body in Rivette's *La Belle Noiseuse* is a filmed body rather than the painterly body it stands for, in part because so much of the film is spent showing the contortions of the body through movement and time, as well as the emotional repercussions of the naked body for the various characters (which is formed through the narrative). The final painting – denied to the gaze of the film's audience – operates in this *extimaté* fashion, for that which is most intimately constructed (the relationship between artist and model, the exposure of flesh, the history of emotions and relations) is the unrepresentable (for the audience) and the most feared (by both artist and model). It is this same *extimaté* quality that *Blow Up* plays with, at first with the lack of it in the fashion shoots early in the film (these are merely cultural constructions of the intimate body); then through the tense conversation between the photographer, Thomas, and Jane when she comes to ask for the photographs; and finally to the deconstruction of the image to produce the questioned body in the bushes. The grainy photographic image – so impossible to read – has the same status of the extimacy of the body for the viewer as does the painting in *La Belle Noiseuse*. It is made invisible precisely because of the excesses of the gaze forced upon it, and in doing so the flesh of the body becomes *extimaté*. In quite another way, and as noted in a different context, the figures of the Delacroix women in Godard's *Passion* are defined by their resistance to the motionless quality of the body that they have in the painting, but at the same time disrupt the cinematic shot in which they are a part. They reflect the character of the director and his inability to finish the film, because the bodies themselves rebel against the elements of the film. We find this same theme in another Godard film, *Armide*, based on the music of Lully. In this short film, Godard poses the naked cleaning women – whose disruptive freedom is in contrast to their economic position in society – with the automatons of the muscle-builders. The rigid men are in effect motionless compared to the flow of the anarchic women. As such they exhibit what Cixous sees as the quality of *écriture feminine*, to *voler* – to steal and fly. The women's bodies fly from the phallocentric order, stealing gazes and power.

This whole process of the body, with its motions and resistances, is part of what we might call the *lacanomy* of film. By this term we mean to refer to three interrelated aspects: the economic drives as defined in Lacanian psychoanalysis; the libidinal economy of Lacanian theory; the anatomy in/of psychoanalysis. Clearly this is much wider than the specifics of corporeality and the discourses of cinema, but it can be brought to bear on precisely these areas. This will take us a step closer to considering the idea of a cinematic libidinal economy, and a few notes should help locate some of the issues at hand.

Economic Drives

In psychoanalysis the idea of the drive is part of what Freud termed the economic processes of the psychic apparatus. These are the three processes of the mind making up a metapsychology (the other two being the dynamic, the system of flows of pressure and drives, and the topographical, the 'structures' of ego, id and super-ego, and conscious, preconscious and unconscious). The economic deals with the levels of psychical energy and excitation, the aim being, Freud argues, to keep these low and balanced. An imbalance in the discharge of this psychical energy can result in mental instability. One of the important aspects of the theory is that this psychical energy, and its economic management, can be released through the body as well as mentally (as in, for example, dreams and parapraxis). Two examples of this playing out of the mental in the physical are innervation and abreaction. Later we will consider the ways this issue is dealt with in terms of hysteria.

Drives,[3] Freud states, lie on 'the frontier between the mental and the physical' (Freud 1977: 168), which is particularly relevant to the concerns here. His most famous designations are the sex drive and the death drive, although there are others such as the ego drive (the motivation towards self-preservation) and the scopic drive (which was considered earlier in Chapters 1 and 2). These drives are based on certain antagonistic relationships and contexts. They are motivated by desires which cause psychical and somatic conflict because either they offer too excessive an action for other drives, or they are in opposition to the edicts of the moral structures (for example, the super-ego), or the aims of the drive are counter to those of other drives.

Lacanian Libidinal Economy

Lacan specifies drives as one of the four fundamental concepts of psychoanalysis and, like Freud, he deliberates on a number of the ramifications of these forces on the psychical and corporeal. In the following chapter we shall pursue the issue of drives further (in terms of ideology, culture and love), so for the moment we can restrict the discussion to a couple of points central to the concerns here. The libidinal economy in Lacan's works can be seen to be a reference to his treatment and analysis of desire, for in this we see both the centrality of desire to psychoanalysis, and the use of it as a critical tool.[4] For the sake of expediency here, we shall focus on desire and the body, for it is in this that we witness some key points in terms of cinema.

There are desires of the body and desires for the body – both of which find representation in cinema. The body's own desires, including those represented on the screen and the spectator's own body, are diverse, ranging from those fundamental ones (hunger, thirst) to the more abstract (the physical improvement of the body as desire, or the sexually voracious body as cultural construction, for example). These desires are part of the economy of the drives because they are also the nexus where the corporeal needs and psychic demands meet. Cinema both produces and satisfies (but only in a restricted sense) such desires, feeding into the wider libidinal economy of desire and the Symbolic order. The body's desires can be shown in forms of excess (the eating scenes in *La Grande Bouffe* (Ferreri 1973) compared to the sexualised eating scenes (in a sense the conflation of sex and eating) in $9\frac{1}{2}$ *Weeks* (Lyne 1986) and *Tampopo* (Itami 1986)) or denial (the ravaged bodies of desire in *Naked* (Leigh 1993)); as culturally defined through repression of desire (the body transformed in *The Sheltering Sky* (Bertolucci 1990) which moves from an alienated European form to one metamorphosised in the desert; compare this to the hybridity of Lawrence's body in *Lawrence of Arabia* – dressed in Arab clothes, but still has impossibly blue eyes), or through a total disregard for such cultural repressions. No matter where such representations of the body's desire are located on such a spectrum, they retain their impetus through the libidinal economy of cinema. The same can be said for the other axis, the desires for the body. Cinema, of course, sets this up constantly, and to understand more fully how this operates within cinema, both in itself and along with the body's own desires, we can now turn directly to the issue of the cinematic libidinal economy.

Cinematic Libidinal Economy

There is a type of economy which drives the material of film – *Drives* as in the sense found in psychoanalysis: a process caught somewhere between demand and desire, devised in the conversion of energy and the qualities of release. This is not simply narrative or diegetic systems (although both of these are often part of the processes involved), but rather the intersection of the filmic reader, the textualities of the film, and the cinematic discursive practices. In one way this is an exploration of the *construction* (by, for example, the spectator or culture), rather than the readerly attributes, of film. The emphasis here is on a particular type of cinematic economy – one driven by the corporeal – which will be designated as libidinal, although clearly film is constituted by a multiplicity of drives. This is the force of the body as it drives the narrative, the diegetic, the discourse, the demands, the desires, and passions of the film and its spectators. The idea of the libidinal economy that we will be concerned with here is derived, in part, from Lyotard's figurings, primary amongst these being his idea of the *dispositif* and his rereadings of the concept of investment from Freud and Lacan.

For Lyotard, the conceptual figuring of *dispositif* is a negotiation of philosophy (largely Kant and Hegel), Marxist theory, and Freud. It is not a
concept to be comfortable with, as is also true of so much of Lyotard's book
Libidinal Economy (1993). Yet it is this discomfort that also gives much
depth to the points that Lyotard is making in both a broad sense and in
terms of the effect on the reader of his book. As a project – the critique of
Marx and Freud and the plausibility of such a conflation of theories – it is
difficult to assess the success of *Libidinal Economy*, and even a retrospective
Lyotard seems ill at ease with it. However, it does offer some possibilities
for our study of a particular type of film discourse, as one of his concerns is
with the systems of power and its manifestations. When Lyotard poses the
question 'How does *force* [*puissance*] give rise to *power* [*pouvoir*]?' (Lyotard
1993:19) he is concerned with an interplay between the social (its histories
and practices) and the subject who is formed by, and operates within, it,
and how these two must always be seen as distinct. The cinematic body as
discourse, we can argue, operates as a site in which these distinctions and
connections between force and power are played out. To rephrase this
question in variable permutations: How does the body, located in cinematic force, give rise to power? How does force give rise to corporeal
power in cinema? How does force give rise to cinematic power of/over the
body? and so on.

The status of the cinematic body may vary in its emphasis, but it will
always be present. When we watch films we are almost always watching
bodies; even the absence of the body in the frame (the sweeping panoramas
of a Ford Western; the unending road of a road movie such as *Mad Max*
(Miller 1979); the immeasurable distances of empty space in *Alien*) necessarily implies the human body. It is the smallness, the finiteness, and often
tenuousness, of the body that allows such landscapes to have these dimensions. It is worth recalling Bazin's point that cinema is all about locating
bodies in spaces. There are certain types of films which invest heavily in
the collocated body – that is, the body foregrounded and made pre-
sentational. The body of Bruce Willis in *Die Hard* (McTeirnan 1988)
is continually hunted by the composing shots of threat and violence: it is
stripped of clothes, made vulnerable, collects cuts, bruises and other
wounds; it is defined by its fluids (sweat, blood, spit), its muscles, and its
efforts. It is constantly placed against hard objects (elevator shafts, roofs,
walls) and sharp surfaces (broken glass features as a recurring motif of the
ease in which the body can be injured), as well as being threatened by other
bodies; it is filmed in closeup to emphasise the vulnerability of skin, and in
longshot to position it as fragile against skyscrapers. Ultimately it is this
clash of bodies that signals the ideological function of the body in this film
(and its sequels). It is the Americanised body – that of the supposed
normal (American) man against the foreign bodies (the viral?) of the

Ubermensch. In the third film of the *Die Hard* series the diegetic significance of the Willis body is further emphasised, this time in the contrasting ideologies of white and black American, with the characters themselves drawing attention to this difference. In these sorts of examples the body is never taken away from its contribution to the driving forces − the libidinal economy − of the film. However, even in films where the body seems far less emphasised, forgotten as it were, there is still a libidinal economy at work. One way of approaching this is through an anatomy of the body and its libidinal economic forces in film.

Skin

The skin of the body performs many functions: it is, for example, the barrier against the world and other bodies; it is the defining surface of the body and, consequently, the subjectivities; it designates age, race, life style, even class; it represents the line of interaction between the body/subject, other subjects (and their bodily representations) and the world. Lyotard describes the libidinal skin as being made up of 'a patchwork of organs, of elements from organic and social bodies. . .like the track of intensities, ephemeral work' (Lyotard 1993: 17). Film not only utilises these functions of the everyday skin, it constructs them, emphasises them, makes them signifying practices in the filmic narrative, as well as the wider cultural and social contexts. It is necessarily libidinal skin because it contains the potential, as well as the actual, intensities of a practice that contains both the social and the individual. This discourse of skin is possible because of both the apparatus of film (the closeup, slow motion and time-lapse photography, which can be extended to include the extraordinary effects of make-up and costumes) and the libidinal economies that the filmic discourse has developed. Some specific examples will help illustrate this.

Pierced/sliced skin

Piercing skin, or the threat/promise to do so, carries a variety of connotations, including abjection, pleasure, fear, and power. Sometimes these are all contained within a single puncture (the vampire's bite for example); other times they are all present, yet represent a division of subjects and their bodies. There is a scene in *Chinatown* (Polanski 1974) where the main character, Jake Gittes, has a knife inserted into his nose before it is flicked violently to slice the nostril. The knife is held there in a gesture of power and pleasure for the sadistic criminal (played by Polanski) and abjection and fear for Jake. The viewing subject watching this scene is located somewhere between the power and powerlessness of the two characters, wishing to avert the gaze, but unable to. However it is the flick of the hand, the cutting through of the nose, that makes this a slice of the filmic discourse of the body, because this is the moment that reflects the dark permutations of the film itself, as well as the possibility of all films to do this. It is not simply enough to have the force to inflict pain on the body, but it is the capacity (the power of the libidinal economy) to demonstrate that power. It is of that same order as the razor slicing the eye in *Un Chien andalou,* or even the slime-covered Ripley in any of the *Alien* films. Yet we may want to distinguish these discourses from, for example, the viewer-imagined ear-slicing in *Reservoir Dogs* (Tarantino 1992). It not simply a distinction based on being shown the slicing of skin as opposed to the cuts and pans away to allow the viewer to imagine the scene. What is involved is a playing out of certain bodies as they become the *punctum* of the scene, or even film. This is also the case when we compare such specific – and perhaps unexpected – scenes within a film's narrative and when there are excesses of sliced and pierced skin, such as those found in the slasher film. The expectation that there will be acts of cutting in such a specific genre undercuts the *punctum* effect, reducing it to the level of the *studium,* that may be achieved in these other examples where the lacerations are less expected.

What perhaps makes the shower scene in *Psycho* so cinematically fascinating is that it actually manages to do both these seemingly oppositional things at the same time: it contains the excess of the slasher film, yet the body is never actually pierced; the shock is invested not simply in a brutal death, but in that it is Marion (the central character of whom we expect to invest the narrative direction) who is killed; and the length of the sequence is much longer than we would normally expect, or perhaps want. It is these moments in film that illustrate Lyotard's idea of the cut: 'There are no holes, only invaginations of surfaces. That is why when we cut open, we affirm only that which is, the vast coiled skin, where slits are not entries, wounds, gashes, openings, but the same surface following its course after a detour in the form of a pocket' (Lyotard 1993: 21). It is this preservation of the skin which makes the cut and tear so much more powerful and shocking, for in this affirmation of the subject's skin rests its *extimacy.* In such a reading the cut and slashed skin remains part of the body – that is, the skin is preserved by subsuming the wound. In doing so the cut becomes part of, and then defines, the subjectivity.

Stretched skin

Skin's connotative values also include power through its tightness. The stretching of Sarah Conner's skin over muscles in *Terminator 2* (Cameron 1991) is much more than an accentuation of physical power. The comparison must be made to the continual references to the body of the terminator, for it is Schwarzenegger's body – its skin's tightness over muscles that seem altogether too large – that is the nodal point between the human and the non-human. Of course skin is a referential point in a great many science fiction and fantasy films about the non-human made to be human. In *Alien* and *Aliens* (Cameron 1986) it is the piercing of the skin, which is more than human, that reveals an *extimaté* relationship of the body between the two non-human entities (the androids and the aliens) and Ripley. This *extimacy* is played out to its *unheimlich* extremes in *Alien Resurrection* (Jeunet 1997) as Ripley's body becomes alien to herself, being more powerful, more physically defined, yet still human (which also works as the corporeal contrast of Sigourney Weaver's physicality to Winona Ryder's fragility). Because it is through the eyes that replicants are revealed in *Blade Runner* (Scott 1982) as not being human, then other parts of their bodies must not give away this secret; their skin acts more like skin than the skin of humans. The final scene as Deckard and Batty fight across rooftops, culminating in the slow-motion death of Batty, is filled with examples of how Batty's skin replicates the human (bleeding, sweat, the traces of tears) through the closeups and lighting effects.

Lips

There are moments in film where lips are offered in such tight closeup that their discursive qualities are emphasised and demanded. These qualities include intimacy, secrecy, passion, and transgression. The whiskered lips of Kane in *Citizen Kane* as he whispers the words 'Rosebud' fill the screen, marking the moment between life and death. These are not sensual lips, but ones drawing a lonely breath for the last time. The lips of Michael Corleone in *The Godfather II* (Coppola 1974) also whisper death (as did his father in the first film), but this time the intimacy is one that also alienates and repulses through its loss of innocence. The lips of Lawrence in *Lawrence of Arabia* are blistered and cracked, not simply because they have been exposed to the desert heat, but because they represent, as much as Peter O'Toole's blue eyes and fair skin, the foreign West to the Arab world order. It is these lips, speaking the native language, that mark the similarities and the differences of cultures in terms of threat. It is the lips of Mia in *Pulp Fiction* which we experience first as they voice commands to a bewildered Vincent. These unkissed lips, as we witnessed before, are continually foregrounded as signifiers of threat. Recall the scene in the diner – it is her lips (and perhaps fingers) that control, demand, and threaten. This time the peril is located within social violence of organised crime and forbidden sexual desire. The unresolved debate as to whether it was a foot massage (the other end of the body to the lips and, supposedly, much less intimate) which led to the man being thrown out of a window, forms part of the cinematic libidinal economy, not simply because it is an integral part of certain narrative devices, but because it underlies the possibilities of violence, sexual desire, transgression, trust, and betrayal.

The Tongue

The tongue, like lips, combines the sexual and the speaking. This has been used in films in a number of different ways, and sometimes much of the whole libidinal economy is premised on a slip of the tongue. The Rabelaisian excesses of the alien in *Killer Tongue* (*La Lengua Asesina*) (Sciamma 1996) contains a sexualised discourse, as well as one on generic parody (of, for example, science fiction films of the 1950s, prison films and road movies of the 1970s, and perhaps even spaghetti westerns of the 1960s). The invading tongue in the woman's body is at first abhorrent, then assimilated, and finally loved. Its presence is only accepted once it begins to speak, for this is the moment it begins to be 'humanised', and then participates in the aims and desires of her. Part of this form operates at the level of cultural threat and difference; we find the same sorts of Hispanic *contra* white America politics played out on the body in *Perdita Durango* (de la Iglesia 1998) when gangster killer Romeo Dolorosa and Perdita plan to kidnap and torture two American teenagers. In such films the white bodies are represented as repressed (sexually, culturally, ideologically), whilst the Hispanic are overtly sexualised and unrestrained. This representation of the Hispanic is parodied somewhat in the films of Almodovar and, particularly in terms of the blindness of masculine desires, Bigas Lunas (for example, *Golden Balls* 1992). The loving lick of the alien against Ripley's skin (in a combination of child to mother, as well as lover to loved) is initially repulsive, as with the killer tongue. But it also sets up a relationship between Ripley and the aliens which combines a strange acceptance of their histories and needs for one another. By the time we arrive at *Alien Resurrection* there is a symbiotic relationship between mothering-obsessed Ripley (continually searching for child substitutes – the cat in the first film, the child in the second, having revealed she had lost a child years before) and the reproductively driven aliens. The tongue caress, and nuzzle, by the alien seems to present a logical conclusion for both their desires. Another inflection of the metaphoric use of tongues and speech is the betrayal of tongues in *The Name of the Rose* (Annaud 1986). The black tongues of the dead monks, as well as the long speeches (perhaps more true of the novel than the film), position tongues as central to the diegetic force of the film.

Fluids

In a scene in *Blood Simple* (Coen Bros. 1984), Ray, after discovering the murdered body of Marty in the office, starts to wipe up the pool of blood. The spectator is usually spared these sorts of acts – even *Pulp Fiction* does not go into great detail in the cleaning up of the car after the accidental shooting – but here we are confronted with what is the nightmare of such a task. The blood doesn't soak into the cloth very well. It spreads further and further across the smooth floor. The blood covers Ray as a guilty signifier, defying easy closure and concealment. The fluid here comes to define the scene as well as the whole narrative track, involving the spectator in every part of the operation, stopping us from making a clean and easy getaway. Spilt blood leads to more and more blood and acts of violence. It also defines the cinematic body, for it is the evidence of that body's presence, and it binds Ray's body to that of the murdered body. *Blood Simple* actually plays with these relationships, shifting truths about them in typically neo-*noir* style; so, the body turns out to be still alive (which in turn produces more nightmare scenes), the photographs of other 'dead' bodies turn out to be fake, and Viser, the detective, at the end turns out to be a case of mistaken identity. Fluids in these bodies, like the events themselves, are revealed to be insecure and unstable signifiers of what they seem to mean.

Apart from death and woundings, another of the dominant depictions of bodily fluids in cinema is the sexual − a dualism tied heavily to a Freudian backdrop of the sex drive and death drive. There are other examples of fluids: the extreme closeup of a saliva-dripping tongue as it licks a face in *Performance* (Roeg 1968), which signifies sexual freedom and an anarchic distance to cultural repression; the dripping nose of Bree Daniels in *Klute* (Pakula 1971) to signify fear; the dribbling mouth of James Cole as he hunches on the floor in *Twelve Monkeys* (Gilliam 1996) to signify madness; the sweating body in *Die Hard* to signify both masculinity and fear, as well as the purely physical. But such examples tend to be individual in style and intent, rather than what we find in the broader depiction of sexual fluids.[5]

Censorship denies the representation of these fluids in mainstream cinema, so they are posited there by implication.[6] In their absence these fluids come to define the body as something more dangerous, less socially controlled and controllable. Here is a bodily function deemed too shocking to be allowed in mainstream cinema, so it comes to be represented as the other, in much the same way blood was in film before the 1960s − a convention broken in the USA, significantly, by the rise of cult movies by small, independent film-makers in Hollywood. The filmic representations of such sexual fluids are more threatening to the social order because they show a beyondness to the body. They cross the boundaries between flesh, body and subject because they represent subjectivity through the acts of flesh, merging the two into a different type of body, that of the unrestrained.

The *Mise-en-Scène* of Flesh: The Cinematised Body

It is now time to focus more specifically on how the cinematic libidinal economy is formulated in terms of power and discourse. This is part of the spectacle of the body, which we can link to the body of the condemned. That is, it is held up not simply as a corporeal function, but rather as an identification of the institution of power and force over the body, and at the same time the body's potential to resist and disrupt these structures of power. In film the body becomes invested in a particular type of relationship to power and the formation of subjectivities. In this way we edge closer to considering when it is that the subject becomes a body, and how the body can be positioned as flesh. For it is in these configurations of power and force that so much of the sensibilities of the body are formulated and enacted.

The Body of the Condemned as Spectacle

In *Discipline and Punish*, Foucault (1987a) details the relationships between social institutions and the body, and how these relationships construct subjectivities and positionalities. A key part of this analysis is the idea of power, and as we are concerned here with the notion of a filmic discourse and its powers, it is worth recalling one of Foucault's key points about the nature of power: 'The exercise of power is not simply a relationship between partners, individuals or collective; it is a way in which certain actions modify others. Which is to say, of course, that something called Power ... which is assumed to exist universally or in a concentrated or diffused form, does not exist. Power exists only when it is put into action' (Foucault 1983: 219). (In such an interpretation we also witness a certain resonance with Lyotard's ideas of force and power.) The sorts of actions that Foucault has in mind are the ones he has previously analysed, including discourses of sexuality, madness, prisons, and medicine. Our concern here will be to consider how the body functions in film within the same terms of power that Foucault is articulating. In doing so we are confronted with two types of bodies − the body on the screen, and the body of the spectator. Rather than distinguish these two, the ensuing discussion will argue that they are inextricably linked in the formation and operation of the cinematic libidinal economy. Indeed this operation of the textual with the psychical (and corporeal) is precisely what this economy is all about. This link can be seen to be acted out within the domain of what Foucault called the political technology of the body, which is a knowledge of the body outside its functioning and a control beyond its subjection (Foucault 1987a: 26). The sorts of relationships that exist within the body on the screen and the body of the audience, as well as the cultural body (which we shall take up in a later chapter), and this political technology are in constant flux, determined by, and determining, power and knowledge. The cinematised body operates both within and beyond this political technology, offering compliance and resistance.

According to Foucault, the most effective use of the scaffold (or indeed any public display of punishment) was its status of the spectacle. It was the body on display that allowed the power structures to be manifested and reinforced within the social order. It was the visual display of the punishment that manifested the control of both body and soul of the people by the state. It was the spectacle in which the power was invested and maintained, rather than any specific torture or punishment. The body became the surface on which social control was played out, not simply in the torturing of it, but through an exerting restraint over its rights. The body became a property once it was incarcerated because it was restricted in its space and time. It was this line of thinking that brought Foucault to argue that the soul was the prison of the body (Foucault 1987a: 30) and to formulate the idea of power/knowledge, in which was also found the determination of truth.[7]

This model of the tortured, punished body held up for public display, determined through power and knowledge, has its equivalents in film. Cinema provides culture with a form of the spectacle of the body as it has been invested with these actions of power, truth and control. At one level, in order for the body to be filmed, and for that film to exist within the social order, there must be an assertion of power over the filmed body. (This is one of the ways in which the absence of sexual fluids, except in sexually explicit films, can be seen as an exertion of control over the body.) It is important to recognise, however, that this is not simply to say that the body, located within a filmic discourse, is rendered powerless and submissive; rather quite the opposite is the case. The cinematic spectacle of the body is ultimately an interplay between these conflicting positions of the 'tortured' and cultured body, and the polymorphic sites of bodily resistance. Film offers a continual outpouring of bodies that, in the desultorous manner, are manipulated and exploited, and yet also resist and subvert. It is the deconstruction of the power-knowledge structures that makes the spectacle of the filmic body so compulsive to watch. This is the case not just with those bodies that are excessive in their disposition (Ripley's powerful alien body in *Alien Resurrection*; Frankenstein's monster's body in both the Hammer versions and Branagh's film with its closer allegiance to Shelley's novel; the body of Nosferatu as it reflects a dark social unconscious) but those that operate within a more closely aligned cultured body. Bardot's body in *Et Dieu Créa la Femme* (Vadim 1956) is a highly phallocentric and phallocular one, yet it is this same quality that allows it to resist the cultural through a challenge to the moral structures of the social order – that is, it has excess only in, and because of, its gender and the ways in which that gender has been constructed. The closeup of luminous skin to signify feminine beauty (Ingrid Bergman in *Casablanca*; Greta Garbo in *Camille* (Cukor 1936)) would seem to be a form of film spectacle which demands so much of the body that it is tortured (too pale, too smooth, too readily demonstrative of pain), and there certainly is a level at which this is a product of the power structures of the phallocularised gaze. At the same time, however, this skin resists because it becomes more than human skin; it is an impossibility through its seamlessness. Or rather it is, in Lyotard's terms (via Liebnez), an *incompossibility* – the meeting of impossible worlds of perfect skin and harsh realities. So this single sign holds both the tortures of feminine beauty as well as a resistance to it. The character of Catherine's body in *Germinal* (Berri 1993) holds the same sorts of contradictions but in quite different ways. The feminine is constantly sublimated by the cinematic libidinal economy through the male miners and the viewer's own expectations. That there is no questioning that a woman should go down into the black, dangerous mines is never raised in the discourse; and yet when one of the men says that if she wants to be a worker she should remove her shirt like the men, even though the miners do not sexualise her body (or even draw attention to its difference), this is what the images themselves provoke.

Foucault's concern with the body and systems of punishment leads him to assert the following: 'the body is also directly involved in a political field; power relations have an immediate hold upon it; they invest it, mark it, train it, torture it, force it to carry out tasks, to perform ceremonies, to emit signs' (Foucault 1987a: 25). We can add to this list that cinema itself is part of these power relations – it *cinematises* the body by positioning it within specific structures, and in doing so participates in these processes such as investing the body with particular traits, training it to represent certain relationships, marking it with specific effects and meanings, and emphasising its signifying possibilities. These cinematised bodies are also producers of knowledge – of a knowledge about the body, and about other fields of knowledge. In order to understand better this idea of the cinematised body we can turn to some specific examples of the assertion of power over the body, and the body's resistance to these assertions, beginning with the altered body.

The cinematised body is necessarily altered, even if the actual operation of this is hidden. Indeed, altering the body functions ideologically in the same way that semiotics speaks of the transformation of what is cultural to appear 'natural'. Within what is defined as the most stripped field of intervention – the documentary – there is an altering of the body as it is preserved, positioned within a history, contained, juxtaposed (often with other bodies it has never encountered). In this sense we are dealing with the mechanics of the body in film, a rendering of it into a textual form which crosses all other modes of representation. However, more literally there is also the altering of the body as a theme, and although these two processes of the force of altering the body by filming it, and dealing with corporeal manipulation and change, may seldom (if ever) interconnect, the two are not as distanced from one another as may first appear. For it is this intersection of the body on film and the body in film that creates the cinematised body.

When dealt with as a theme, altering the body is often presented in terms of a threat or as more desirable, and so fits into a larger cinematic discourse on the body.[8] This threat originates from a number of different sources, of which two examples will be considered here: the altered body of desire; the body as political site.

The body can be altered in terms of its desiring functions in any number of ways: it can be made more desirable, as is evident in, for example, the female characters in musicals. The lead women in *My Fair Lady* (Cukor 1964), *Grease* (Kleiser 1978), and *Strictly Ballroom* (Lurhmann 1992) are all transformed into desired bodies. Or, in a different manner, when Orlando changes from male to female in *Orlando* (Potter 1993) the body is seen as more desirable by male characters. This may well seem like an obvious point, but what is significant is that this site of desire is actually stated – it becomes a point of relationships. Or the body can be made less desirable: Frankenstein's creation is the altered body, once desired, now abhorrent; *The Fly* (Neumann 1958; Cronenberg 1986) deals with similar issues of science-altered bodies. A totally different example is *Raging Bull* (Scorsese 1980) where the masculine body becomes firstly too violent (and then gone to waste) through its alterations. The body's socio-cultural status can be brought into question through altering the operations of its desires. *Some Like It Hot* (Wilder 1959) sets up such questions of gender and sexuality for both a number of its characters and audience; it can be posited as altered desire (*The Crying Game* (Jordan 1992) and *The Last Seduction* feature trans-sexuality as potential sites of desire which emphasise the alteration of the male body; *Kiss of the Spiderwoman* (Babenco 1985) traces desire as it shifts against gender and sexuality); it can be altered by desire that becomes an obsession (*Apocalypse Now* (Coppola 1979) relies on the altered body of Brando to physically demonstrate the force of an obsession; the *Godfather* cycle utilises physicality to signify obsessions); it can be an altered state of desire (*That Obscure Object of Desire* (Buñuel 1977) parodies masculine desire by constantly thwarting it, in part by making the desired body lack consistency).[9]

Clearly not all these categories, and the examples given, possess the quality of a threat; in fact some of the desires represented in these films rely precisely on the alteration of the body to create desire. However, desire itself becomes problematised in all these films (and clearly the list could be continued), often in a threatening way because the alterations take place at the level of the corporeal. In doing so the cinematised body reflects the challenges to the political technology of the body (even if it often exists *in potentia*). Even in those examples where the transformation of the body is seen as a triumph (notably, in these examples listed above, the musical) the issue of the desires of the body (as distinct from those for that body) is seldom resolved. The altered body is often presented in such films as satiated, but the body in the musical is caught up in a never-ending repetition of undesired bodies altered to desired ones, only to be picked up in the next cycle of musicals with the same sorts of transformations. This generically driven cinematisation of the body connects the films through transposition, and in doing so presents the body as unstable. Even musicals that are self-reflexive about their generic status, such as *New York, New York* (Scorsese 1977) and *All That Jazz* (Fosse 1979), contain elements of the altered body and threatening desires. In *All That Jazz*, for example, we find the desirable (altered) bodies of the dancers contrasted with Fosse's autobiographical character with his death-obsessed, pill-ridden, alcoholic body. The perfection of the dancers' bodies contributes to the threatened existence of this other body, somewhat ironically presented in terms of spiritual angst surrounded by very physical bodies.

Perhaps a much clearer example of the altered body as threatening desire is where the difference of the body is also that which is specifically desired. The *femme fatale* of film *noir* is a good example of this. It is not simply that these women are beautiful and highly desirable for the male characters, but that they are also a body from the city (their dress, make-up, movement, speech, hair all signifies the urban). It is this urban difference that often makes the body an altered one, and one that is desired. The inverse model of this can also work on the same principle; the body altered to be more located in nature becomes desired for that difference. *Cat People* (Tourneur 1942) does this quite literally, but other examples include *Sirens* (Duigan 1984) (which utilises Lindsey's painting style to depict the Bacchanalian women); the beach scene in *Dr No* (Young 1962) (which contrasts the civilised James Bond with a Botticelli rendering of Honeychild Rider); the forest scene in *Manon des sources* where Ugolin spies on Manon. That all of these examples are specifically women should not be too surprising given that within a phallocular dominated system examples of desired bodies from both culture and nature are often constructed from a masculine perspective. There are, of course, masculine equivalents, and we can find many examples in science fiction (such as *Terminator*) and action films. We still encounter the phallocular gaze, only this time it is directed at the male body as site of desire.

The altering of the body as a political site has been manifested in many ways. This type of process recalls much of Foucault's works on the prison, medicine and sexuality.[10] Two types will serve as examples for this manifestation of the cinematised body. The first example is the politically dispossessed body, which has an underlying premise that the body is always positioned in terms of a political history of ideas and conflicts. The most literal example is that series of films produced in the US in the 1950s (that is, the beginnings and developments of the Cold War), reflecting a cultural paranoia about communism. Films such as *Invasion of the Body Snatchers* (Siegel 1956), *Them* (Douglas 1954), and *I Married a Monster from Outer Space* (Fowler Jr. 1958) locate the ideological take-over not within the psychological, but in the physical. It is the foreign/alien force manifested in bodies which look the same that carries the greatest threat. The body is thus articulated as a double threat: it is the ultimate disguise if no differences can be detected; and it is seen as the weakest part of the human subject (contrasted with curious ideals about indomitable spirit and strength of mind!). This is subjectivity rendered as flesh, with the body becoming the ideological site of control.

A different sort of politicisation is with the classing of the body, notably the idea of working-class identities. The British director Mike Leigh demonstrates this in a number of his films, with *Naked* serving as a good example. Not only do we find the body as signifier of class (through accent, dress, or where it is located socially; its occupation is usually physical in nature, or often unemployed) but also it serves as a tableau of the destructive forces of the social order. The speech-impaired, limping, and bruised body of Sophie is a transformation of the body as class. In a similar way, the body is made abject through class and race in *Trainspotting* (Boyle 1996), only in this example the body is embedded in the antisocial processes of heroin and presented with ironic twists. Begby's vicious nature, manifested directly through his violent body, is never directly tracked back to class or racial issues (it is posited as psychotic behaviour), just as Spud's loss of bodily control in the bed (and then as the contents of the sheet are thrown over the room and people) is not directly linked to these sorts of reasons. Instead it is the voice-over of Renton which provides the link between the body and ideological contexts. His outburst on the Highlands, declaring that the English are 'wankers' but the Scots are worse because they were colonised by them, self-reflexively tracks the body into a political site. Similar comments can be made about positioning of the body in terms of race, with a subtext of the non-white body as other (that is, in this case, altered) to the white body. Spike Lee's films deliberate on this theme in depth, not simply in a binarism of black and white, but cross-cultural conflicts and differences. The riot in *Do the Right Thing* (Lee 1989) is motivated more particularly than between black and white, perhaps as closely as specific neighbourhood variations on the wider themes of black Americans and Italian-Americans.

The Perversions of the Cinematic Body

Another way in which these sorts of issues are played out is through the gendering of the body. Once more there are many ways in which this type of body altering has been dealt with, but to keep the range tight here the example of perversion will be considered. The perverse body, like all the bodies considered so far, is not simple to categorise. We cannot safely speak of a perversity which is inherent or stable – all depends on culture, history, code structures, acts of reading, psychic relationships, etc. Even the very notion of perversion is problematic, implying as it does a sense of the 'normal'. Freud, who has had such an enormous influence on how the twentieth century tackled such issues, points out that deviations from what a culture describes as normal, healthy sexual desires and activities are very common. He states: 'No healthy person. . .can fail to make some addition [to their sexuality] that might be called perverse to the normal sexual aim; and the universality of this finding is in itself enough to show how inappropriate it is to use the word perversion as a term of reproach' (Freud 1984: 74). This is how the term is employed here – totally without a sense of moral categorising or abhorrence. Instead, the emphasis is on that which is declared in the etymology of the term, to turn towards difference.

It is part of the cinematic libidinal economy to invest all cinematised bodies with the propensity for, if not actuality of, perversion.[11] The perverse body is produced at any number of different levels and forms, each one a variant or invention independent from, and yet interconnected to, a cultured notion of the perverse. If we narrow the field to perversion and gender, we are still left with a fluidity of form and interpretation, for theories such as psychoanalysis, queer theory, and feminism have all, in some ways, argued that it is the difference in gender that contributes to the production of ideas of perversion. That which is other (and othered) always retains the potential to be seen as perverse. Even within the gender divisions themselves there is a sensibility of the perverse; masculine discourse, for example, can readily produce a sense of the perverse masculine within itself and for itself.

Does this then leave us with a term so unstable as to be critically impossible? If perversion is so relatively defined how can use be made of it to determine something like the perverse body? Lacan offers some interesting points which will assist us in all this. Lacan, in keeping with his Freudian backdrop, negotiates perversion via the scopic drives – of seeing and being seen. He argues that it is not the drive that is perversion, but 'what defines perversion is precisely the way in which the subject is placed in it' (Lacan 1986: 181–2). The cinematic equivalent here is this positioning of the subject (either the subject on the screen or the viewing subject, or both) into a situation which is a beyond to the everyday, which becomes the perverse. At one level this is part of the aim/desire of watching films, which may sound very Foucauldian in intent. As Lacan argues, 'the pervert is he who, in short circuit, more directly than any other, succeeds in his aim, by integrating in the most profound way his function as subject with his existence as desire' (Lacan 1986: 206). It is the operation of the cinematic libidinal economy which allows the viewing subject to merge these qualities of subjectivity and desire. And yet still the question must arise as to whether such an operation covers all cinematic experiences, and if so, is the cinematic economy fundamentally one of perversion? The initial response is, of course, no, as the experience of cinema is far more heterogeneous. Yet, defined within Lacan's sense of desire, subjectivity, demand, and positionality, there is a sense of perversion through the exchange of phantasy for reality in watching a film that must run through the entire cinematic experience. This is not simply the morally or ethically perverse of a social order (such as the representation of gay love in a homophobic culture, or interracial love in an apartheid system), but the cinema's capacity to challenge reality by representing desire, and the viewing subject's psychic responses and interactions to this. Any apparatus (of which cinema is one) which can produce the sorts of effects that Lacan attributes to the perverse (desire as existence and function) operates within that paradigm, even if this is a broad spectrum. Given this, it is perhaps useful to once more attempt to distinguish between a representation of the perverse body, and this broader sense of the cinematised body as perverse in its relationship to the viewing subject (and, consequently, this subject's perversity in its relationship to the cinematised body).

This notion of the perverse body can be seen to be presented in many ways, the issue of gender being but one of many, even if it is a fundamental one. Certainly the cinema of Greenaway, Lynch and Cronenberg leap to mind as ones populated by the body made perverse. However, it is far too problematic to group these together – which illustrates the wider difficulties of ascribing a cinematic perversion which encompasses all variants and forms. Greenaway's *The Cook, The Thief, His Wife, and Her Lover* (1989), Lynch's *Blue Velvet* and Cronenberg's *Crash* (1997) all evoke notions of culturally defined perversions, often played out through the body. All three films link eroticism with violence, positioning those characters (the thief in *The Cook*, Frank in *Blue Velvet* and perhaps all the main characters in *Crash*, but certainly James and Catherine Ballard) as sexually perverse. Yet at the same time, all the films rely on the device of voyeurism and seduction to link what the spectator is doing to what is happening in the films. This is also found, at another level, in *Rear Window*, for the perversion across the courtyard inverts and parallels the perversions of the bodies and relationship between Jeff and Lisa. Their scopic drive, and panoptic position, draws them into more perversions, which they themselves acknowledge. They find themselves willing a murder to have taken place, demonstrating disappointment when they seem to be wrong.

The lovers in all these examples are all watched and become watchers – that is to say, they occupy the liminal site of recognising the perverse sexuality and gendering of the Other, but then become part of it. This is in keeping with Freud's point that the one force which directly opposes scopophilia is shame (see, for example, Freud 1977: 69–70). However, it is this post-voyeuristic relationship that redefines the character's propensity to the perverse. The characters in *Crash* are destined to continue to play out the perversities until the inevitable end; Jeff, in *Blue Velvet*, attempts to return to a normality, but this is presented as another form of perversion (one of a hyper-real suburbia); the lovers James and Catherine close *Crash* with the words of 'Perhaps next time'. This sense of a cycle is perhaps more heavily inscribed into the relationship of perversity and subject's sexuality and gender than may first appear to be the case. There is a resistance to closure because the body itself cannot find stasis (literally death, but there are a great many other variants). Even in a situation where such a 'return' should be impossible through a lack of desire, the insertion of the abject, and a type of cultural/historical abhorrence – such as that of the Jewish woman from a concentration camp and the Nazi guard, in Cavani's *The Night Porter* (1974) – the compulsion to repeat seems impossible to deny.

These orders – the political body and the body of desire – illustrate Foucault's points regarding the panopticon and the watched body.[12] This is the body as it is displayed, but it is also the play of power over the body. As Foucault puts it: 'Power has its principle not so much in a person as in a certain concerted distribution of bodies, surfaces, lights, gazes; in an arrangement whose internal mechanisms produce the relation in which individuals are caught up' (Foucault 1987a: 202). This panoptic effect can work in three different ways in cinema: it can be represented within the film itself (the systems of surveillance, the sense of being watched – nothing can be hidden from the camera after all); this can lead to the cinema forming part of the panoptic effect for the spectator (the sense that the film being watched is actually watching you through its representations, as well as its techniques); and cinema can work against the panoptic effect, either by exposing it (so once we become aware of panopticism we can resist it) or operating at a subversive level to it. Within all of this is the body, resisting or complying, subverting or being contained. Its movements from flesh to body to subject, and back again, are filled with the potential of resistance and compliance. And each body on the screen holds all these qualities at the same time.

Kristeva (1982) speaks of the *corps propre* (one's clean and proper body) and abjection in a detailed analysis of the operation of the body and mind, and their textual and cultural significations. What we find in all these examples of the cinematic body is an interplay between the idealism of the *corps propre* as it is positioned as part of the Symbolic order and its cinematic representations, and the body which must take in the impurities, including those of vision. This is not simply a case of the body on the screen compared to the body of the spectator, but more a process involving the Symbolic ordering of the body and the corporeal and psychical interventions on that. Both the politicised body and the body of desire attain that particular status because they represent bodies which have been transformed from some sense of the *corps propre* into a type of corporeality. In this way they are further inflections of the wider process of the cinematising of the body itself. The culmination of this in cinema is that we can speak of a corporeality of the filmic discourse. Film is driven in, by and through the body. Not a simple body, but one that resists and demands, is socialised and resists any social conformity, is disempowered and subversively all powerful. It is a discourse of corporeality which is constituted of flesh, body, and subject, and in turn comes to constitute them. Cinema's relationship to the body is much more like the operation of the symptom as it manifests disguised signs as marks on the corporeal.[13] Cinema's discourse is the discourse of the body.

5

The Ideology of Love: Film and Culture

That cinema is a cultural phenomenon is beyond dispute, but what do we mean when we say such a thing? What is meant by the assertion that a film is produced by, read in, and gains meaning from, its cultural postionings? There has been a wide and diverse range of film theories that have attempted to deal with these sorts of issues. These include: theories devised out of a Marxist tradition, where the emphasis is on the ideological processes in different aspects of film; feminist film theory, where the emphasis is on the formations and explorations of gender, sexuality, and power; and certain psychoanalytic approaches to the film text, which see a melding of different influences, including, for example, Althusser's blending of Marxist philosophy and Lacanian theory, and Kristeva's intellectual lineage of psychoanalysis, feminism and cultural theory. The complexity of the issues involved, and the diversity of approaches, makes summary neither practical nor desirable. Instead the focus here (and in the following chapter) will be on some possibilities for locating cinema within cultural contexts and processes. To this end the following discussion will focus on a particular example – that of love – in order to work through some of the ideas on cinema and culture. The issue will be how cinematic formations of love can be analysed to interpret relationships between film and cultural contexts. This, in turn , will allow us to consider how certain critical movements argue for a type of intertextual exchange between culture and text.

Cinema and Its Discontents

At one level what is to be argued here is that particular relationships which exist within cinema and cultures are motivated, and organised, by a type of discontent. This is a discontent that is fecund and vibrant, an unsettling relationship based on slippage and challenge, where film's cultural underpinning can be seen as a seismic one. This is so because the operation of ideological and cultural processes is also the formation of subjectivities and subject positions. At the very least, the heterogeneity of the film and its spectators ensures this. Part of cinema has always had this function of problematising, of foregrounding difficult issues, of questioning, of allowing, sometimes even forcing, its audience to look at situations (histories, cultures, attitudes) differently. Even within the most 'conservative' examples we can find moments of this cultural discontent. This is not to say that all films question the cultural order, or that they attempt to erode the ideological frames in which they are produced and/or are read. Films have been as sexist, racist, misogynistic, politically biased, etc. as any other cultural production. Therefore they can conform to, and confirm, the dominant ideological paradigms. But rather than focus on those moments of film that attempt to settle into the major ideological contexts in which they are produced and/or read, the concern here will be how film (and the film viewer) problematises such contexts, working at the level of discontent. This discontent operates not necessarily within the politics of the film, but in the gestures of the spectator as he/she engages with the film.

Much of the theory that attempts to position texts within social, historical, and ideological contexts does so from one of three broad paradigms, or combinations of them, producing different theories on the social realities of the text. (This is perilously close to over-generalisation and is intended as summation and backdrop rather than a model that is deeply accurate.) The first type examines the production of the text within socio-cultural and ideological contexts. This includes the classic Marxist idea of base and superstructure, with the base being the economic conditions of production, and the superstructure the manifestations of the culture (including texts) and its ideological dimensions. The most obvious difficulty with this approach is that it has an inherent implication of reflection between the two structures, and argues that we can determine ideological operations and reflections as they are apparent in the film. The two dominant issues of interpretation in this sense are that the superstructure emerges from the base structure; and that analysis needs to be directed at the influence of the superstructure on the formation and function of the base structure. Another conceptual aspect of this approach is the relationship between texts and history, drawing on the conflict-based model of the dialectical process. The second type deals with the interplay between texts and social order, with each affecting the other in different ways. This is the ideological and revolutionary force of the texts themselves as they resist, alter and challenge the ideological contexts. The writings of Pierre Macherey are a good example of this, in which he argues that art has the capacity to expose and criticise ideological systems. An example of this is the text's capacity to analyse and foreground processes such as reification (Marx's idea that relationships between people can be constructed in terms of the objectification of the subject, so leading to alienation). The third type is really a conflation of different theories, not homogeneous in either style or direction. This would include feminist theory as it analyses the politics of gender, postcolonialism and its critique of cultural politics (such as in Edward Said), the combinations of Marxist theory and psycho-analysis (such as in Althusser and Homi Bhabha), and Kristeva's analysis of culture in a blend of ideological analysis and the formations of the subject, the analysis of language systems in terms of their ideological effects, etc. In short, this third paradigm is concerned with the complex network of relationships between culture, ideology, and the subject as active (as well as passive) social agent.

In order to better understand how we might approach the idea of film and its relationship to culture, as well as the operation of concepts such as ideology, power, and the role of the spectator, we shall now turn to love. This is not an attempt to resolve the myriad complexities of these concepts in the analysis of film; rather it is an example in which we witness different sorts of cultural forces coming into play. The creation and function of the cinematic sign of love can reveal much about the theoretical concepts, and how film operates within cultural contexts.

On Love

Love is one of the primary processes of cinema, not just at the level of repre-sentation (of which it occupies a central role in a great many films), but also as a type of cinematic drive which in turn produces an amatory econ-omy (as distinct from say the libidinal economy of Lyotard). It is precisely this amatory economy – this drive in, through and by cinematic love – that forms a key domain in film's cultural contexts and processes. In other words, that cinema deals with, and constantly returns to, love locates it as part of a cultural order. In this relationship film contributes to (through participation, challenges to, reformulating) a culture's discourses of love. This idea of the amatory economy will help us remain close to the central issue of cinema's cultural functions, while allowing a discussion of how film produces a type of discourse within this larger order. Furthermore, this sec-tion will be concerned not simply with the representation of love, but also how love can be seen as a metaphor for cinematic epistemologies. To this end the motifs we will consider are the kiss and true love. Before we turn to these, however, a further comment is needed on the idea of the cinematic drive in these terms of love and culture.

The Amatory Drive

The drive, as we have observed elsewhere, is what psychoanalysis describes as a primary process in the operation of the unconscious, as well as the formulation of the subject. It performs this second function particularly through the formation of certain relationships between the unconscious and conscious, as well as between the subject and his/her existence in the Symbolic order (that is, in effect culture). To argue that there might be something called the cinematic drive is tied up with all these issues; at one level it is part of the operation of the cinematic apparatus as it manages, performs, and produces narrative effects. That is to say, the cinematic drive is the force which binds the different aspects of film together as they move towards certain points of representation and meaning. A simple example of this is how lighting, sound, camera angles, and character dialogue are brought together in the cinematic drive towards a certain diegetic construction or interpretative point. At another level we can speak of the cinematic drive performing those qualities of desire, in which we find the space where spectator and film meet.

The cinematic drive can be split into two primary strands, with variations stemming from each of these. The first is what we shall designate as the semiotic drive, which contains within it the properties of film the spectator draws on to make meanings, construct intertextual and transpositional connections, understand code structures, etc. The semiotic drive in cinema is heavily invested in the whole set of film elements that are produced in the film and in the watching of it. It is important to note that this drive is not simply the film and its constitutive elements (such as the narrative processes), but also includes the act of constructing the spectating position. The second drive is even more firmly located in these performances, but derived this time from the act of spectating – that is, from the spectator himself/herself. To distinguish this from the sorts of drives that psychoanalysis designates as the scopic, we shall refer to it here as the *spectral* drive. This contains all those attributes and qualities of the spectating position, including the sexual drives, the body of the film spectator, the cultural order of the spectator, etc.

The movement of the drive, for Lacan, is always one of outwards from the source (subject or film here) and then back. Lacan (1986: 178) constructs the following diagram to illustrate this; next to it is a modified version which positions cinema and spectator within the model (see Figure 5.1).

What these diagrams show is the ways in which the drives move out from, and then return to, the (cinematic) rim. This presents us with a number of issues, not the least being how different aims are fulfilled, or merged, through this action. The arching loop, which represents the drives of the spectator and the cinematic, is what we as spectators do with the elements of a film as we watch it; as well as what those elements do to us. There is always a return back to the rim of film/culture because no matter how divergent these drives of the spectator are, they are ultimately always grounded within the representations and devices of the film and its cultural

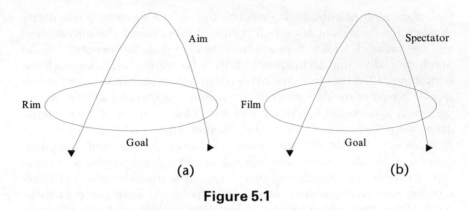

Figure 5.1

contexts and production. This loop, then, is the movement of the cinematic drive in conjunction with the drives of the spectating subject (and so necessarily contains both the scopic and spectral drives) as they come to form the act of spectating.[1] All of this is shaped and determined in various ways by the cultural basis to which it returns. One final point on this, and then we can begin to locate some of this material within some specific examples.

Lacan's emphasis on the scopic drive – which, as we have noted, is integral to this model – is that it is motivated by desire. Its awareness is derived from the introduction of the Other, transforming the scopic into the voyeuristic, which in turn ties it to pleasure. In other words, the scopic drive, through this attribute of pleasure, comes to formulate the subject itself; subjectivity becomes defined through the drive. One aspect of this which is of particular interest here is what this scopic drive is attempting to achieve. As Lacan puts it: 'What the voyeur is looking for and finds is merely a shadow, a shadow behind the curtain. There he will phantasize any magic of presence' (Lacan 1986: 182). This is very much a description that can be applied to cinema. The images presented are shadows which become invested with different properties by the spectator. This is an issue to which we shall return in a later chapter; for the moment we shall turn our attention to love and, to commence, with the kiss.

The Kiss

The kiss operates as a declarative sign of love, and as such should enjoy a certain stability. The kiss, after all, functions to confirm love, to show love, to signify love. Yet, in all of these operations and declarations, the kiss also has a 'darker' side; for every cinematic kiss that closes the film and signifies 'love' (or more a notion of true love, as discussed below), there are other kisses which destabilise perceptions and knowledges, run counter to the epistemes of the text, and challenge the character's and our own capacity as readers to generate certainty and meaning. Herein lies the operation of the cinematic kiss, for it is at the same time both absolutely certain and fixed, and always uncertain and fluid. To some extent this is a generically determined reading process. The kiss in *film noir* is destabilising and dangerous, and the spectator recognises this function, moving it from a signification of love, to one of seduction and betrayal;[2] just as the kiss in the Romance genre often carries with it a sense of confirming love. Yet in both these genres the kiss brings with it an instability of certain knowledges (about events within the film, about love, about the meaning of the kiss itself) that has been challenged. The kiss in *Double Indemnity* (Wilder 1944) between Walter Neff and Phyllis Dietrichson would seem to have, as its underlying intent, deception and power, and yet the spectator is encouraged to read it otherwise, as having some quality of (romantic) love attached to it. Similarly any kiss between Cathy and Heathcliff, in all the film versions of *Wuthering Heights*, or between Rick and Ilsa in *Casablanca*, are read not simply as a confirming of love, but a reminder of the problems that such a love contains. So it is with the kiss between Finn and Sam at the end of *How to Make an American Quilt* (Moorhouse 1995); it comes just prior to Finn's voice-over about her doubts and certainties of marriage, signalling both her return to the relationship and a sense of awareness about what might be involved. This kiss is marked against the one that does not take place between her and Leon in the truck in the fields. This absence of a kiss which signifies, essentially, a disruption of the romantic ideal of love (and a connotative value of disregarding the conservatism of tradition and marriage – in short, the irresponsible kiss of passion against the expected kiss of marriage) allows the other kiss to confirm her love for one man and not the other, yet there is still the undercurrent of ambiguity. Such polysemic readings and dangers are sometimes integral to the narrative itself (such as in *noir* and romance films), and this difficulty of reading the kiss becomes part of its attraction. The fatal love in, for example, *The Grifters* (Frears 1990) and *Prizzi's Honour* (Huston 1985) is continually posited as part of the relationship between the characters – and the kiss reminds us and them of this, rather than usurping it.

What this suggests is nothing especially surprising, for the kiss is notoriously difficult to understand, and even more difficult to fix with any certainty. For a signifier that is supposed to confirm, the kiss is fundamentally unstable in its meaning structures. This instability is part of its function both narratively speaking and in terms of the spectator's relationship to his/her cultural contexts. The signifier of the kiss almost invariably leads elsewhere, always towards another set of connotations and events. This is why something like the kiss provides us with an insight into how certain cinematic epistemologies operate within cultural contexts. How, for instance, does the spectator make sense of cinematic signs, and how does he/she cope with their instabilities? This quality of instability is derived from at least three sources that can be illustrated through the kiss: the resistance to knowledge; the kiss as *différance*; the drive towards resolution.

The kiss operates outside of knowledge, no matter how carefully it has been mapped and coded. Even though popular culture abounds with notions that the kiss confirms or denies love, and it is to the kiss that the lover most often refers as a defining moment of love, there is always an underlying insecurity on the part of the lover (and spectator) in his/her capabilities to actually understand the kiss. Part of this is contextual, for the diegetic and extra-diegetic elements contribute to the instability as much as they might confirm any interpretations. It is also to do with the cultural construction of the kiss as a sign that extends beyond its own parameters. This is especially true of those moments in film where the act of kissing is foregrounded as a defining moment of subjectivities and cultural orders/ideologies. Some examples will help illustrate this.

One type of the foregrounded kiss is where the character(s) are being redefined in their subjectivities and the kiss marks the moment of transgression and/or metamorphosis. This often takes place in films dealing with a character's questioning of his/her sexuality. *When Night is Falling* (Rozema 1995) invests the kiss with both resolution and further ambiguities, for it is the initially tenuous kiss between the two women that suggests that Camille, the conservative professor of Calvinist religion, is beginning to acknowledge her own decisions about her subjectivity defined through sexuality. As is often the case in such scenarios, with any sense of resolution there are also further ambiguities and questionings. Compare similar kisses in, for example, *Lianna* (Sayles 1983), *Desert Heart* (Deitch 1985), *Personal Best* (Towne 1982), *My Beautiful Laundrette* (Frears 1985), *The Hunger* (Scott 1983), where the instability of the redefining subjectivities is manifested in the kiss itself. In all these cases the pursuit of some sense of knowledge about the self (and the formation of the subject position) is channelled into a need/desire to confirm sexuality. This is almost invariably located within a conflict between the subject's sense of the self, and the cultural order of sexuality and morality. However, the kiss actually destabilises, creating further issues to be dealt with. These are kisses that necessarily disquiet and unsettle.

Part of the reason this takes place is that so much is invested into a single moment – the kiss on the screen becomes a synecdoche of nothing less than a redefining of what that subject's relationship to himself/herself and the cultural order is. In this we witness further the relationship between the filmic kiss and culture. Most, if not all, such kisses are problematic to the character because he/she must reflect on the cultural ramifications of the changes that such a kiss signifies. The kiss between Camille and Petra in *When Night is Falling* symbolises a turning away from heterosexuality, marriage, and a Christian morality; the kiss between Johnny and Omar in *My Beautiful Laundrette* is a resistance to the ethics of the Anglo-Indian community as well as the type of masculinity enforced in the violent world of gangs; the kiss between Vivienne and Cay in *Desert Hearts* involves giving up the security of a socially respected teaching profession; the incestuous kiss in *Close My Eyes* (Poliakoff 1991) signals the willingness and knowledge of brother and sister that they will transgress the social edicts. All of these films declare their social agenda, so can the same be said of something like the kiss between Deneuve and Sarandon in *The Hunger* which operates more firmly in the genre of vampire and fantasy, so that the social agendas are much less overt? At one level the difference is invested in narrative ramifications (if the character does this, then he/she will be radically changed in the social status of themselves and in relation to others) as distinct from the same sorts of actions taking place in different cultural contexts. However, the kiss still carries the connotative values of a resistance to knowledge, as well as an investment in a certain type of knowledge of the self-reflexive subject, and instability whether it is located in a form of social realism or the fantastic. All of this, in turn, positions the spectator in an interesting site of hypocrisis, formulating certain knowledges and questioning others.

Such kisses (and it is noteworthy that all these examples are concerned with a gay and lesbian theme) also demonstrate the operation of *différance*. Clearly the attribute that distinguishes these kisses is difference, in this case the difference of same gender (other examples might include race and class, which is the case with *My Beautiful Laundrette*). The act of the kiss is not different in itself (still lips and tongues coming together), and often its representation, although emphasised (through extreme closeups or slow motion), is not different. Nor should we take the easy route and say that the difference is in the fact that it is two men or two women that are kissing. The difference of the *différance* in such kisses is invested in the transformation of subjectivities as they are located within cultural contexts. This is what makes these kisses distinct from those emphasising the sexual, such as *Bound* (Warchowski Bros. 1996), where the difference of the subject in his/her cultural context is often absent, replaced instead with an investment in the erotic.

The other part of *différance* in this equation is the deferral of any resolutions of both sexuality and love. The first kiss, foregrounded and isolated, usually marks a crisis point that defers any sense of confirming pleasure or security. Instead we often find guilt and an emphasis on a sense of transgression. This deferral operates within the cultural contexts of both the filmic order and the wider diegetic orders of production and reception. The kiss as cinematic signifier is particularly good at playing this role, for in every moment when it declares love as unbounded and never-ending, there is an equal force which problematises and stretches beyond the act and into an unknown future. In such cases the kiss cannot resolve, it can only make promises, some of which are never fulfilled. This is the kiss as it defers meanings, constantly leading to points as yet unseen or negotiated. The idea of the temporal nature of the kiss illustrates this. At what point do we acknowledge that the kiss has taken place? In the anticipation (and where does this start? When the characters first meet? When they acknowledge each other? In the moment before physical contact is made? Or even within the generic field which provides the initial frame of interpretation?); in the actual contact of skin on skin; in the after-effects as they shape the future of the lovers? Similarly, the power structures of the kiss create ambiguities and questions. How does one distinguish between the kissing and the kissed? Is there a sense of gift, submission, power, or control? Such questions shape the future relationships, as well as the redefining of the subject positions of the characters and the spectators.

Another factor in the *différance* of the kiss is that culturally (and by this is also implied cinematically) the kiss is used to connote change. It is often positioned as a catalyst, driving the amatory economy, the characters and diegetic formations into new orders. Such kisses signify an alteration in the social order as well as the character's own subjectivity, for nothing remains the same afterwards. It is more than acknowledging love or passion, it is a point of transition which will often mark a transgression of the social order (and consequently often discontent). When Vincent, in the scene in *Pulp Fiction* where he stands looking at himself in the mirror of Mia's bathroom, states that he is involved in a moral dilemma he cannot mean the morality of the social order which provides and maintains the law – for that is a moral code long since abandoned by him. He must instead be referring to that same moral and ethical code system that opens the film; is it morally correct to have someone thrown out of a window because of a possible or potential sexual indiscretion? Vincent is more concerned with his own moral structures – and preservation of life – than what the cultural order may determine as acceptable. In terms of the model of the drive referred to earlier, Vincent's return through the arc of the loop is away from those ethics he sets himself, and then back again. Interestingly, this is quite a different trajectory to what we see operating in Jules, whose action of the loop is determined by the spiritual revelation of being saved from the bullets. His drive is firstly outwards in an antimonial fashion, and then back towards a culturally sanctioned life. Vincent, in this moment in front of the mirror, is engaging in a moral code that exists extropically. This is the ethics that Lacan speaks of when he states: 'Moral action is grafted on to the real. It introduces something new into the real and thereby opens a path in which the point of our presence is legitimised' (Lacan 1992: 21).

The moral reflections of Vincent at this point reveal the process of the grafting on to the Real because it is the only time we witness any sense of moral deliberation by him – and it is a deliberation centred initially, and finally, on the kiss. For all the other times he is seemingly devoid of any moral direction.

The absence of a passionate kiss between Vincent and Mia is significant because it marks a particular inflection of their relationship. (The closest they come to a kiss is the one blown to Mia by Vincent, and even then her back is turned.) On the one hand it signifies a diachronic moment – that they have not yet reached (and possibly never will reach) the confession of love. It can also be seen to be acting in a synecdochic fashion, indicating the type of relationship they are engaged in. In one sense conservative social codes indicate that the kissless relationship is not romantic, and therefore either platonic or invested more in lust than love. It also gives us an avenue back to the qualities of *noir* cinema, which *Pulp Fiction* seems to play with.

Within the generic structure of *noir* cinema, with its convolutions of morality and ethics and its constant playing with ambiguities and gender politics, *Pulp Fiction* picks up these ideas and caresses them along. Vincent is the killer, the efficient and dependable agent of violence. For him death is not the issue, it is simply the following and enacting of a system of law. Witness when the gun accidentally goes off in the car, killing the teenage boy in the back seat. There is no shock for him, no disbelief that a relative innocent has just been brutally slain. The death is meaningless – it is a pulp fiction death. In *noir* death does have a meaning – often the entire sequence of events and character interrelationships is based around a death or the possibility of one – yet the meaning exists outside of that death. It is, as far as the death itself goes, just as meaningless. The killing is only ever invested with meaning through the supplements of morality, passion, and gender. This is also why the kiss is such a volatile signifier in this genre. Because so much is invested in mistrust (to double dealings bound, as Shakespeare put it), then the ambiguity of the kiss makes it the almost perfect *noir* signifier. The effects of this – the ambiguities, the emphasis on misreadings, the divergences of the loop in the drive – on the spectator, and the broader notion of the cultural order of reception, is part of the positionality of love and its discourses in the relationship between film and culture. Another point where this takes place is the cultural idea of true love.

True Love/Breathless Love

The cultural construction and attitude towards a concept such as true love, and film's role in such matters, are part of the wider cultural discourse on love specifically, and the relationships between film and culture. Film has become one of the dominant textual forms in presenting a cultural discourse of love as it constantly performs, creates, and deliberates on acts of love. The idea of true love serves here to illustrate further such relationships between a cultural paradigm and its textual manifestations. The 'true', 'truth', etc. are difficult and complex enough in themselves, but when they are combined with something as equally complex as love, the difficulties are only increased. For the construction of 'true love' seems to be initially motivated by a need or desire to resolve a certain type of feeling – a love greater than other forms, because it is true. But the contiguity of the terms more often than not actually draws attention to the problematic nature of both 'true' and 'love'.

As with the kiss, true love is supposed to confirm the existence, direction, and function of the amatory economy, place events and people within a frame of reference that is constant and discernible, operating, as it does, through cultural constructions. Yet there are always elements of instability and slippage that make its very status problematic. Textually speaking this is not unique to cinema, having a long tradition in other textual forms. Two issues that perhaps make cinema different are its fundamental position in the formation and representation of love in culture, and that it has developed at a time when there has been a fundamental questioning of notions of truth and meaning. Truth, as Lacan says, 'is a word of ill repute, a word banished from polite society' (Lacan 1985: 120), which is certainly a reflection on the modernist/postmodernist and poststructuralist philosophies of the twentieth century. Cinema accommodates and contributes to the amatory discourses because of its position (as popular, as 'art', as diverse, etc.) in culture, which includes the performance of love and the deconstruction of it. The configuration of true love is often one read in reverse – that it is the love part that confirms the sense of 'true' – rather than what might at first appear to be the case. This has certain cultural and ideological implications, for in this sense truth is confirmed through the amatory economy.

Another part of the equation of the cultural construction of true love is sacrifice, and it is the depth of that willingness to surrender that which is most desired – often the love itself – which demonstrates love. This again is part of the generic formation of high Romance, and its durability is due in no small part to the cathexis of emotions involved. To illustrate this we can consider how a film such as *Casablanca* constructs, and draws on, the idea of true love in order to formulate specific cultural positions and interpretations, for it is very much a text located within the long tradition of high Romance.

Casablanca sets up the need for sacrifice from its very opening moments, even if the desire for it comes later. The stasis of the city, of the world, is what defines every action and every character. It is only through some form of sacrifice that changes can be brought into this world order. There are at least five manifestations of this romantic notion of love as sacrifice: (i) the sacrifice of one's personal feelings of love for love; (ii) the personal sacrifice for world peace; (iii) the sacrifice of history and the past for the future, as well as a sacrifice of certain choices for the future; (iv) the sacrifice of truth (Rick's obvious lie of 'She doesn't love me' is still such a sacrifice, even if it is acknowledged as false); (v) the sacrifice of desire for love. The sorts of demands made within this order of sacrifice is a classic romantic agenda – of the individual for the other, which includes another person, group of people, social order, or ideal. In short, the sacrifices are directed primarily towards a cultural order outside of the self. In *Casablanca* the sacrifices are seen in terms of the world community.

To read this underlying ideological current of the social order that requires sacrifice through love we can turn to Kristeva. Part of her (philosophical) concerns are for an interpretation of Hegel's and Heidegger's notions of *cura*, or care, and how this operates in the formation of the social subject. We can note that the representation of these forms of love in films such as *Casablanca* (that is, high Romance) is a manifestation of *cura*, as well as a demonstration of cinema's contribution to this in the social order. In other words, by representing care as a social need, films also participate in the social construction of this ideology. *Cura* is the 'basis on which *every* interpretation of *Dasein* [Heidegger's term for Beingness] which is ontic and belongs to the world order' (Kristeva 1984b: 128). This is precisely the sense we find in *Casablanca* – each character's sense of worth and beingness comes to be invested in their capacity to demonstrate *cura*, which is sharply contrasted with the Nazi (and Vichy) ideology.

We can trace the manifestation of the ideology of care even further by considering another passage from Kristeva: 'Care is the repression of social practice as *objective* practice, and its replacement by the resigned expectation of a meaning – social or transcendental – always anticipated, never attained ... The subject then attributes meaning to the world, which he thereafter considers a corollary to himself, a kind of system of signification' (Kristeva 1984b: 130). This is the ideology of love in *Casablanca*. Taking each point in terms of the film, we see:

The repression of social practice The social practice is always subjective due to the repression of the idea of the objective, for each character intervenes in the social world order through their acts of love and sacrifice. It is the personal, subjective intervention that challenges the abject ideology of Nazism.

The resigned expectation of meaning Each character is resigned to an expectation of meaning – indeed, each act of love is seen as a socialised form of meaning. Love is used to make sense of the world; it is contrasted with the meaningless, unchanging world of Casablanca. (It is also noteworthy that Kristeva's 'expectation of meaning' involves a sense of the temporal – something Casablanca lacks until love as *cura* is invested in it.)

Social and transcendental acts   Meaning through love's sacrifice in *Casablanca* is both social and transcendental. The actions of Rick, Ilsa, and Victor all involve a combination of social and transcendental meanings (and we can add the final acts of Captain Renault to this list as well). This means that the (romantic/sexual) love for the other becomes the love for freedom, peace, noble ideals, and virtue through the enacting of sacrifice, which is *cura*. This, in turn, is fed back into the love for the other in a cycle typical of romance ideology. But such a cycle means that, just as Kristeva points out, the meaning is never attained. The actions of love and *cura*, through these personal sacrifices, are what allow meaning to be attributed to the world, which is then part of the self. In *Casablanca* this is demonstrated by the world order becoming meaningful to Rick only after he asserts his sense of *cura*. This is also what Marxist theory sees as the anchoring of the subject to the mechanisms of the State. It is Rick's *cura* (which here comes to stand for both sacrifice and love) that relocates him back into the ideology of the cultural order – an action we witnessed in the same manner (but with quite different qualities) with the loop of the drive of Jules in *Pulp Fiction*.

The choices presented to Rick, in particular, revolve around the romantic and the political/ideological. He can have one or the other, but not both. Somewhat ironically, the fact that he chooses the political over the romantic ends up repositioning him as a romantic hero within the wider cultural order; the character becomes an icon of the romantic hero in Classical Hollywood cinema. It would seem that at one level Ilsa, as a woman, is denied such choice; it is men who make decisions about world politics, ideological struggles, and even love. This is overtly stated in the scene where she tells Rick to think for both of them. She seems to be placed as an antithetical companion to politics, caught between the desiring gaze of two men – one an empty moraliser, the other an impotent father. At another level (or perhaps more accurately from a different interpretative stance) she is a much more active agent than either of the two men, again through this ideology of *cura*. It is she who exerts power over them, possessing far more knowledge (about the men and the past) than either of them. She is also far more causal than the men, offering a sense of action within a social order seen largely as deterministic. Compared to the narcissistic musings of the men, she is the one who allows a manifestation of *cura* to take place. The centrality of her in terms of the exchange of the two letters reveals this.

The exchange of letters is based on a system of power and knowledge, gift and denial. The control of the letters becomes part of the manifestation of *cura*. For as each letter is given and then denied, denied then given, there

is a demonstration of sacrifice which is directly tied to the social construction of love. Each of these acts is motivated through love, just as each one
becomes more than its initial signifier of escape. And central to all these
exchanges is Ilsa.

The sense of the gift in *Casablanca* is a common feature in romance, and
this film interweaves the other ideologies into this signifier so that it
becomes part of the scenario of sacrifice and love. It is worth comparing it
to another film that utilises this structure only to undermine it. In *Manon
des sources* there is a series of ritualistic gift givings, some intended as love,
others interpreted that way. The circle involves three characters: Manon,
Ugolin, and the teacher. Ugolin leaves birds in Manon's traps to signify his
love – a series of gifts that become undone when he clumsily declares
his love through the prompting of his uncle. Manon gives the lost knife
back to the teacher, which is a gift to show her interest in him; and he
gives it back, which is a gift exchange that Ugolin observes and becomes
distressed over. The final gift is one that is not intended, and becomes a
signifier of Ugolin's madness. Manon's hair ribbon is found by Ugolin
and then sewn on to his breast in a scene that is eerily silent and visually
disturbing. These gifts are not of the same order of sacrifice that are postu-
lated in *Casablanca*, yet they come to signify the same sorts of love. *Cura* finds
no ready place in these loves, in part because the entire narrative is centred
on a culturally corrupted order. The village, including Manon, are still
living the consequences of the events portrayed in earlier years (and
shown in the earlier film, *Jean de Florette* (Berri 1986)). The water Manon
gives to the village is part of this system, and yet is also the one real manifestation of *cura*. For this reason it is the gift which locates her back in the
social order, giving, as noted in Kristeva earlier, meaning to the world
order, as well as making it a corollary to the self. The initial images of
Manon as a wild, primitive and ethereal spirit, unable or unwilling to
engage in speech, give way to the socially inscribed repositioning of her
(through dress, language, and the adoption of social conventions, including romance and love).

The gift, like the kiss, is revealed to have an investment in portraying
love, but possesses too much ambiguity to do so without confusion. In his
book *Given Time*, Derrida investigates the idea of the gift, commencing with
a proposition vital to his concerns: 'the gift is the impossible. Not impossible but the impossible. The very figure of the impossible. It announces
itself, gives itself to be thought as the impossible' (Derrida 1994: 7). Part
of the reason for the impossibility of the gift for Derrida is that it must be a
part of the economy of our culture, and yet always remains outside of it.
Any gift, argues Derrida, can never be given without incurring a sense
of debt,[3] and places us within a circular pattern of 'payment and
discharge of debt' (Derrida 1994: 12). This is also part of what Derrida sees

as the negation of the gift once it is given and acknowledged: 'There is no more gift as soon as the other *receives* – and even if she refuses the gift that she has perceived or recognized as gift. As soon as she keeps for the gift the signification of gift, she loses it, there is no more *gift*' (Derrida 1994: 14–15). In our language – including that of cinema – the gift and the kiss are strongly entwined. We speak, for example, of giving someone a kiss, and of receiving one. It has become part of the ideology of the exchange. Similarly, the gifts in *Manon des sources* incur debts, even if the participants are not aware that an exchange of gifts has taken place. Furthermore, once they become aware of the gifts, each of the signifiers of the gift is altered in its meaning. In some ways these gifts, with their sense of debt, contain transgressive qualities; each contains an element which requires the giver to relinquish part of their subjectivity (Manon's secrecy, Ugolin's confessions of his love).

The idea of a transgressive gift of love is demonstrated in quite a different fashion in *Les Yeux Sans Visage* (*Eyes Without a Face*) (Franju 1959). The story of a surgeon who kidnaps women so that he can remove their face in order to sew it on to his daughter (who was disfigured in an accident), is constructed as horrific. Yet all of his actions are presented as motivated through love, even if this is a version of perverse love ultimately driving towards madness. The film replicates this action with the doctor's assistant who, through her love for him, helps trap the victims. Love drives the horror, but it is always preserved as the amatory gift even at its most abject. The abject gift of love (another woman's face, the sewing of the ribbon into Ugolin's breast) presents overtly these attributes of the impossibility of the gift. They also present an antithetical model to the romantic notion of love and *cura*, for the abject love is also antisocial in its actions and results. However this impossibility is not always so abject, and often underlies the whole scenario of love as gift. The exchanges we witness in *Casablanca*, for example, signify the same sorts of impossibility without the terror.

This relationship of ideology to love (in this example true love formulated through *cura*) is, of course, far more diverse than is found in high Romance. We have, for example, already seen the complexity of the kiss once it is invested with a sense of otherness and social transgression. Our final example will show how these aspects can operate within these ideological orders, and yet also transgress them. This is the version of true love found in *A bout de souffle*.

Even the film's title – breathless – suggests both its form and themes; this is a breathless rendition of breathless love! In these terms it is a love closer to *jouissance* than the romantic for it is driven by a certain passion, even in its moments of tenderness. Interestingly, this sort of division is what is found in both Freud and Lacan when they discuss the drive and love; as Lacan puts it: 'On one side, Freud puts the partial drives and on the other love . . . The drives necessitate us in the sexual order – they come from the heart' (Lacan 1986: 189). The drives in *A bout de souffle* carry the events and characters, particularly Michel whose actions are motivated by a type of excessive desire that overrides social and personal constraints. His *jouissance* positions him outside of the Symbolic order, unsettling and disrupting the conventions. In this way he is a motif of the whole New Wave movement, which was a type of cinematic *jouissance* as it openly transgressed the established discourses of narrative cinema. Love sits between acts of *jouissance* (such as pure passion) and its Symbolic manifestations.

In many ways *A bout de souffle* is a classical love story in its themes, but it deconstructs this in its emphasis on the differences of love. Here the male, Michel, is seen as excessively sexual, passionate and socially irresponsible – an antithesis of Rick and Victor in *Casablanca*. Patricia is invested with these responsibilities, including nurturing and motherhood. This observation of the traditions of a form in order to disrupt them is typical of the New Wave films, and in particular Godard. Although Truffaut is less extravagant in this issue, many of his films still portray disruptions of these systems of representing love. The development of Antoine Doinel in the series of films *Les 400 coups* (1959), *L'Amour à vingt ans* (1962), *Baisers volés* (1968), and *Domicile conjugal* (1970) demonstrates a cycle of the character's movement in and out of positions of responsibility, almost always instigated by issues of love and passion. A different sort of example, still from the French New Wave, is Jean-Pierre Melville's film *Le Samourai* (1967), which takes the emotions out of its lead figure, only so that it can represent his social and personal unravelling through the intervention of love.

The very masculine perspective that many of these films are derived from often led to a construction of love that was threatening and violent. Lacan, in dealing with the issue of transference in psychoanalysis, voices this sort of process in terms of the other: 'I love you, but, because inexplicably I love in you something more than you – the *objet petit a* – I mutilate you' (Lacan 1986: 248). Such mutilation in *A bout de souffle* takes place on a number of levels: Michel treats Patricia terribly, often with arrogance, partly because he doesn't understand others generally, but women particularly.[4] Patricia wants to be free – she states this quite literally – but her freedom is tied up with the death of Michel – a death which is presented in quite a comical way. His mutilation through love is directly physical. We certainly don't respond to it as if it is tragedy – especially when Patricia adopts Michel's Bogartesque swipe of the lips. This comic underpinning once more shows how the film sets up the conventions of high Romance, only in order to undercut them.

Michel Mourlet, in the New Wave's own journal *Cahiers du Cinéma*, wrote an essay entitled 'In Defence of Violence' which begins: 'Violence is a major theme in aesthetics. Past or present, latent or active, it is of its nature at the heart of every creative act, even at the moment it is being denied' (Mourlet 1986: 132); later he adds that 'cinema is the art most attuned to violence'. The actual conceptual points being made here are of less interest than the fact that they are made within this context. It could never be argued that the films of the New Wave were especially violent, or even that they demonstrated an aesthetics of violence (as we might wish to argue is the case with Peckinpah, Tarantino, John Woo, or Scorsese). Mourlet's argument, furthermore, is not specifically directed towards the New Wave, but to cinema overall. The important point is that this essay, and others like it, does reveal something of the position of violence for that cinematic (and theoretical) group. In these terms we circle back to an ideological function of the representation of love. Michel's death may well be somewhat parodic, but it is still a signifier filmed with a certain fluidity, tied to an act of love. It also captures another part of Lacan's commentary on love when he states: 'Love rarely comes true, as each of us knows, and it only lasts for a time' (Lacan 1983: 170).

This last line from Lacan is, of course, a nod to the cultural construction of love. It comes from a Lacan who acknowledges the positioning of love is both psychical and cultural. What we observe from all this is that cinema's investment in love is part of a largely cultural order, and any investigation of it leads us to an analysis of the wider issues of cinema and ideology. The example of love is quite specific – even if it covers a wide and diverse set of issues – but it does serve as an example of how we might approach cinema's cultural and ideological connections. We shall pursue more of these issues in the following chapter, which has as one of its primary concerns cinema's capacity for social disruption.

6

The Carnivalesque: Film and Social Order

Artifice is at the very heart of reality.
(Baudrillard)

Film and Constructions of Social Order

Films, like other narrative processes, establish social orders which are constructed from a variety of sources, including the social order of the created world, the socio-historical contexts which the film draws on, the critical contexts of its reception, and the social contexts of the spectator. These orders are all played out within what we might call the architectonics of social orders. Such architectonics (the systematised ordering of knowledges and formations of contexts of meaning) operate within themselves to give relational points to events, people, histories, ethics, etc. within the film and outside of it. Part of this process is the construction of boundaries which delimit and establish the hows and whys of narrative events and objects. Such boundaries, often unacknowledged (as they operate largely at a level of invisibility within the textual fabric and act of reading), most often do not function as restrictive practices, but as moments where difference is mapped in order for it to become part of the spectating process. For when we watch a film we continually oscillate between the film's social world order, the social order it is derived from, and our own. Perhaps such boundaries are limitless, or form part of the unrepresentable, or are ephemeral and specific to a film. But some are more persistent and recurring than others, and the overall structure of such boundaries is common to all films. Of these types some examples include: the boundaries within the films themselves (the represented social order); the boundaries between the film's world order and the wider social environment; and the boundaries between these two social orders of the film and the spectator. The movements and connections between these boundaries, and how the film spectator engages with them, tells us much about film and its relationship to

109

social orders. They are also part of what may be termed shifts in the status of different ontologies.[1] These will be quickly mapped out now so that we can move on to explore more on film's capacity to disrupt and challenge such architectonics.

The first of these boundaries operates within the film itself. A social order is set up in the diegetics of the film, most often paralleling in some way the historical and ideological order which produced it. This is almost inevitable because even in films that try to represent a social order beyond their historical moment, we still find reproductions of systems such as gender relations, power structures, systems of discourse, moral practices, etc. This boundary of a diegetic social order can be established quickly because of such parallels, and the audience maps out the familiar even in the most unfamiliar of landscapes. The function of this is at least twofold: created world orders can be made sense of because of this operation of the familiar; the films are able to produce dramatic effects by playing with such relationships. The horror films made in the 1980s and 1990s by people such as Wes Craven and Sam Raimi presented an over-familiarised social setting (middle-American suburbia) so that the terror was more intense because of the established and strongly recognisable social contexts; Hitchcock positioned his characters in the ordinary and everyday to make the social disruption more perplexing, one of the best examples of this being *North by Northwest*. It is the absolute bewilderment of Roger Thornhill that makes the threats more sinister. It is not surprising that in such examples we find a strong demonstration of Freud's theory of the *Unheimlich*; for the uncanny contains that which is overly familiar, as well as the hidden and strange.

Even the most seemingly trivial of signs can link the film's narrative order back to a social context beyond itself. This may operate specifically within a social domain (for example, Big Ben or The White House have particular cultural connotations) or it may be intertextually driven. In *A Clockwork Orange* (Kubrick 1971), for example, the rendition of the song *Singin' in the Rain,* within a context so far removed from its Gene Kelly origins, does not negate those roots – if anything they are strengthened precisely because of this dark and sinister moment. Murder, rape, and torture are seeming impossibilities within the 1950s musical, which makes the scene in *A Clockwork Orange* more shocking and disturbing. Once such a reference is made, we may pursue more connotations, such as the idea that it is a song which originates from a scene depicting a form of madness (albeit out of romantic love); and it is the watchful gaze of the policeman that halts Kelly's dancing and singing – but not his feelings – just as Alex *seems* to be halted in his antisocial acts by the panoptic gaze of authority. Such intertextual references vary in how they relate to connections between social orders (either film to film or film to social contexts), but there is usually some point at which we can see this in operation.

Furthermore, the trace lines that allow such intertextuality to take place cannot operate solely within the textual field; it is a cultural ordering of things that allows, establishes, and maintains such connections. In other words, the sorts of links made between films are more often played out within a set of cultural paradigms than just the textual references that seem to set them up.

This is an important point because, as we have noted elsewhere, the range and degree of intertextualities are significant modes in the production of meanings. This class of intertextual references, which are played out almost entirely at the level of the social, may appear the same as those which are predominantly textually driven, but their distinction lies in this basis, and emphasis, of a cultural drive. How a culture organises such links (that is, for example, how they become established as legitimate readings of a film) reveals much of that culture's ideological operations. For example, the Western *Ulzana's Raid* (Aldrich 1973) is often positioned as a culturally driven intertextual reference to the USA's involvement in the Vietnam war. The intertextuality here is at least threefold: the generic (Westerns and War films); the historical (the events of the Vietnam war − that is, the event as text); the metaphoric/allegorical (the symbolism of images and narrative within the film itself). In these terms the 'meaning' of *Ulzana's Raid* is seen to be developed in at least two of the levels of the film's textual order. However, the interpretation of all such signs is dependent on this intertextual cultural context. This is emphasised further when the idea of a generic history is mapped out, with such a film marking a genre being redefined by a current social context. This is part of the relationship between the film's created social order, and the wider cultural contexts.

Part of the function of this created social order is to provide the moral contexts in which the narrative of the film takes place. In many cases it is the portrayal of a character (or set of events) which operate outside of the moral context which is used to define them (that is, the spectator is given the social order through its oppositions). This is a very common device, delivering narrative force as well as building up the film's social order. The sociopathic and psychopathic Hannibal Lecter in *Silence of the Lambs* does this at the level of social order (which is the diegetic Symbolic) by running counter to all of its moral codes, and at the level of the psychic order by entering into the (mostly repressed) memories and emotions of FBI agent Starling. In both cases Lecter exposes the moral order and social organisation by being a more extreme version of what is portrayed. He is presented as a natural product of such a social order, not so much an aberration but more a variation on the morals represented. His capacity to operate for most of the time as a reasonable, sensitive and even enlightened person allows him to function (diegetically speaking) as a reflection of the social order as it is transgressed and warped. That the depicted social order is closely aligned to a recognisable one (late capitalist USA with hierarchies of order and power, male dominated, etc.) means that his transgressions operate within a double context of crossing the boundaries of his social order, and crossing the boundaries of the culture which produced the film (which includes much of its audience). In a curious way Agent Starling also acts transgressively as it is her gender which is used to question some of the hierarchical structures of power.

This relates to the second type of carnivalesque disruption of social orders, which involves those between the film's social order and a wider social environment. (We have already encountered much of how this takes place in the previous chapter, so a few short examples will suffice here.) At its most simple level this is when film challenges the Symbolic, perhaps most clearly demonstrated in terms of morality and ethics. What can be represented, and how things are represented, always remains an area of contention. The abjection and violence in Pasolini's *Salo*, the sexual politics of Bertolucci's *Last Tango in Paris* (1973), the reflexivity of sex and death in *Peeping Tom*, the problems of paedophile acts in *Lolita* (Kubrick 1962), and the horror of fascism in *Triumph of the Will* (Riefenstahl 1935) all represent, although in quite different ways, the challenge that films can present to the established social order. What is useful to ask is how might this be different (or the same) from the example of boundaries presented above. This is a difference based on the disruption of a social order within the film, and a disruption outside of the film. In one sense it could be argued that this is part of the function of film within its social context. Film often represents what happens when the social order is challenged, disrupted, or inverted; and watching this is part of the pleasure because we know that what is being played out has a certain reality, but one that is textually based. However, even the most ardent supporter of propaganda (to take a specific example) recognises that there are strict limitations on any text's capacity to change people's attitudes towards social orders, such as moral and ethical actions, quite apart from changing the orders themselves.

Outside of this is another process which would see film's disruptive operations as a necessary part of the evolution of the social world order. By exposing that which is transgressive, film also reveals the ideological operation of moral and ethical codes, of representations of gender, race, of the systems of power. In short, the interaction between the social order and film is played out as part of a meta-carnivalesque (see below) which attempts to produce knowledges about that very order and how it functions. Such an interpretation is located between the idea that texts represent and/or reflect the ideological order (almost in the classical Marxist sense), and that they have the capacity to actively intervene in it (as the theories of Brecht, for example, argue).

The third type of boundary − that between the filmic order and the spectator's − is the one where we will often witness different individual relational contexts brought to bear. For in the boundary between film and culture there is a clear delineation between textual world orders and other types (such as the social) in which connections can be made or seen; in the boundaries within a film itself there is a common point of ontological existence, so that even if the boundaries are broken or transgressed this very act becomes part of the film's textual order. However, the spectator and the film always operate at a unique and individual level, even within these larger contexts. For the spectator acknowledges the textual world order of the film (and all its specifications), and operates within at least one of the cultural orders. These include the cultural order of the production of the film (that is, the historical and ideological moment of the film's genesis); or the cultural order of the reception of the film (that is, a film watched within the context of its cultural reception); or the cultural order of the critical analysis of the film (that is, how a film is positioned critically − such as art-house, popular, obscene, sublime); or the cultural order of its interpretation (that is, that films are seen to mean specific things in various contexts).

There is a beyond to all of these, which is the spectator's own position within those different, but ultimately interconnected, cultural contexts. For no matter how powerful such contexts are (and they do have a great force) there will also be microcosms of spectator positions, some derived from these contexts, others products of individual histories and psychical sites. White, racist skinheads watching *Romper Stomper* (Wright 1992) may well observe all of the social contexts with which the film engages, but their reactions to it are most likely to be quite different from those of other parts of the audience that do not share their political views. Such a spectator may see no irony in Hando as a tragically heroic figure, while others will see nothing but vicious fascism in the character. Such interpretations are heavily influenced by the other social and textual contexts, but there must also be a point where what the spectator sees, and how he/she reacts, is derived from the unique position of their subjectivity. This is the interplay between the Lyotardian Grand Narratives of cultural contexts, and the explosion of countless little narratives, some of which are sustained while others quickly fade away. These little narratives allow deviation and difference, rather than the sense of identity figured in the Grand Narratives. These meta-narratives challenge all narrating positions in their production of a multiplicity of positions and perspectives.

It is not so simple to say that certain films will match certain spectators, and so the different textual, cultural, and individual contexts will match, ideologies are made more compliant, and then pleasure is derived. At the very least such an equation is problematic at the level of pleasure, for that which is pleasurable might be obtained precisely from a position of antagonism or difference. One of the things that this idea of textual and spectator positions does reveal is how dynamic the act of watching films is, and how impossible any alignment within this process is. Part of this can be read in terms of phenomenology's concept of quasi-judgements. These are related to the distinctions made between those actions and events in a text, such as film, and those that take place in the outside 'real' world. We do not race out of the theatre and call the police when Norman Bates stabs Marion in the shower, yet our emotional reactions of horror and fear demonstrate that at least on one level such events mean something. The fictional quality of these judgements gives them a quasi-real status, but in doing so disallows a binarism of truth and fiction. The question then arises as to what is the relationship between the textual world order of quasi-judgements and socio-historical events. Clearly this is something that is mediated to a large part in the act of reading/spectating.

Of course these three types of boundaries (not forgetting that there are always others in operation) work as part of a larger matrix, from which we derive the relational contexts and readings of social orders. It is also important to remember that they all work *in potentia* and in-process; that is, the persistence of such orders (and their operation) means that the spectator comes to expect them (even if it is at a disguised level), and they can never be strictly defined systems or characteristics. By this is meant that the interaction with all social orders (from the created world order of the films to the lived world order of the spectator which repositions the signs of the film) is a constantly changing one, never fixed and certain. A specific example will help to illustrate how we can observe all three boundaries and positionalities in operation, and this quality of the social order in-process.

An often cited film to illustrate the cinematic 'attachment' to outside events and histories is Rossellini's *Rome, Open City* (1945). There is a certain ease to which we can map these sorts of connections: the immediacy of the represented events of occupied Rome by Nazi Germany (and the knowledge that such events took place); the filming of sequences on location (as opposed to the relative artificiality of studios); the grainy quality of filming and the documentary style of the film material; the constant reminders of actual places, events and, in their sense of anonymity, people, etc. Interwoven with this are the narrativised sequences – the children, the romance, the subterfuge, the resistance to oppression and evil. It is this relatively seamless matching of the two orders that gives so much power to *Rome, Open City*. If we were to draw up a spectrum of the film's engagement with the boundaries between its own social order (the events and diegetics of the film) and that of the outside world (Italy in the last years of the Second World War, or Rome as interpreted by Rossellini), then we find specific sequences in the film where the two are most carefully acknowledged and negotiated. Which is not to say that this is not taking place more or less all of the time, but there are points where such issues of the diversity of social orders are foregrounded. In those scenes the constructions of the filmic signs are positioned outside of the ontological orders of both the historico-social context and the created world order of the film. One such example of this is the shooting of Pina.[2] It is not simply the emotional construction of the act (the callous murder of a pregnant woman; the death of a figure who represented romantic love; the killing of a mother), or the idea that these sorts of things take place in war, or the quality of newsreel footage that the scene evokes, which makes this sequence a collocated junction of the different boundaries of social orders. In part it is the style of the way in which it is filmed – the action is much faster, the camera moves far more quickly than it does in most of the film, Pina runs in a disturbing fashion and is swept up by the priest in a motion almost too rapid. Such a visually distinctive set of constructions positions the whole event as neither part of the careful pacing of the film, nor the deliberate realism of the social context. It has a sense of disruption in both social orders (that is, the film's as well as the historically located ones). It also disrupts the social order of the spectator, as he/she must renegotiate this scene as something beyond the film's narrative and historical orders. Such actions by the spectator ensure the in-process of the boundaries of the social orders because it marks out the differences of the ontological orders, and the unique position that film has in representing and creating them.

Dialogism and Social Inversion

The act of watching a film is in itself a participation in a type of carnivalesque – that moment where the social restrictions and constructed orders, the established laws and hierarchies, are forgone and the potential for inversion is allowed. In some ways this cinematic carnivalesque does operate like much of the other forms of this social release (the *carnivale*, the Gay and Lesbian *Mardi Gras* parades) in that it can been seen as a type of hegemonic control. For although the social order might be challenged and usurped for that period of time involved in watching a film, what is represented and experienced is still restricted within a larger context of the Symbolic and its Law, as well as an adherence to specific formats of the cinema itself. So even though we witness all kinds of social disruption when we watch films (murder, unrestrained sexuality, immoral acts, comic interventions on life, people breaking into song and dance) the sorts of boundaries discussed above must be negotiated and maintained. It is important to recognise that the carnivalesque can be located in either the formal aspects, or the thematics of the text, or, perhaps as is most often the case, in both. Considering how variations on these three become articulated in film will help us move towards understanding another facet of cinema's relationships to social order.

To grasp the idea of a cinematic carnivalesque we also need to take into account Bakhtin's idea of dialogism, particularly in terms of Kristeva's readings. This inflection towards Kristeva's interpretation is important because it accommodates a broader perspective than the original linguistic one of the Russian Formalists and (although to a lesser extent) Bakhtin himself. Kristeva is interested in the social and psychoanalytic dimensions of dialogism, as well as the textual. When she links Bakhtin with Benveniste in terms of discourse and social practice, extending the dimensions of dialogism to include 'both subjectivity and communication' (Kristeva 1984a: 68), the emphasis shifts from an almost purely textual concern, to one which necessarily includes the subject in his/her social contexts. So at one level dialogism means a discursive practice, bound up with the positionings of the subject in terms of specific social practices. At another level it is a multiplicity of languages, opposed to monologism in its resistance to certainty and authority, offering alternative systems of meaning and knowledge. Part of this operation is what Kristeva, via Bakhtin, describes as the polyphonic. Once more her emphasis is on the literary, but the fecundity of the ideas makes them of interest to film studies. The polyphonic is, as the term suggests, defined by its multiplicity; it is that which, according to Kristeva, incorporates carnivalesque structures (Kristeva 1984a: 71).

At this point we need to ask if the very terms of 'dialogism' and 'polyphonic' are suitable for film; after all their origins and theoretical intent are firmly based in the literary. To answer such a question we need to recognise that film, perhaps even more than its literary counterparts, has even greater dialogism and polyphony, at both its level of discourse, as well as in its visuals. Together these represent the filmic structure of the carnivalesque. If, as Kristeva puts it, 'Dialogism is not "freedom to say anything," it is a *dramatic* "banter", . . . an *other* imperative than that of 0' (Kristeva 1984a: 71), then film has, potentially, a continual flow of this banter at all the levels of its narrative – the structural, social representations, the visual, etc. The sorts of films that most readily fit this description are those that operate where images, dialogue, narrative, and representations are both enfolded and yet resistant to one another. In other words, film has the potential to set up dialogic and polyphonic processes within individual strands (such as within the images) or across strands (such as image against sound, social context against dialogue). Some specific examples will help to illustrate this.

The carnivalesque is resistant to definition – a resistance premised at least partly on the mutability of the form. However, there are often certain attributes that mark the carnivalesque in film, or styles and themes that we come to recognise as part of this other order. Similarly, certain directors leap to mind when the term carnivalesque is used. Fellini, early Rivette, Buñuel, Jeunet and Caro, Polanski, Pasolini, Cavani, certainly Godard, Greenaway, Cronenberg, Wertmuller, Gilliam are all examples of directors where we find a recurring engagement with either carnivalesque themes or styles, and often both. Such a list is not intended to suggest homogeneity in the films themselves or between the directors, for such an idea would edge towards a sort of generic ideal, and this would be a difficult line to defend. That said, it is possible to indicate some of these recurring points, all the while acknowledging that there is more often difference than similarity. Another significant point within this context is that we might wish to speak of different types of carnivalesque, sharing some qualities, but markedly different in others. To give an idea of the sorts of qualities that can be seen as constitutive of the carnivalesque the following list is indicative, but by no means comprehensive. Similarly, these features are common in formations of the carnivalesque, but they are not exclusive to it, and their function will vary in many ways according to the filmic contexts. Such a list of features includes the following.

(a) Representations of excess
This is often expressed in terms of the body and its distorted engagement with the world, such as eating, drinking, and sexual activity. In this way the carnivalesque is used to play on what are seen as normal, healthy activities, and pushes them to extremes. Ferreri's film *La Grande Bouffe* is the perverse narrative of how three men set out to eat themselves to death, but does so with a sort of calm deliberation. It is this calmness within all the excesses that makes the whole process more carnivalesque, perhaps even more than the actual eating. Compare this to the almost hysterical carnivalesque of Robinson's *Withnail and I* (1987) which presents a continual flow of excesses, especially in terms of drinking and attitudes towards sexual difference. (The opening scene captures this when 'I' sits in the sordid coffee shop watching a greasy, runny egg squirt from bread, and reads about trans-sexuality; but there are almost continuous images of this type throughout.) The sexuality in *Last Tango in Paris* is not necessarily excessive (although it did challenge many of the filmic and social conventions of both mainstream and art-house cinemas at its time of release), but the way that sexuality is treated, and the contexts in which it is played out (an aging man and young woman, the demands for total anonymity, the brutal force of the sex contrasted with the almost naive romantic love of the young couple, the entwining of images of sex and death), gives it some sense of the carnivalesque. One of the defining qualities of such excess in a carnivalesque context is the almost matter of fact attitude of the participants.

In all these examples of eating, drinking and sexual acts there is an almost detached manner in which most of the central characters act. Excess is not seen as such in the carnivalesque, but rather as the natural order of things in this inverted social order.

(b) Dream-like qualities to the narrative sequences and settings
Rather than a theme (although of course it can be thematic as well), this quality is most often played out in the style of the film. Carnivalesque cinema will often not distinguish dream-like sequences from the everyday, or may establish only a rudimentary sense of the outside world before creating this other, phantastic region. Polanski's *What?* (1973) has only a brief opening and closing sequence of the outside world before locating the Alice-like woman into the house filled with madness and Art. The frame-tale device is almost mechanical in its position in the narrative. Similarly, the various house scenes in Rivette's *Celine and Julie Go Boating* (1973) contain a mixture of Art, fiction, the cinematic, and dreams, none of which are distinguished within that world order. The frame is abandoned here, which is a construction common to most of Rivette's films. Such orders reflect what Kristeva sees as part of the transgressive quality of the carnivalesque, which succeeds 'because it accepts another law' (Kristeva 1984a: 71). These other settings have their own internal logics and laws, which may well be a sort of Borgesian law of breaking all laws!

(c) Themes of social disruption
A point such as this highlights one of the difficulties of attempting to articulate the carnivalesque. At one level almost all cinema could be said to deal with socially disruptive themes (and for that matter a great deal of cinema could be said to be excessive, dream-like, etc.), so does this make all cinema carnivalesque, and if that is so, does it then make this particular aspect redundant as a critical tool? Or do we limit our classification of this strictly in terms of films that demonstrate a specific use of such a theme within a sensibility of the carnivalesque? Furthermore, are we primarily concerned with the *representation* of social disruption, or cinema's capacity to disrupt the social environment of the spectator? There are no short answers to such questions (in some ways these are the questions that this entire discussion is about), but part of our negotiation of them must include the idea that certain films invest more in this disruptive quality, be that thematically, in their style, or both. The representation of a socially disruptive event (such as revolutions, wars, political instability) is clearly not in itself carnivalesque, although there are certain films that might be considered as such. Costa-Gavras's *Z* (1969) with its mix of cinema *vérité* and innovative narrative style, and a specific political currency, is a good example of a film

that challenges the monologic approach to political commentary and the thriller. The idea that film can be socially disruptive at a political level (derived at least in part from the theories of Brecht) is a force that drives much of Godard's work.

Another way of approaching this idea is to consider film's disruption of social practices through different carnivalesque devices and structures. Established social practices such as sexuality, gender roles, the positioning of the elderly or young, are often challenged in the cinema through excess, the fantastic, the grotesque, etc. What this potentially achieves is a polyphony of ways of thinking about such social practices – that is, film has the potential to reinscribe the social by making it other to what is normally experienced. Gilliam's *Brazil* (1985) works on both levels of representing a socially disturbed world, disrupted in different ways; and a perverse paralleling of the bureaucratic world of late capitalism. In doing so it has the possibility of challenging the spectator's own sense of his/her position in the bureaucratic schema of things.

(d) Dark comic humour

The carnivalesque is often infested with a humour that is derived from the compulsive and repulsive. *Withnail and I* details the carnivalesque through its Rabelaisian humour, piling one comic moment on another to produce a sort of despair that is almost trivial in its origins, but all-encompassing to its main characters, especially in Withnail, who is one of the best examples of a reinvention of the Rabelaisian figure in contemporary cinema. In this film we see the operation of the doubling effect, not so that there is a carnivalesque moment to be contrasted with one from the rational, monologic world; rather there is a polyphonic discharge where the images and events challenge each other within the carnivalesque.[3] The dark representation of Uncle Monty in such homophobic terms is undercut by Withnail's laments as a lover towards I at the very end of the film (note his emphasis on Shakespeare's 'and I love him'); the bravado of Withnail is always contrasted with greater masculine violence (in the pub, with Danny the drug dealer, with the bull in the field, with the poacher) that results in a comic excess. The film's narrative is derived from, and propelled by, the polyphony of comic compulsions and repulsions. In a similar way Wertmuller's films play out a warped version of recognisable stereotypes so that the carnivalesque comic is only a slight twist on normal relationships (*Swept Away* (Wertmuller 1975) is an example of this in terms of gender roles). Almodóvar's characters – such as the kidnapper and the porn star in *Tie Me Up, Tie Me Down* (1990), the mother and daughter in *High Heels* (1991), and the television presenter, Andrea Scarface, in *Kika* (1993) – work in a similar way at the level of the carnivalesque because they present extremes of certain cultural and gender types.

Another way of approaching this sort of carnivalesque attribute would be to examine how certain combinations of elements actually transform the essential quality of the relationships, acts, or social orders. This dark humour of the carnivalesque can transform violence, for example, into an order of excess. *Lock, Stock and Two Smoking Barrels* (Ritchie 1998) takes the acts of violence (both the literal acts of killing and torture, as well as the implied) to such an extreme that it becomes more about excess than blood. In doing so the darkness of the humour does not function as a form of relief from the violence for the spectator (as is so often the case in thrillers and horror films), but rather it feeds into the transforming of the signifiers as moments of excess.

(e) A resistance to laws
Part of the drive of the carnivalesque, that is, its reason for existence, is to invert the laws of the social order. As Kristeva points out: 'The carnivalesque challenges God, authority, and social law; in so far as it is dialogical, it is rebellious' (Kristeva 1984a: 79). Often this is done in a fashion that is so absurd and extreme that the very discourse created is the defence against censorship. The form feigns to declare itself invalid by presenting antisocial ideas (in a mainstream sense) through the comic, the parodic, and the excessive. However in doing so the carnivalesque allows itself the capacity to provide resistance to the laws (the moral and ethical as well as the legal) which operate both within the created world order and the outside social order of the viewer. Once more it is important to recognise that one of the distinguishing features of this is not the establishing of an alternative system of laws, for the carnivalesque more often attacks the existing social codes without offering other possibilities except the comic and excessive. There are variations to this, but generally speaking the anarchy of the Marx Brothers in *Duck Soup* (McCarey 1933), for example, is more carnivalesque in these terms than Altman's *M*A*S*H* (1970). For although both films have a sense of political satire, *Duck Soup* is more directed as satirising other anti-war films than producing something like an anti-war sentiment as found in Altman's film.

The idea of resistance to laws can be also be taken at a formal level, with some carnivalesque texts demonstrating a concerted effort at breaking down established structures. One way of interpreting this is through Kristeva's ideas on dialogue. She states: '*Dialogue* appears most clearly in the structure of carnivalesque language, where symbolic relationships and analogy take precedence over substance-causality connections' (Kristeva 1984a: 72). Once films break down the substance-causality connections – that is, the fundamentally given of narrative sequences – then there is a direct challenge to the laws of narrative itself. *Last Year at Marienbad* pushes such laws to the extreme so that all the usual constructions of narrative (past, present, future; cause and effect; time as measurable and constant structure; the memory of the narrating position as reliable; relationships between characters stable unless the shifts are marked out, etc.) give way to the Symbolic ideas of narrative, and analogies of cause and effect. More tentatively, we might argue that the early use of the jump-cut works as a carnivalesque interruption of the laws of narrative and editing. To include such an interpretation would suggest that the carnivalesque can be found in small elements of a film, and not always developed in all aspects of the film. In this sense we might read the jump-cut as carnivalesque in *A bout de souffle*, but resist the idea that the entire film can be seen as such. It operates as carnivalesque because it mostly works outside of any narrative attachment. When there is a jump-cut there is not necessarily a corresponding relationship to changes in events on the screen or the characters' emotions. It could be argued that this is precisely what the jump-cut is — at least in the hands of Godard — but to see it as carnivalesque is to invest it with this sense of resistance to the law of montage.

(f) Figures of the grotesque
Part of the historical tradition of the carnivalesque is the grotesque. There are differences (one is not always the other), nor can they simply be seen as subcategories of each other. However, the connections are often present, enforced as much by the shared histories as by specific textual references and reading practices. Lynch is one director whose films seem bound to the figures of the grotesque. Films such as *Eraserhead* (1978), *Blue Velvet*, and *Wild at Heart* (1990) in different ways demonstrate connections between the grotesque and carnivalesque. *The Elephant Man* (1980) works less like these, even if its theme is, almost literally, about a carnivalesque character, because it sets up the differences within the film itself, whereas the other three examples contain a world order devised of the carnivalesque itself. *Lost Highway* (1997) returns to the figures found in *Blue Velvet* (the bewildered young man, the sexually alluring and mysterious woman, the threatening older man with pathological gangster attributes), but locates the figures of the grotesque in a much less black-and-white scenario. These character types are something like an embodiment of the darker drives, a sort of Hollywood version of the Freudian drives of sex and death. In a different way Cronenberg's films have a recurring image of the grotesque, often based on the body made abject. These films combine a type of technological grotesque to produce the carnivalesque of the body. His visions of the body transformed into a machine resist the comforts of seamless mergings found in some science fiction cinema, and instead play out the grotesque. *Crash* is one of the best examples of this, although *Videodrome* (1983) and *Existenz* (1999) demonstrate similar ideas and attitudes. Compare these to *The Terminator* (Cameron 1984), for example,

which has the merged body/machine and, although threatening, is never of the same order of the grotesque. What makes these sorts of manifestations of the grotesque different in such carnivalesque settings is, like with the representation of excesses, they are not seen as such by the subjects in the films. There is fascination, perhaps disturbance, but not the revulsion or resistance found in horror or thriller genres.

(g) Liminal spaces

We have noted above how certain films establish dream-like settings where the elements of the carnivalesque are played out. There is also the division of spaces into liminal zones where social inversion operates within the world order. Once more, one of the distinguishing features of this is that these spaces are not in themselves always marked out as difference. For this reason, something like Alex Proyas's *Dark City* (1998), where there are explanations offered to the social inversions of the city, has a different sense of the carnivalesque from that of the dark recesses of cities such as those found in *City of Lost Children* (Jeunet and Caro 1995) or *The Cook, the Thief, His Wife and Her Lover* and *A Zed and Two Noughts* (Greenaway 1985) where the warped social environment is the norm. In different ways these sorts of films rely on the viewer recognising the particularity of the created, anonymous cityscape and urban environments, and at the same time seeing distortion and inversion of their own. The city is a particularly strong motif in these terms, but there are also equivalent rural regions. The crop-dusting scene in *North-by-Northwest* has a certain carnivalesque feel about it, one character pointing out the strangeness of dusting where there are no crops. Fellini's *City of Women* (1981) plays with both the rural and the urban to mark out a phallocentric version of a feminine carnivalesque. It is the quality of the familiar and the strange which makes these regions liminal, because to occupy a site which crosses the two social orders of the film and the spectator there must be nodal points of recognition and disjunction.

(h) Historically recognisable but distorted time periods

As with the invention of disturbed and strange spaces that at once connect and disconnect to regions outside of the film, the carnivalesque also plays with temporality. It does this in many different ways (*Last Year at Marienbad* as cited above can be seen to be doing carnivalesque things with time). Apart from the more obvious temporal distortions, another way cinema constructs the carnivalesque is by creating times and scenes that have recognisable historical currency (perhaps even veracity within the social order) and then inverting or disrupting this sense of the period. Cavani reworks elements of Nazi Europe in *The Night Porter* by positing the enormity of the tragedy into a single relationship. And it is in this relationship that the carnivalesque is played out in sadistic and masochistic terms. Similarly, her *Beyond Good and Evil* (1977) mixes historical figures (such as Nietzsche and Lou-Andres Salome) with sequences of carnivalesque dance that are also found in the woman's act in *The Night Porter*. Other examples of this distorting of time periods include Pasolini's Middle Ages in *The Decameron* (1971) and Chaucer's England in *The Canterbury Tales* (1971). Jarman's *Caravaggio* (1986) plays out the jarring effect of including modern artifacts (such as a watch) on historical figures.

All of these devices work at different levels in the film text. In doing so the carnivalesque cinema sets up an alternative to the cinematic 'language' of both form and content. It reinvents itself as a double to that which is seen as the cinematic discourse. This doubling effect is important because it textually distinguishes and connects (often through a type of intertextuality) the dialogic and polyphonic processes to the cinematic paradigm, rather than posing it as difference. In other words, such processes provide a way of considering cinema as a socially disruptive force in itself. To understand further how this takes place, we can now turn to another aspect of disruption.

The Reality Effect

Film's connections to reality have produced a long tradition of ideas on what this relationship might be, how it differs from other textual forms, how it shapes the very processes of the cinematic apparatus, etc. Part of this issue is, of course, to do with 'realism', but the implications of it resonate throughout the very idea of cinema itself. By considering this relational context of reality and realism we shall be able to speculate further on some of the connections between film and its social orders. For in these connections and contexts are formulated textual practices (notions of the real and realism) as well as cultural attitudes and acts of reading.

Much of the theorising of film and ideology has been based on figuring the relationship between cinema and reality.[4] A significant reason for this is not that a realist mode has anything more particularly invested in the cultural processes of ideology, but rather that it can appear to have. The realist mode *appears* to be more real, which is more motivated (in a semiotic sense) and attached to 'reality', and so has a certain relationship to ideology. Part of the reason for this is that ideology itself operates as if it is part of the natural order, and in doing so makes the cultural appear natural. Here we see one particular inflection of film's relationship to its materiality. All film strives for this sense of 'reality'. Even the most fantastic of films, such as *Un Chien andalou*, *Twelve Monkeys*, or *City of Lost Children*, produce a sense of reality within their textual order of things. However, this sense of reality, and how it operates, what effects it has, what textual motivation drives it (and allows it to exist), varies dramatically across films, film forms, and genres. If this is so, we at least need to try to make sense of the relationship between reality, realism, the real, and all of their effects, if only in terms of their social implications and textual systems.

One way of approaching the issue of the construction of reality in the text is to consider its function against its form. This is to argue that realism operates as a certain function within the text, independent of its proximity to any sense of outside reality. Something has the attribute of realism if it fulfils this function and not necessarily if it is realistic. So, for example, time travel has a level of (and investment in) realism in *Twelve Monkeys*, even if we do not accept it outside of the parameters of the film. Barthes, in discussing what he terms the reality effect, asks the following question: 'is everything in the narrative meaningful, significant? And if not, if there exist insignificant stretches, what is, so to speak, the ultimate significance of this insignificance?' (Barthes 1982: 12). His answer is the reality effect, and these additions give a sense of reality to the entire narrative. In the example of *Twelve Monkeys*, it is the elaborate machines, the dehumanised scientists, the special effects, that have this insignificant signification to produce a sense of the reality of travelling through time. In themselves these signifiers are meaningless and insignificant to the overall narrative of the film; but in their insignificance they come to construct reality.

Barthes's idea of the reality effect is premised on a whole new formulation of *vraisemblance*, and, he argues, represents a total break in the traditional systems of realism in a text. In film we encounter a specific development of this reality effect. The key to this effect is the new order's intention to 'alter the tripartite nature of the sign so as to make the descriptive notation a pure encounter between the object and its expression' (Barthes 1982: 16). Or, to disentangle Barthes's semiotic language, the reality effect we encounter in cinema challenges the old textual order of the relationship between sign and referent so that we actually have to devise new strategies for understanding and analysing the textual construction of realism. In a different way this is what Lyotard argues in his analysis of postmodernism. He draws specifically on cinema to work through 'the effects of reality, or if one prefers, the fantasies of realism' (Lyotard 1984: 73). Lyotard's 'equivalence' (a dangerous term here) to Barthes's idea of a totally new relational context of the sign to realism is found in postmodernism and 'the withdrawal of the real' and participates in 'the business not to supply reality but to invent illusions' (Lyotard 1984: 123) – which also operates as a more than useful definition of cinema's relationship to realism and reality.

There are a number of different orders of reality which come into play when we watch a film. There is the reality of trees and chairs and tables, or what phenomenology calls the *lebenswelt*, forming part of the natural attitude. This is the 'reality' we would usually associate with the term; the reality of our everyday existence. There is also what might be called the 'socio-reality', or that reality formulated in and through the social order of things. This is an ideological-based reality which is continually asserted as if it is part of the first order of objects and the everyday. This is how ideological 'reality' must operate if it is to escape scrutiny, and in doing so allows ideological systems to function within the everyday. A third order is produced from this which we will call 'epistemic reality', or that reality which produces and is produced by systems of knowledge. This is the construction of reality as if it is a knowledge-based process, and so 'truth'. As with socio-reality, this version of reality ends up producing interpretations which are not necessarily based on any actual reality. It is part of what Nietzsche pointed out in regard to truth when he said that truth is just a metaphor that has forgotten its status: 'truths are illusions of which one has forgotten that they *are* illusions' (Nietzsche 1964: 172). The fourth version of reality is 'psychical reality', which comes close to what Lacan called the Real. This is the reality that is formulated out of the interplay and differences between the unconscious and the conscious mind. The unconscious – driven by desires and drives – has a different reality from the socially orientated conscious mind, moderated by the actions of the super-ego and the ego ideal.[5] It is also the reality of the split subject as he/she negotiates a position of subjectivity in the Symbolic order. As Lacan puts it: 'What is refused in the Symbolic order re-emerges in the Real' (Lacan 1993: 13), which allows him to *attach* the Real on to that which lies outside of the reality constructed in the cultural order. Such a construction is well suited to explore the cinematic constructions and operations of the Real.

What such a model suggests is that all the forms of reality listed so far contain within them a constructed set of interpretations which are driven not simply by their constitutive elements (the trees-and-chairs part of them, so to speak) but by the desires of the subjectivities through and in which they operate. This suggests a fifth level of reality, that of the subject's reality. This is derived from the subject's position within all these other orders of reality, and the sorts of impacts that that has on how we construct, accept (or deny), and participate in the other orders. Gender, race, class, sexuality are all influences on how this subject reality is formulated and engaged in. The final version of reality we are concerned with here is filmic reality, which is constructed out of at least two very large orders. The first are the realities of a film derived from that particular film's narrative, style, history, position in the industry, etc. That is, this is the reality of the film's constructed world order, and how that order, in turn, is intertextually connected to lots of other films. The second order is the construction of a film's reality out of a culmination of elements from these other realities.

What this interweaving of different realms indicates is that film's reality is derived not simply from its textual order, but from a complex interplay between a vast and subtle series of factors, including the social, subjective, epistemological, and psychical. The point where all these meet is in the spectating position – where the film is realised through, and combined with, the spectator's levels of reality. What this also means is that film's relationship to 'reality' is far more complex than at first might seem to be the case. We can return to a specific example in order to illustrate this: one that is seen to have a particular relationship to Realism (as a textual order) and reality, that is the film *Rome, Open City*.

The sequence that will be the focus here is one touched on earlier, and comes mid-way through the film. The Nazis have raided the block of flats where the two resistance fighters have been hiding out; the priest Don Pietro has been called by the local children to the scene and, under the pretext of visiting a sick old man, enters the building just as the Nazis are commencing their search. Don Pietro discovers one of the children with a gun and bomb, threatening to use them against the Nazi troops; Don Pietro hides the weapons in the old man's bed (after knocking him unconscious with a frying pan) and fools the soldiers. After this scene the camera returns to the crowd on the street below. Francesco and Pina, separated by the Nazis, recognise each other and call out. Francesco is forcefully placed on a truck with the other prisoners and Pina, hysterical with grief, runs down the street after the truck, only to be shot by the Nazi troops. Don Pietro gathers her fallen body up from the cobblestones, and her son is pulled from her body, before there is a cut to the convoy of trucks and the prisoners.

One of the interesting things about this whole sequence is how it interweaves various combinations of oppositions. The first set of shots (the priest and the old man) is presented in an almost Classical Hollywood style. There are rapid cuts of the priest and small boy coming down the stairs as the Nazis come up; there are odd angles and strong use of bars (from the stairs) to heighten the tension and operate metaphorically for entrapment and danger; there are extra-diagetic sounds and parts of the narrative that only become clear afterwards (how did the priest manage to pacify the old man? what was the strange sound of metal as the shot of the Nazi officer looking into a doorway occupies the screen? These sorts of questions are only resolved when the boy holds up the frying pan and exclaims how hard the priest had hit the old man). All of these elements produce strong narrative effects and the comic, almost high farce. There is also the sense of triumph, as the priest has outwitted the Nazi, saved the boys, and perhaps helped the resistance fighters to escape. The following shots in the street actually reveal that they have not managed to do this, and the contrast is remarkable as the tone moves from the comic (Pina's slapping of the Nazi guard) to the tragic (her death on the street). The filming in this second sequence becomes much more like newsreel footage, particularly when the priest gathers up Pina's body. Here the lighting, the pace and the camera's movement all contribute to a style that comes to define Italian Neo-realism as oppositional (or at least different) to the Classical Hollywood tradition.

Having described these two scenes (and it is interesting that they are located in the film next to one another because so much of their effect is derived from this positioning and its force of contrast) in this way, it is also important to realise that such effects (of narrative and style, of realism and Hollywoodism, of the comic and tragic) are all derived from an inter-play of the versions of reality detailed above. In other words, we need to take into account how such scenes are produced in the act of watching the film via the different realities that the spectator draws on. The first of these – the reality of objects – is based here on *Rome, Open City* as a 'record' of events and spaces at the end of the Second World War. Much is made of the fact that the film takes place on the streets and in the buildings of a Rome that existed at a (historically established and defined) point in time. This gives the status of the film a particular relationship to that first order of reality of objects, because it suggests that the objects are somehow more real than the artifice of objects in other films. This is the relation-ship denoted by the code system of 'documentary' and even 'docu-drama'. However, once we bring to bear the socio-reality (of both the Italian Neo-realists and the generations of spectators which follow) and the epistemic reality, then this relationship shifts from one of reality to realism. What is meant by this is that it is the realities of the social orders and systems of knowledge which construct the relationships of reality within a form known as realism. Here we begin to approach Baudrillard's ideas of the simulacra, and this is an issue to which we shall return in a moment.

These orders of reality, and the formations of realism, operate in the sub-ject's reality (derived in part from the psychic realities, in part from the social and cultural contexts of the reader, and in part from the reading competence), and this is how we, as film spectators, negotiate sequences like this one in *Rome, Open City*. There may well be this construction of differences in the sequences which produce the comic and tragic, the nar-rative style of Hollywood and the documentary style of news footage. However, it is not enough to see these interpretations as constructed simply out of the film itself. It is the *conflation* and intersection of realities which produce these filmic differences and emotive effects; it is in the space of the spectator's construction of the film, which necessarily contains and often sustains such realities, where differences are formed. This is the case because within each of these realities there is a vast amount of contra-diction and heterogeneity. No realm of reality is uniform in either its mate-riality (that is, what it includes as 'real') or its interpretative gestures (that is, what a 'real' element means and how it is understood to have that status), or its status of significance.

The questioning, and questionable, status of such versions and structures of reality raises the issue of how *items* (such as objects, people, events) pro-duced in them retain any status of the real and realism. Of course most often they do not, and this is precisely how cultures distinguish between a murder in a film and a murder that takes place in real life. At one level this quasi-judgemental status is apparent, and the demarcations, whilst slippery, are recognisable most of the time. It is part of how the spectator comes to take up certain viewing positions or at least pretends to (the hypocrisis). How-ever, part of this whole process involves deliberating on the relational con-texts between reality (its effects and models) and simulacra. One of the key theorists in recent times on the simulacra is Baudrillard and it is worth recalling some of his points on this.[6]

For Baudrillard the production of signs in postmodernity (and cinema is the art form born in postmodernist times) involves signs that are more real than the real — these are the hyper-real which produce, or are produced out of, 'an esthetic hallucination of reality' (Baudrillard 1983: 142). Bau-drillard, like Lyotard, argues that the production of signs more real than the real constitutes an essential part of the production and analysis of post-modernism. In doing so they come to question the relationship between signs and what they refer to (in much the same way as we observed above with Barthes's notion of the reality effect). This is related to a complex interplay between reality, simulation and representation: 'The hyper-real transcends representation only because it is entirely in simulation' (Baudrillard 1983: 142). This is precisely what we find in cinema's rela-tionship to reality, and its production of the effects of realism. The cine-matic sign is more real than anything we find in the world, and in this quality we discover a shift in the fundamental relationship of signs to what they represent.[7]

The Disruptive *Dispositif*

We have already encountered the term *dispositif*, but its operation will be considered in a slightly different manner here. Film's capacity to disrupt social orders is premised on its position within the social orders themselves. In other words, film disrupts because of its presence as part of the social orders of its creation and reception, as well as its capacity to influence the formation of the spectating subject. It is where these elements of the different social orders, the formation of the subject, and the formation of a spectating subject, meet that forms the *dispositif*. This, in turn, provides the force for the disruption. We have already noted the three key aspects to this (the fundamental aspect of film as a social process; the capacity of cinema to disrupt through forms such as the carnivalesque; the relationship of film to different structures of reality). For this last section we shall be concerned not with attempting to bring these elements together, but to note some of the possibilities of their interactions and, in doing so, acknowledge the open-endedness of such operations.

Lyotard's use of *dispositif* emphasises the *positif* aspects – it is the investment and cathexis of processes which lead to a positivity. In this way we witness a similarity – a contiguity is perhaps more correct – with the manner in which Kristeva posits the operation of the carnivalesque and its rupture of the thetic as a creative and enriching experience. A point – and it is a significant one – where such a comparison runs into problems is that much of the carnivalesque is socially disturbing, and this quality in itself is not inherently positive (no matter how broad such a description is in the sense of the *dispositif*). What all this suggests is that we need to look at those filmic moments where the social disruption has positivity, so that there is a recognition of a disruptive *dispositif*. One way of doing this is to trace some of the points Kristeva makes regarding Menippean discourse,[8] considering how these might be applied to the cinema.

To summarise Kristeva's interpretation, Menippean discourse has the following qualities:

1. Both comic and tragic, serious and carnivalesque
2. Politically and socially disturbing
3. Highly inventive in its philosophical and imaginative constructions
4. Freedom in its use of language, partly because it operates outside of the mainstream language structures
5. Elements of the fantastic, often combined with 'macabre naturalism'
6. 'Adventures unfolded in brothels, robbers' dens, taverns, fairgrounds, and prisons, among erotic orgies and during sacred worship'
7. Lack of distinction between virtues and vices
8. Use of madness, dreams, *doppelgangers*
9. Eccentricism in language
10. Strong use of contrasts, and sudden changes and transitions
11. A fascination with the double
12. An exteriorisation of 'political and ideological conflicts of the moment'
13. It emphasises the spectacle
14. It resists logical sequences and structures

(see Kristeva 1984a: 82–5)

As with all such listings, it would be impossible to find any one text that fulfils all its elements (although any text must have a number of the qualities to be recognisable as Menippean); similarly the fluidity of some of the elements makes them impossible as precise reference points. However it is worth pursuing the idea of a Menippean cinema, for in such a form rests the possibility of a disruptive *dispositif*. The brief comments and film references below are indicators of the richness of such a film form, and demonstrate how certain directors' works recur within this field.[9] (Some of the points have been conflated below more as a point of economy, rather than implying they are the same.)

1. Both comic and tragic

To make this different from other variations of this combination, the tragicomedy for example, we need to note that in a Menippean cinema the two axes resist opposition and become fused so that sometimes it is difficult to tell one apart from the other. This means that rather than the tragic and the comic seeming to be separated by a thin line, or that they are opposites to one another, in Menippean cinema one can actually replace the other in its functions. Films such as *Blood Simple, Lock, Stock and Two Smoking Barrels, Reservoir Dogs*, and *Pulp Fiction* do this by creating a world order where the use of graphic violence forces the spectator into the difficult position of simultaneous anguish at the violence and perverse laughter at its excess. It could be argued that the laughter that takes place during and after such scenes, in, for example, the accidental death of the adolescent in the back of the car in *Pulp Fiction*, and in the torture of the policeman in *Reservoir Dogs*, and in the hunting of Abby by the private detective in the final scenes of *Blood Simple*, are all cases of an emotional release caused by the tension of the scene. What should make us resist this reading as the sole cause of such laughter (for it is almost certain that it does form part of the reason) is, firstly, that each of these scenes is mirrored by other scenes of violence and the comic, so that these are part of a larger order of diegetic organisation. This in turn gives the sequences not a shock value (found, for example, in the shower scene of *Psycho*), but a sense of a continuum of such events. This continuum (an unending stretching forth of the conflation of the comic and tragic, especially in *Pulp Fiction* which presents the narrative in a cyclic effect) is related to the second point, which is that the images in themselves do not mean anything. That is, they provide evidence of the casual nature of violence in these worlds, which has the effect of removing tragedy from violence. The way it is reinserted is through the signifiers of the innocence of the victims. The excess of the violence gives these victims the status of the *pharmakos*, whose punishment is greater than any possible guilt. But even this is undercut by the lack of remorse. The difference in the final scenes of *Blood Simple* and *Blade Runner* serves as an example of this.

Both are stylistically very similar, with the darkness filling the screen, an almost homage to *noir* techniques, and the pursuit taking on excessive proportions. The main difference is how death is treated; the sheriff laughs and jokes at the irony of mistaken identity as he dies, but Roy Batty in *Blade Runner* philosophises about the same ironies of identity and loss.

2. *Politically and socially disturbing; an exteriorisation of*
   'political and ideological conflicts of the moment'
The idea that these films have a capacity to disturb the social and/or political orders is in one way demonstrated in their reception. This is not simply a case of looking for films that have incited riots or caused social upheaval. The idea of disturbance is more subtle, often imperceptible at the time. It can be of a wide social consequence (*Salo* for example), or it can have an impact on a small group or even the individual spectator. However, what distinguishes the Menippean/carnivalesque cinema from films with a social agenda is a lack of social responsibility. Examples of the first type, where films explore particular social and political issues, would include Eisenstein's *Battleship Potemkin* (1925) which has specific State-led agendas, *Naked* with its attack on Thatcherite politics and alienation, *My Beautiful Laundrette*, which explores both interracial relationships and gay sexuality, and Troche's *Go Fish* (1994) which examines lesbian relationships and their social contexts. These agendas set such films apart from the Menippean, which may share those same sorts of interests and disruptions, but do not always have a uniform or clearly delineated position. *Belle de Jour* cannot be read as a film about the repression of sexuality and childhood trauma (in the most Freudian of senses), because it undercuts its own perspective on these. Severine/Belle explore the power of sexuality without resolution (as both the opening and closing scenes demonstrate). As Kristeva puts it: 'the Menippean experience is not cathartic; it is a festival of cruelty, but also a political act' (Kristeva 1984a: 84). Similarly, Buñuel's *The Discreet Charms of the Bourgeoisie* (1972) shifts the ironic mode too often for it to be a film simply about the excesses and immorality of the middle class.

3. *Highly inventive in its philosophical and imaginative*
   constructions
Many of the films already referred to demonstrate these qualities, integrating different ideas and systems of thought into their narrative structure and themes. This can also be seen when film explores its own attributes; *Citizen Kane* is as much, if not more, about the investigation of cinema's philosophy and imagination as it is the story of a newspaper owner. Cinema's capacity to bewilder is also the quality that allows it to be inventive in

these terms. The inventiveness of a shot or composition, which may make it appear 'meaningless' can be what it means; this in turn becomes part of the cinematic philosophy. The image of the two heads of the prisoners as they emerge, screaming, out of the rain-soaked ground in *Raising Arizona* (Coen Bros. 1987) means little (their escape will be established), yet its inventiveness carries with it a sense of how cinema can disrupt itself and its own narrative processes.

4. Freedom in its use of language, partly because it operates outside of the mainstream language structures

Here we need to interpret this in terms of film language (as distinct from Kristeva's sense, which is more directed at the *parole*) and one such example would be film's language of temporality. *Pulp Fiction*, with its disregard of the temporal organisation usually found in Hollywood cinema, demonstrates such freedom. Another example, far less complex in its use of temporal structuring, is *The Devil's Advocate* (Hackford 1997). Almost the entire film works outside of the narrating frame's temporal order as the lawyer Kevin Lomax glances into the mirror, but this is not revealed until the final scenes. There is a hint of this given in his shudder, but this is not explained when it first takes place. The split second of the shudder takes up the entire journey to New York, madness and death, and it is in that moment that the festival of cruelty takes place. Here, time is used to restructure the film, as well as feed in to the idea of temptation, second chances, and human weakness.

5. Elements of the fantastic, often combined with 'macabre naturalism'

Certain cinematic forms immediately leap to mind in terms of such qualities, including surrealism (such as Cocteau's *Blood of a Poet* (1930) and all of Buñuel's works) and expressionism (*Cabinet of Dr Caligari* and, later, Fassbinder's *The Bitter Tears of Petra Von Kant* (1972) and Herzog's *Even Dwarfs Started Small* (1970) demonstrate in different ways such combinations). Similarly, some directors have a style which makes use of the fantastic and this macabre naturalism, often to provide social and political commentary. The films of both Almodóvar and Bigas Lunas demonstrate these elements located within excesses of sexuality and corporeality. The characters are obsessive about the body and its sexual functions, often to the point of being antisocial (and so fulfilling that other quality of the socially disturbing) with little or no regard for the cultural conventions. Almodóvar's *Tie Me Up, Tie Me Down* and *Live Flesh* (1998) produce their macabre qualities from the violence of love; Lunas's *The Tit and the Moon* (*Teta y la Luna*) (1994) and *Golden Balls* (*Hueros de Oro*) (1993) utilise the fantastic wanderings of the male protagonist to examine the obsessions and excesses of masculine desires, especially in terms of the body.

6. *'Adventures unfolded in brothels, robbers' dens, taverns,*
   fairgrounds, and prisons, among erotic orgies and during
   sacred worship'

These settings were used in original Menippean literatures to present the fringes of 'normal' society; they were the liminal zones that edged and undercut the pretences of the orderly and harmonious in culture. As discussed above, the liminal spaces are often used to parody the operations of the social, warping the moral and ethical structures so they are still recognisable, yet estranged. Many of these spaces, subsequently, have become a form of shorthand for these qualities, and film will utilise the connotations of the space to establish a break from the normal social order. It is the intrusion of these spaces into the social order which presents a more carnivalesque usage, rather than the protagonists visiting these areas. Many of Jacques Tourneur's films have this quality of the intervention of the carnivalesque, often presented metaphorically as part of the supernatural, including *Cat People* and *I Walked With a Zombie* (1943), which locate the macabre in the everyday. In a different way, his *Out of the Past* (1947) has the intervention of a carnivalesque (prisons and crime) as it emerges from a repressed past. A film that plays with this whole structure of disintegrating divisions between the real and the fantastic is *Celine and Julie Going Boating*. The two women take it in turns to visit the strange house until they understand the narrative within that world order. They then rescue the small girl held captive, but in doing so allow the fantastic world to intrude into their everyday existence in Paris when the characters follow them. There are other examples which illustrate these sorts of liminal social zones, where violence, madness and unrestrained sexuality are part of the order: Ken Russell's *The Devils* (1971), with its theme of religious mania, is an example of a combination of the orgiastic and sacred worship; *Belle de Jour* mixes the setting of the brothel with Belle's unconscious so that they become synchronous states; *The Cabinet of Dr Caligari* utilises the fairground atmosphere to confuse madness with the carnival; the series of women in prison (for example, *Caged Heat* (Demme 1974)) use the interplay of socially constructed sites of perverted law to represent transgressions of violence and sexuality.

7. *Lack of distinction between virtues and vices*

The problematising of ethics and morality is a key function of the Menippean form, for it offers very few (if any) solutions to these dilemmas, producing them instead. Part of this use in the films is premised on the blurring of

virtue and vice. Sometimes this is played out openly, with the social conventions declared, such as is found in Jancsó's *Public Virtues, Private Vices*
(1976), but in such an example the lack is actually not derived from a cultural irony or hypocrisy, but from the diegetic lack of moral distinctions.
Pasolini's cinema often holds this very quality up for careful scrutiny,
avoiding a moralising position, and allowing the images themselves to problematise the culturally established differences between the acceptable
and the forbidden. One of the best examples of this is *Theorem* (1968)
which uses sexual desire as a metaphor for class structure and morality.
This is part of the strength of this form of cinema; for rather than moralise,
it proposes ideological positions that constantly question those very processes of moralising. This whole issue is also significant in terms of Lacan's
ideas on the relationship between the Real and morality.[10]

8. *Use of madness, dreams,* doppelgangers; *a fascination*
with the double

Many of the films already cited so far contain attributes such as madness
and dreams. Sometimes these are foregrounded (such as *The Cabinet of
Dr. Caligari* emphasising madness, the dream-like qualities of Tourneur's
Cat People, and *Twelve Monkeys*, which contains both) so that the status
itself is used as an organising principle of the film's narrative. At other
times these aspects are presented without mediation or explanation. *City
of Lost Children* and *Delicatessen* (Jeunet and Caro 1991) offer nothing by
way of explaining the strangeness of the worlds we witness. The use of *doppelgangers*, as with many other of these devices, varies in its sense of the carnivalesque. *The Double Life of Véronique* (Kieslowski 1991) is much less
Menippean in its use of the double, as is Fellini's *Toby Dammit* (in *Histoires
Extraordinaires* 1967). For whereas the first of these has a languid, almost
accidental double, the protagonist in *Toby Dammit* is tortured and, eventually, driven to madness and death by his double. Véronique's double
exists in a sense of the possibility of alternate lives (in a similar way to
Helen Quilley in *Sliding Doors* (Hewitt 1998)); but Toby Dammit is never
given the possibility of escape.

9. *Strong use of contrasts, and sudden changes and transitions*

These aspects can take place at both the level of content/style and theme,
and it is not uncommon to find both taking place in the same film. It is
important to remember that part of the Menippean form (and hence a
carnivalesque operation) is a resistance to clear-cut distinctions (as in,
for example, moral and ethical acts). As such, the sharp contrasts made
often operate within the created world order's own perspective. After all,
it could be argued that Ethan in *The Searchers* (Ford 1956) demonstrates

these characteristics, but we would be reluctant to describe this as carnivalesque, except within a strict generic sense of a disruption of the Western codes. For this attribute to function within a carnivalesque capacity, the contrasts and transitions must work within a form that already resists many of the expected qualities of film. *Un Chien andalou* does this, drawing surrealism's desires for the shocking and instability; another of Buñuel's films which illustrates this is the final scene of *Simon of the Desert* with its abrupt change to mid-1960s images of modernity. A more subtle example is *Badlands*, which at first sight might seem far from carnivalesque. However, one of the ways in which this film utilises contrasts is between the narrating voice of Holly and the actions seen on the screen. The almost matter-of-fact, flatly delivered explanations of why and how certain events took place, are often completely undermined by the shown actions of Kit. Far more than an unreliable narrator, this voice works against the image (and vice versa) so that what are posed are a number of different narratives, each as plausible as the others, operating within different temporal zones as the story switches from the action taking place to what has supposedly happened, and what might have happened.

10. An emphasis on the spectacle
Cinema, by its very nature, is spectacle, but the nature of that visual effect and composition is far from homogeneous. So we must distinguish between the different senses of the spectacle in order to indicate what it might look like in the carnivalesque. For example, there are differences in the sort of spectacle of excess found in a Cecil B. de Mille production, the spectacle of special effects found in *Armageddon* (Bay 1998), and the baroque details in *The Cook, the Thief, His Wife and Her Lover* or the chiaroscuro visuals in *Prospero's Books* (1991). Of these perhaps the last examples from Greenaway best represent the carnivalesque usage, although it could be argued that *The Ten Commandments* (de Mille 1923; 1956) has a dimension of the carnivalesque in terms of its excess; and *Armageddon* (like other films based on powerful visual effects) pushes, to excess, the whole use of special effects by its dependency on them. However, in Greenaway's films (and this is the case for most, if not all, of them) the spectacle becomes emphasised in a different way, for it can run counter to the narrative processes (that is, visuals appear with little or no direct correlation to what is happening in the narrative itself). The visuals can also consume the narrative, making what is seen far more important that what is understood by them. Often the spectacle in Greenaway is just that, and any sense of diegetic depth is resisted as it passes quickly out of view. It is this quality of the emphasis, rather than just the spectacle, that can give the images a carnivalesque quality.

11. The resistance to logical sequences and structures
This aspect follows on from the idea of the spectacle, for one of the ways
cinema best resists logical structures is through the image. The constructs
of montage and *mise-en-scène* are used to develop logical sequences, and to
structure images; yet it is precisely this attribute that makes them equally
effective in resisting such procedures. This is well demonstrated in a film like
Un Chien andalou, but there is something equally carnivalesque in the tightly
constructed montage of the shower scene in *Psycho*. As with visual excess
(and the spectacle) this scene sets up a resistance to logical sequences, even
though the sequence itself is highly structured. This happens because of the
tightness of the structure, rather than because of it. In short, Hitchcock
deconstructs the montage effect by taking it further than is usually found.
In other examples of this type we might wish to designate a carnivalesque
quality to those moments where the resistance is used but not explained
(as would be the case in flashbacks, or the epiphany of Kevin in the mirror
at the beginning of *The Devil's Advocate*).

A different sort of example to this idea of resistance is Lynch's *Lost Highway* and *Wild at Heart*. Both films contain many attributes of the carnivalesque listed above, and it is fairly straightforward to see how they resist
logical sequences (particularly *Lost Highway*). However, a different way of
considering this would be the generic link which both films establish and
then break. The road movies of Hollywood in the 1970s tied their narrative
structures quite literally to the road. In a linear metaphor the journey of
the protagonist (almost inevitably male until *Thelma and Louise* (Scott
1991)) starts in the city and ends somewhere on the road, often in the
hands of authority (such as *Vanishing Point* (Sarafian 1971)) or opposing
ideologies (as in *Easy Rider*). Even the *Mad Max* trilogy, which in the first
film resisted closure, works towards an end to the road. This film form has a
strong, logical sequence to the narrative overall, and it is this convention
that the anti-road movie *Lost Highway* resists.

From this sense that film can both establish its discourses and undermine
them, sometimes at the same time, we move towards a consideration of
meaning structures and cinema. This will, inevitably, involve a similar
division – a construction of devices which attempt to establish meaning,
and an undercutting of them by other processes and cinematic invention.
It is to these points that we must turn our attention.

7

Film and Meaning

There are many ways in which we might approach the idea of meaning in film. However the main concern here is not what films mean, but how they come to be seen as meaningful, how there is a generation of signs which take on the appearance of sense and hermeneutic value, how our perception of them is arrested so that we feel, as spectators, that meaning is to be found, or needs to be worked at. To this end, the chapter is divided into three parts: the first section will be concerned with mapping out a particular approach to how meaning appears in films; the second section will take up this issue from two different perspectives, shifting away from the point of the film's reception, to issues concerned with the cultural production of meaning; the final section will take up some points from Derrida, examining how meaning 'frames' are generated in order to make interpretative gestures. Each of these positions is used to illustrate the volatility of meaning, and how ultimately we need to look to the mechanisms which declare something to be meaningful in order to understand the relationship of cinema to meaning. The following chapter will consider in more detail the challenge to, and even collapse of, such relationships.

Towards a Phenomenology of Cinema

Of all the theories of meaning and interpretation which have developed in recent times, such as semiotics, psychoanalysis, feminism, cultural theory, and deconstruction, the place of phenomenology has been the least explored. As a movement its importance is perhaps not as clearly stated because it has operated as a backdrop to some of the other, more highlighted, theories. Certainly the psychoanalysis of Lacan, the semiotics of Barthes, the feminist psychoanalysis of Kristeva, and Derrida's deconstructionalist methods all share some sort of relationship with phenomenology (be it supportive or, at times, antagonistic). Some of these points have already been considered in the course of this book, but in order to work through the idea that phenomenology might provide a model for considering how meanings operate in the cinema, we shall consider some

137

fundamental ideas from the works of Husserl, Ingarden, and Iser in terms of the film texts.

The first general point that we observe in such an approach is the emphasis on the act of reading. Phenomenology is concerned with how the subject produces understanding (that is, interpretative gestures) about the world around himself/herself, and the relationships which determine, and are determined, by this. In terms of the text, a phenomenological approach considers how the act of reading/looking is part of these processes, and participates in the construction of the relationships. Phenomenology distinguishes what it calls the *lebenswelt* (life-world), or the world of everyday existence, from other realms, such as the textual and psychical. The *lebenswelt* determines, and is determined by, the 'natural attitude', and part of phenomenology's task, according to Husserl, is to allow us to work beyond that position to investigate the *eidos* (the fundamental essence) of the object, event, sensation, etc. The methods by which we can arrive at this perspective (for in phenomenology it is much more about the positioning of the subject rather than some sort of Platonic ideal) are detailed and complex, and would lead us too far from our main concerns. However a few selected concepts will illustrate what a phenomenological approach looks like, and also allow us to explore it in terms of film and meaning.

To arrive at the *eidos* of the phenomenon, phenomenology argues we need to bracket off the object of investigation, to take it out of the natural attitude and strip it to its core. This is eidetic reduction, and fundamental to it is the idea that the act of consciousness is composed of two parts, the *noesis* and the *noema*. The *noesis* is the act of consciousness itself, and the *noema* is the object to which that consciousness is directed. The other significant part to this is that consciousness must be seen as being intentional, of having a direction. When we are conscious, we are conscious of *something* (we think something, we dream something, we feel something). The act of *noesis* is always directed towards some object, thought, event, etc. Phenomenology, largely via Husserl, describes at length the sorts of mechanisms and processes involved in performing this type of analysis, moving from the subject's position in the *lebenswelt*, through this idea of phenomenological suspension (the bracketing or *epoche*), through eidetic reduction, to a point where the relationship between *noesis* and *noema* is seen as part of a specific relationship between subject and object. This is what is called the transcendental egological state, or the focus on what consciousness itself is. This provides us with the first set of ideas about phenomenology and film.

Essentially we can approach the analysis of cinema through phenomenology in two ways. First, phenomenology can be used to examine cinema itself, its *cinemaness*, or that which makes cinema, cinema.[1] The other approach would be to consider cinema as a form of phenomenological investigation – that is, that cinema itself provides us with a type of eidetic reduction; that watching a film allows the spectator to observe the *eidos* of a subjective or cultural phenomenon, such as love, horror, history, or care. As our primary concern here is to examine the idea of meaning-producing systems, we shall focus on the second of these, commenting whenever possible on the first. And to keep the discussion focused, a specific example will be considered, that of revenge. Before doing so we require one further note on the idea of meaning (from a phenomenological perspective) itself.

   Ruthrof (1992), in his study of the relationships between language and meaning, suggests three sources to explain the occurrence of slippage (or, as he puts it, fuzziness) in meaning. These are *propositional opacity, modal opacity,* and *semiotic opacity.* The first of these is 'a semantic opaqueness inherent in the way in which the meanings of words and their combinations in expressions and sentences are circumscribed'; the second is 'the opaqueness introduced into language through enunciation' (Ruthrof 1992: 28); and the third is the slippage through the meeting of different sign systems and the socio-cultural surroundings in which we encounter the text (Ruthrof 1992: 75). Furthermore, Ruthrof allows for the intervention of these opacities in texts through the reader actively constructing speech situations. Although his interests are with the literary text and the spoken word, Ruthrof's ideas on opacity and meaning can be usefully employed in the study of relationships between the film text and the spectator. We find the same phenomena of opaqueness present in cinema through a combination of processes, including the missing parts of the image and narrative (see below), the activity of the gaze from the spectator, his/her cultural contexts, and the gaze emerging from the screen itself. Propositional opacity in film includes the formation of meanings and slippage through its constitutive elements (camera angles, lighting, sound, sharpness of image, etc.); modal opacity is formulated in the meeting of the gaze in everyday life with the gaze we adopt to watch films. Physiologically the same (except perhaps in levels of intensity), these gazes operate in vastly different terms of determining meaning and producing opacity in them. And semiotic opacity is the variation we encounter between the differing cultural contexts of the created world order of the film, the spectator's cultural context, the culture of the critical environment, etc.

The Eidos *of Revenge*

Our concern here must not simply be the cataloguing of films which feature revenge as an integral part of their narrative. For this would lead us closer to a generic formation rather than developing the idea that film can be interpreted as devising a type of eidetic reduction. Herein lies the double agenda of meaning in this context: that by examining film in a certain way we produce a type of interpretation about a cultural (or textual) *noema*; and that this whole process is in itself a system of interpretation, for it can be seen to reflect cinema's relationship to the production of meaning(s). These two hermeneutic functions are not necessarily compatible, it must be stated, for one suggests film's use as an interpretative 'tool', whilst the other makes demands which require us to distinguish how such knowledges are produced. This means that if we are to consider how cinema might allow an eidetic reduction of revenge, so that we come to understand what revenge is in both a cinematic and wider cultural context, then the caveat must be that any knowledge produced from this already has a frame surrounding it. What we may arrive at is much less an understanding of the *eidos* of revenge, and more a semiotic sense of its cinematic operations. This signals the impossibility of a phenomenological reduction, without at least some acknowledgement of the interpretative frames themselves, and the problems of attempting to arrive at essences. This is precisely the issue to be taken up in the following sections of this chapter.

To refine the example here we shall borrow from Klein's notions of the good object and bad object (Klein 1988), where she determines that the inter/intrapsychic relationship between a subject and various objects shifts from the totally positive to the totally negative (Klein's example being the breast for the child is good if it is given, bad if it is withheld). Revenge in most films is represented as mostly good or bad, with the occasional taint of the other. Revenge comes at a cost to those who enact it, no matter how 'pure' the motivations seem. Part of this is the delineation of revenge as a specific phenomenon, as distinct from, say, murder, theft, obsession, the immoral. This is its *eidos* compared to other, similar emotions and actions, for it is, comparatively, what makes revenge revenge and not any of these others.

In cinema there are, invariably, three parts to revenge: the causal sequences, the acting out, the revelation. The first of these refers to that sequence of events which justifies the revenge if it is seen as part of the good object, or makes it seem perverse if it is the bad object. It is in this element of causality that the overt ideological properties of the actions are often embedded. The long production of Vietnam war films (particularly in cases such as *Rambo* (Cosmatos 1982) and its sequels) contains many examples of the causality of revenge being ideologically driven, which in turn is supposed to justify the actions. In this sense Hollywood in the 1970s and 1980s produced many examples of revenge films, all premised on a causality to give the acts of revenge a sense of the good object. Three of the main motives often found in such films of this period were patriotism (with films such as *Rambo*), rape (for example, *Lipstick* (Johnson 1976), *Angel* (O'Neill 1984) *Straw Dogs* (Peckinpah 1971), *Deliverance* (Boorman

1972), and from a quite different perspective *Fatal Attraction* (Lyne 1987)), and urban crime and the individual policeman's (for it was almost always a man) fight against it (*Dirty Harry* (Siegal 1971)). The popularity of such films ensured sequels, but in itself this ongoing process of the return to revenge suggests that the act is something that is part of a continuous cycle. This quality constitutes part of the eidetic structure of revenge – it is not resolvable, even if death has been delivered. The *Nightmare on Elm Street* films (along with a great many other slasher films premised on revenge) utilised the supernatural to continue the cycle of vengeance; *Rambo*, and other war films of this type, utilise the need to rewrite history; *Deliverance*, which lacks the supernatural or cultural histories, closes with a nightmare of the body breaking the surface of the water. In this case the act of revenge has become part of the unconscious.

In such scenarios of the good object(ive) of revenge, the causal events must always be extreme (often in terms of violence and violation), unjust, and highly personalised, with an ineffectual response from the social order (such as the legal system). This allows the events to become focused on an individual, who comes to stand, in a synecdoche fashion, for all types of revenge. In this sense we witness another part of the *eidos* of revenge, particularly in terms of Hollywood cinema – it reflects the individuation of a subject through the ineffectual mechanisms of law and social order. Without this textual legitimation the acts of revenge would be seen as antisocial and anarchic; but with it the opposite is posited. In such films there is little, if any, sense of a conflict in these terms. The good object(ive) of revenge is marked by triumph, even if the cost (socially or subjectively in terms of the scarring of the self) is acknowledged. This scarring is also part of the *eidos* of revenge, for it marks the necessity of all actions, bears witness to the causal events, distinguishes the agent of vengeance from others in the social order, and serves as a reminder, in the cyclic process, of such actions and causes.

Compare the causality of revenge in other types of films and it becomes evident that such a quality of the investment in the individual through the good object of revenge is not always consistent. Coppola's *Godfather* trilogy stands out as a reminder of the darkness of revenge as a corrupting process, and as such all revenge becomes the bad object, no matter what the motive. All the participants in the acts of violence (including the women) acknowledge the *coda* of the vendetta, and incorporate these aspects we have considered so far – the cyclic process, the individuation, and the scarring. Sonny and Michael are positioned as different, oppositional poles on the axis of revenge; one blinded by the need for retribution, and made violent in a desire for it; the other calmer and made somehow less human by the calculations of revenge. Yet both observe, in their different ways, the same procedures, rendering it a combination of the good and the bad. Revenge in Scorsese's *Taxi Driver* (1976) functions in an ironic and oppositional mode to the celebratory good objects of vengeance. It demonstrates a social order just as incapable as Travis Bickle of distinguishing the violence of madness from the acts of a Rambo or Harry Callahan. Part of this is attributable to the Catholicism of Scorsese's films, for the scarring of these characters is a spiritual one, often tied to guilt.

The bad object(ive) of revenge carries these same eidetic qualities, but such acts are seen as antisocial precisely because they are driven by these qualities. An individual's desire for revenge against a specific person, as well as the law, in *High Noon* threatens the entire social order, and the Marshall's thwarting of it does not in itself rescue that order (which is akin to a scarring of the social order). In *Die Hard 3* it is the desire to avenge a brother's death that motivates the terrorist acts, so combining the issues of the individual against the social order (through terrorism), and the cycle of those acts. The highly symbolic revenge meted out by Stewart on Ada in *The Piano* (Campion 1993) with the cutting off of her finger illustrates how the act of revenge can be more excessive than that which caused it, and the scarring operates within the domain of sacrifice and exchange.

The second part of the sequence is the acting out of the revenge. Because of what has gone before, there is usually no need to justify the excesses of the actions of the person exacting vengeance for the good object(ive). Whilst in the bad object(ive) of revenge the more extreme the acts the stronger the sense of the antisocial and pathological. This brings us to another eidetic point of revenge. The desire for revenge is premised on obsession and consumes all its participants, both good and bad. It is a destabilising process and all reason is forgone in the efforts to gain what is desired. This is part of the cyclic flow of these acts, for each action elicits a secondary order of revenge. When Will Kane throws his badge to the ground at the end of *High Noon* he is acting out his own revenge against the townspeople's apathy and inaction. The irony here of course is that Frank Miller's revenge on the town fails at one level, but succeeds in the flow-on effect of social breakdown. Ethan, in *The Searchers*, is driven to the point of madness by the need/desire for revenge; yet even when it is supposedly satiated, the sense of cycle continues as the closing shot mirrors the opening one. Similarly Ada does enact revenge against her husband's violent punishment, at first by leaving him, then in choosing life. These examples illustrate how revenge can operate symbolically, as forming part of a conscious agent, as well as unconsciously. This is an idea that Freud utilises in his attempts to explain the final acts of Dora in his case study. Unconscious revenge is no less motivated than those acts which are carefully and consciously defined.

The final scene of Ada playing the piano, a metal finger tapping against a key, like the final scene in *High Noon* (a metal badge against the soil) and *The Searchers* (the lonely figure of Ethan wandering into the vast expanse of land), represents the unresolvable nature of revenge. It is part of the *eidos* of revenge that it must take place at the end of the narrative, for it is a force which diegetically drives the characters, and is at its most powerful when its resolution is absent and seemingly impossible. But in this non-closure is located the sense of the cycle, because the protagonist who commences any act of revenge is invariably altered by his/her actions, and this in turn alters their social position and the meanings surrounding all activities. The implication (which is of an eidetic nature) must be that no action motivated by revenge can produce quietus.

The third part of revenge is related to this sense of non-closure, for it is the moment of realisation. Revenge works most sweetly for its enactors in this revelatory moment. Often the whole narrative sequence is based on the lack of knowledge by one party, and the power of this knowledge by the other. The moment of epiphany acts as the closest thing to resolution in the revenge cycle, for it is here that power is asserted, and satisfaction gained. Cinema often draws on this moment, utilising the closeup to mark the point of realisation. In *Mad Max* all of the events which portray Max's revenge for the death of his wife, child and work partner, are prefaced with him letting the bike gang members know who is killing them, and why. Each death he causes produces no satisfaction in itself, it is only the moment beforehand – this moment of revelatory power – which carries with it any sense of gaining resolution. Even so, Max is condemned to a form of madness, and endless wanderings, because he becomes involved in these acts. Similarly, Ethan in *The Searchers* performs vengeance by returning the daughter into the home (with more impact than any of the more overt acts, such as scalping and shooting the dead Indians, which are devoid of any meaning to the white people). This is an ideological revenge, perhaps more insidious in its political dimensions than other demonstrations of revenge in the Western. William Munny in *Unforgiven*, like Max, is drawn into the cycle of revenge most reluctantly; and this is a reluctance derived from the knowledge that it never ends. What overrides this hesitancy is not simply the death of close friends and family, but the seduction of the revelatory power.

We could continue with such examples, but let us return to the point which commenced this section. Do these points on the cinematic *eidos* of revenge indicate a wider social *eidos* on the same subject? Such a complex question resists easy answers. At one level it could be argued that the social relationships of film to culture mean that the production of such texts invariably reflects a certain perspective on the structure, function, and processes of revenge. The almost limitless factors that come into play with such an assertion (where, for example, do we locate the forces of capitalism in the sense of individuation? of the twentieth century as a milieu with historically distinct attitudes towards revenge? and of the religious influences in a Christian culture on the sensibility of the cycle of vengeance?) make any specific resolutions impossible. What we can note, however, is that the *eidos* of revenge in cinema marks cultural and historical perspectives, not in a homogeneous sense, but as a part of the hermeneutic act. This point returns us to the central issue at hand, that of cinema's relationship to meaning. However, before tackling this issue from a different perspective, some other concepts from phenomenology will enable us to consider other aspects of the construction of meaning.

The Appresentation of Terror; the Lacunae of the Orgasm

Part of the emphasis that has developed out of phenomenology, via reception theory and, to a certain extent, the semiotics of Barthes and Eco, has been on the role of the reader/spectator. This shift from an emphasis on certain devices in the text, or the functions and constructions of the artist (in cinema the director would seem the most appropriate figure), and even the cultural contexts, to the creative and active reader/spectator should not be seen as a negation of those other elements. Barthes's notions of the *lisible* and *scriptible*, which are so heavily invested with the processes of reading, rely, at some point, on the intervention of elements outside of the act of reading; but it is the emphasis which sets these sorts of approaches apart. One of the ways phenomenological strategies have dealt with the role and function of the reading agent is by examining the incomplete qualities of the text.

Various phenomenological approaches (the works of Ingarden and Iser are good examples) argue that the literary text is constituted not of completion, of solid and crafted descriptions, but of gaps and absences, the lacunae. The act of reading, within such terms, is pleasurable – desired even – because there is much to do in this filling in of the missing parts. This is also part of the opacity of meaning (Ruthrof 1992) – a quality which actually allows for slippage in meaning and creativity. Cinema presents unique issues in these terms because, at face value, there would seem to be little missing from the images and sounds on the screen. However, apart from the lacunae of narrative that cinema shares with other narrative forms (such as the novel), there are also number of devices that have developed within film that actively promote and rely on these absences, as well as the opacity. We shall consider only one of these, that of appresentation, marking points where others are of relevance, within the specific representation of terror.

Part of the phenomenological method deals with the process of how we continually perform acts of appresentation. The following is a simple illustration: when we look at an object – say a table – we do not see the complete form, and perhaps only three legs can be seen, or part of the top is obscured. We do not think that this is a three-legged table, but rather we appresent the missing parts. This is done through a number of processes, not the least (in this example anyway) being our knowledge of tables and table-like structures. The more 'complex' (a difficult concept in these terms) the object, the more we rely on further and more extensive paradigms of experience and knowledge to produce meaning. Cinema requires its spectators to function constantly within a mode of appresentation, at both the formal and content levels. Sometimes this has an almost entirely pragmatic function, where aspects of the narrative are appresented for the sake of economy. A character boards a train at a station, and is then seen disembarking after a series of shots of train wheels speeding along. The spectator has appresented (this time using the codes of montage and diegetic progression) that the character has taken a journey, and the need to extend images of that journey become redundant.

There are more complex processes of appresentation, one being where the film actually forces a type of filling-in by the spectator, almost against his/her will or desire. This illustrates the idea of *hypocrisis* or feigning (Ruthrof 1992: 166), which is the way in which (for our interests here) the spectator operates within and beyond the boundaries established in the reading/viewing position of the film. In other words, if cinema, and each individual film, sets up certain positions in order to be watched (and this is more than simply perception of course), then the spectator adopts these and alters, resists, changes certain attributes of them. Ruthrof describes this as the feigning of the subject position in the act of reading, and it is a concept well-suited to understanding variants in the spectating event as well. Along with the continual evocations of feigned subject positions that the spectator necessarily takes up in order to watch the film, there is also the 'reader's awareness of the relationship between a statement [for our concerns the equivalent is the image] and its frame' (Ruthrof 1992: 166). Such combinations are created within the space determined by the gaze of the spectator co-joined with that of the film. The capacity for film to cause the appresentation of terror, which should run counter to any sense of pleasure, is a powerful device in the cinematic process. It is one of the ways in which we can understand the operation of hypocrisis in the spectator, and why pleasure and terror can be co-joined. And as a contrasting, but also complementary, idea we can consider how the representation of pleasure (in this case sexual) is also positioned as an absence requiring appresentation and a feigned subject position. Finally, we can consider how the two forms are utilised to create a composite set of appresentations that should work oppositionally, but are textually bound together.

The most effective forms of terror are often those derived from the lacunal qualities. It has been said many times over that the force of the imagination can conjure up far more terrifying images than can be actually shown; so the slow pan up from the torture scene of the policeman in

Reservoir Dogs forces us to appresent a *terrorness* that could never be actually replicated on the screen. Such an idea of *terrorness* (the eidetic quality of terror itself) only ever being possible through appresentation leads us to Kristeva's points on abjection and specular seduction. In her book *Powers of Horror*, Kristeva designates the unnamable terror – the abject drive – as part of the splitting of the subject, and of a recognition of the defiled body emerging out from the subject's own sense of the *corps propre* (Kristeva 1982). But a key part to this is the lacunal threats to that body – it is the fear of the loss which gives so much power to the abject, producing what Kristeva calls the borderliner. Similarly, she opens her essay 'Ellipsis on Dread and the Specular Seduction' by marking the abject's relationship to the gaze as the absent self: 'What I see has nothing to do with the spec-ular which fascinates me. The glance by which I identify an object, a face, my own, another's, delivers my identity which reassures me: for it delivers me from *frayages*, nameless dread ...' (Kristeva 1986: 236). This dread, which leads to so much terror – including the terror within the self, and the cultural construction of images of terror – is located within a struggle manifested in the gaze.[2] For Kristeva it is the model of the hysteric that best illustrates this fear, for in this is the process of being 'endlessly unable to find a sufficiently satisfying mirror' (Kristeva 1986: 236), and so have no sense of reference for the self. As with Lacan's anecdote about his fishing trip with Petit-Jean (as discussed in Chapter 2), to not be recognised by the gaze of the Other induces a sense of a loss of the subject himself/herself.

This more psychoanalytically motivated scene can be brought to bear on the idea of terror and appresentation. The terror of the hysteric's rela-tionship of the image for the self, like the terror created on the screen, is premised on the lack devised out of the requirements of appresentation. The force comes from the inescapable nature of that very relationship which inserts the spectator into the image, reflecting themselves back to the self. What we fear in the appresentation of terror is twofold: that which can be created in our imagination, helped by the elements in the film; and our own relationship to the terror, created in the creative act of appresenting. If the image is complete, the abject made visible, there is still the possibility of resisting it, or of locating the self outside of it. How-ever, any act of appresentation immediately traps the spectator into becoming part of the construction of the terror itself. To appresent terror is to locate the self as part of that creation, and it is this point that sets appresentation apart from the more straightforward idea that the absence of the representation is a textual construction, derived from conventions and textual practices.

What then of the representation of the orgasm through a system of appresentation? Can the same sorts of relationships be said to exist? The social order's moral codes designate the explicit depiction of sexuality into rigorously policed categories. These codes clearly mark out (from culture to culture and across time) what can and cannot be represented, and what categories the representing of the sexual falls into (the acceptable in the public sphere against the pornographic, etc). Already from this straightforward, social (legal) perspective we witness elements of the *lacunae*, for it is these gaps that allow cinema to suggest, imply, and momentarily disclose the repressed of the Symbolic order. There is a beyond to this, which locates the key elements within a different (although not necessarily unrelated) set of processes.

Certain types of the *lacunae* of the orgasm, like terror, often work through metonymy, and cinema's metonymic processes are an inherent part of its discourses. The cinematic metonym is most readily recognisable as an image implying a concept. For example, in *Psycho* the money that Marion steals operates metonymically for all of her social transgressions (sex outside of marriage, lying); yet it is also a metonym for irony (because she chooses to return the money but is still killed), and for the excesses of the punishment (her death is more brutal than any crime she commits). The camera pans out of the bathroom, after the attack by 'Mother', across the room, before halting for a considerable period on the money wrapped in newspaper. This shot provides the metonymic link between the money, its representative values, and the consequences of them. In other words, the metonymic processes of the images are often polysemic, and so their diegetic function can be diverse. The more tightly controlled the representation of an image, the more devices such as the metonym are employed, which is certainly the case with the orgasm. Some of these images become located within a code system so that they operate as a form of established meaning. The closeup of a hand clenching a sheet, the head thrown back, closed eyes, all function as metonyms for the orgasm.

Beyond this, however, there is another type of *lacunae* of the orgasm which functions in a different political frame. This is when the orgasm is not metonymically suggested, but where it is made absent for any number of reasons, including the political and the textual. Such lacunae are paradigmatically linked to other absences, such as homosexuality and interracial relationships. That they are not represented gives way to a social order where their existence seems to be an impossibility, the unthought, or the unrepresentable. Appresenting these becomes a much more politically framed act.

Cinematic Epistemes and the *Dispositif*

Foucault's theories on the episteme will provide us with a good starting point to understanding further the relationship between film and meaning.

By working towards the idea that there might be cinematic epistemes we can also consider some of the ways in which meaning functions cinematically (that is, in and through cinema). Exactly what Foucault had in mind when he devised the idea of epistemes is not entirely clear; more often he (perhaps characteristically) defined them by what they are not, avoiding any direct points of stability. Towards the end of *The Archaeology of Knowledge* he does provide this set of details:

> By *episteme*, we mean, in fact, the total set of relations that unite, at a given period, the discursive practices that give rise to epistemological figures, sciences, and possibly formalised systems; the way in which, in each of these discursive formations, the transitions to epistemologization, scientificity, and formalization are situated and operate; ... the lateral relations that may exist between epistemological figures or sciences ... The episteme is not a form of knowledge (*connaissance*) or type of rationality which, crossing the boundaries of the most varied sciences, manifests the sovereign unity of a subject, spirit, or a period; it is the totality of relations that can be discovered, for a given period, between the sciences when one analyses them at the level of discursive regularities. (Foucault 1986a: 191)

Foucault goes on to argue that the analysis of the episteme is an examination of an 'indefinite field of relations' and is a 'constantly moving set of articulations, shifts, and coincidences that are established only to give rise to others' (Foucault 1986a: 192). This is a rich and complex set of ideas, and even though Foucault himself was later to acknowledge the critical problems of attempting to articulate such epistemes,[3] there is much to be gained by considering these points.

Once more we are confronted with the fundamental issue of cinema's conceptual relationship to something like the episteme. Are we dealing with cinema's cultural position as part of the epistemic formations? That is, how cinema is located within the wider issues of cultural epistemes; how it functions within, and contributes to, them. Or are we dealing with the idea of the episteme *within* cinema? That is, a particular type of episteme which operates within a specific textual order (which is necessarily related to that other order at some level). The answer to these questions is to be found in a combination of the two, for even though they represent quite distinct interpretative approaches, ultimately they converge at a point where one can be seen to depend on the other. For the sake of expediency, and perhaps more directly relevant to the concerns here, we shall commence with the idea of cinematic epistemes.

Foucault's point about epistemes not being knowledge, but rather primary forces and processes in the formation of knowledges (at a particular point in time, to a particular group), corresponds to the idea at hand here. The cinematic episteme is not a unit of meaning, or a specific interpretation of a film (or elements within a film), but rather how something comes to mean something within a film. It is the interplay among all these elements of the production of meaning that constitutes the episteme. Things such as generic conventions, intertextuality-transposition, the notion of the *auteur* as interpretative gesture, the historical positioning of the film (within its own diachronics – such as *Citizen Kane* as technical innovation – and across others – such as the French New Wave as a moment in French and international cinema developments), are all part of the formations of epistemes. These are part of this Foucauldian notion of an indefinite set of relations, sometimes foregrounded, other times quite invisible. It is precisely this fluidity that marks the action of cinematic epistemes, and offers one explanation as to why films shift in their status of meaning. In one sense this is illustrated in the above discussion of the *eidos* of revenge. It would be possible to map out a sort of epistemic development of revenge, noting the (historico-cultural) shifts in production and interpretation, or the shifting emphasis in different epistemes (such as individuation being central to revenge in Hollywood cinema of the 1970s; or the emphasis on the dissatisfaction of revenge in the slasher film).

Ultimately, however, any investigation of cinematic epistemes must be seen as not specific interpretative gestures, but the larger question of how meaning itself operates in film. How, for example, montage and *mise-en-scène* function differently to produce signs which are recognised as meaningful 'utterances'; or how, to take these organising systems even further, the space-time systems, as analysed by Deleuze, are cinematic epistemes. In, for example, the section entitled 'The Powers of the False', in his book *Cinema 2: The Time-Image*, Deleuze progressively divides the cinematic image into the regimes of the organic/kinetic and crystalline/chronic, based on distinctions such as continuity. He argues that the organic is recognised through its systems of continuity and linkage; progression is part of how the image is developed in this system. Yet within the organic regime, Deleuze argues, there are two orders: one which provides the image with a systematic set of connections (the 'real'); and another, premised on contrast, where the links are tested or even ignored (such as in dreams). Deleuze then posits the crystalline regime as that where 'the actual is cut off from its motor linkages, or the real from its legal connections, and the virtual, for its part, detaches itself from its actualizations, starts to be valid for itself' (Deleuze 1989: 127). This sets up a relationship of the different types of images transforming themselves and each other, which in turn allows for the construction of different types of narration. So, the organic narration is one of the reactions by characters to certain events and situations (emphasising the connections), whereas the crystalline does not rely on reaction, for the characters are swamped by 'pure optical and sound situations' (Deleuze 1989: 128) which they struggle to comprehend. Deleuze's example here is 'the Dostoevskian condition taken up by Kurosawa' (Deleuze 1989: 128), but another example might be Marianne in *La Belle Noiseuse* as she finds her body as well as sensibilities confronted with the exposure to Frenhofer's gaze (which shifts between man and artist) to the point where narration itself is abandoned to the force of the purely optical.

Deleuze performs this analysis of these regimes with one central project in mind – to continue his investigation into the position of movement in cinema, as it is defined in the cinematic apparatus, and as it defines cinema itself. This culminates in what reads as a defining moment on cinema and movement: 'Movement which is fundamentally decentred becomes false movement, and time which is fundamentally liberated becomes power of the false which is now brought into effect in false movement' (Deleuze 1989: 143). This point, combined with the ensuing discussion on consciousness and cinema, is where we most clearly witness Deleuze working out what can be seen as the episteme in terms of cinema's time–movement structures and properties. Deleuze, in this construction of orders of the image (movement), operating through time, can be compared to the development of a type of cinematic episteme. This, in turn, can be measured against Foucault's ideas on power and knowledge, which seems to be quite compatible with Deleuze's points on the false and power. Subsequently this will allow us to locate the wider sense of the *dispositif* within this discussion.

When Foucault does shift towards what has become known as the genealogical method, he does so via the analysis of power and knowledge. This is succinctly put in *Discipline and Punish*: 'we should admit ... that power and knowledge directly imply one another; that there is no power relation without the correlative constitution of a field of knowledge, nor any knowledge that does not presuppose and constitute at the same time power relations' (Foucault 1987a: 27). This is not foreign terrain for the cinematic episteme, for to understand how this operates is also to take into account the formation of a power/knowledge within the cinematic apparatus. These are the relationships which operate within the film itself, and within the other epistemic fields (spectator to film, film to culture, director to film, etc.). Power/knowledge (Foucauldian theory merges the terms to suggest a composite as well as a new idea) can be seen as Foucault's attempt to move the analysis of the epistemes into the *dispositif*.

This entire system of relations, including the production of meaning and interpretation, can be relocated within the model of the *dispositif*; not the one of Lyotard – although this is not necessarily excluded here – but a Foucauldian one, which incorporates power/knowledge as the underlying apparatus of the production of meaning. We have already seen how this operates in a number of different ways: in the theorising of the gaze we witness the idea of a struggle between the gaze and the eye, and between competing gazes; in the cinematic body we have seen how the corporeal is constructed within paradigms of power in order for it to produce knowledges, and have a sense of meaning; in cinematic discourse we have noted the relationships between power and the multiplicity of dialogism of competing 'voices'; and in the ensuing chapter we will consider cinematic strategies against the dominant discourses of power/knowledge.

For Foucault the *dispositif* is a much larger construction than epistemes, for it includes these processes within its scheme. It is a disparate and multiple order, including 'discourses, institutions, architectural arrangements, regulations, laws, administrative measures, scientific statements, philosophical propositions, morality, philanthropy, etc.' (Foucault 1980: 194). The underlying critical force of this concept is power/knowledge, arguing, as we have seen above, that one is not possible without the other. What is needed here is a consideration of how cinematic knowledge is produced out of cinematic power, and vice versa.

The above example from Deleuze is one approach to this issue; the production of a relationship between the false and power operates very much within this idea of the cinematic *dispositif*. One of the clearest examples (and it is not distinct from Deleuze's project) is the function of the body as a site of power/knowledge in cinema. The idea of the appresentation of terror and the *lacunae* of the orgasm are both premised on a relationship between knowledge (true/false, the good and the bad, its presence and lack) and the body. From such combinations we find a system of power produced – the power over the body, as well as the body's capacity to both resist and subvert power (that is, the power of the body over knowledge). The appresentation of terror operates through false knowledge (as well as lack), both within the narration and the spectating position (although these obviously do not always correspond with one another) but is driven by a power of the body *against* this. Similarly, the *lacunae* of the orgasm are a form of power over the body, but the knowledge (corporeal knowledge as well as acts of consciousness) of its absence produces sites of resistance. This is why cinema is such a significant apparatus for the study of power/knowledge. This is true in terms of these examples of the body, but also much more widely speaking, such as consciousness, the socio-cultural, the historical, etc. This is the production of meaning within the cinematic apparatus, its production by cinema within the social, the relationship of meaning and the spectator. The combinations and variations of these produce what we shall term the *epistemocine*, or knowledge/power in and through the cinematic apparatus. Another approach to this idea will allow us to understand better how this operates.

The Cinematic *Point du Capiton*

Lacan, in attempting to investigate the relationship between meaning as it operates within the Symbolic order, and the impossibilities of constructing such meanings in the unconscious, uses the idea of the *point du capiton*. These are, literally speaking, the buttons in the fabric of a chair. Lacan's metaphor is beautiful in its simplicity, yet complex in its implications. The fabric of meaning, this unending flow of cloth with its folds, undulations and creases, is impossible to arrest in its entirety, but the Symbolic order produces these moments – the *points du capiton* – which fix meanings (for an instant or for what must seem like an eternity). Although Lacan would never have suggested it, the idea that there is a force effective enough to fix such meanings ties the model to an analysis of power in much the same way as Foucault does in his construction of power/knowledge. Our concern here will be how the *point du capiton* model might be applied to cinema; that is, how meanings come to be fixed in the fluidity of cinema.[4]

One of the fundamental aspects of the formation of such *points du capiton* is need, for a certain type of such fixing moments is derived from a necessity to understand a certain construction in order for it to appear meaningful. This is distinct from the larger orders of the *points du capiton*, which are derived from a socially and/or textually familiar pattern. A straightforward example in film would be the use of certain devices to signify a flashback or some recollection. These devices (such as the fade-out, the black screen, or waves of distortion) fix the meaning of that which follows as belonging to the past, and therefore having a different narrative attachment to the perspective found in the rest of the film. Any point designated as memory must be seen as having a direct link to the first person narrator, rather than the rest of a film which has been constructed in terms of the third person, omniscient. These moments are predetermined through the conventions of the cinematic discourse, as well as the social order in which the films are located.

Our concern here, however, must be with a different sense of the operation of the *point du capiton* in cinema, where meaning emerges out of a series of particular processes. This is acknowledging the construction of a film as one of diverse and complex strata derived from, for example, dialogism, heterogeneous elements from the Symbolic and Imaginary orders, a play of transpositions. This, then, is a consideration of the investment of power/knowledge in the cinematic *point du capiton*.

The *Parergonal* Logic of the Cinematic Frame

So far in this chapter we have considered meaning in cinema from three different perspectives: the idea of meaning itself as an element, contextualised by various textual, intersubjective, and cultural processes; the relationship of meaning to power; and the processes which allow the spectator to 'fix' a meaning or to produce interpretation. This final section will be in effect taking a step back from these three, and will consider how meanings generated within the film are dependent on a relationship to something which is neither within the film itself, nor derived from outside of it (from, for example, the socio-historical conditions, or the spectator's own perspective and reading competence). This is the relationship of constructions of meaning to that liminal space which is neither included in, nor excluded from, the work, but functions between them and in them. This is the *parergonal* logic of the frame.

Derrida offers the following as an introduction and definition to the *parergon*: 'neither work (*ergon*) nor outside the work, neither inside nor outside, neither above nor below, it disconcerts any opposition but does not remain indeterminate and it *gives rise* to the work. It is no longer merely around the work' (Derrida 1987b: 9). Although, in typical Derridean style, the ideas are twofold in *The Truth in Painting* (the investigation of an idea, and the investigation of that investigation[5]), it is possible for us to focus attention on how the *parergon* functions in this relationship to cinematic meaning, its formations and its relationship to power and control. It is necessary to note that Derrida's primary concern (apart from his meta-investigative stance) and designated text is painting, and we must be aware that some of the more specific points made in the two books of interest here – *The Truth in Painting* and *Memoirs of the Blind* (1999) – are directed at the discourse of the painting. That said, there is still much to be gained in considering cinema in terms of the function of the *parergon*.

One of the driving forces in Derrida's study is the idea that the space of the *parergon* has a particular relationship to meaning/truth;[6] one which operates outside of it, and yet is also a part of it. Similarly, we need to negotiate the *parergon* in order to understand what is being produced in terms of meaning – that is, how meanings that come to stand as such (that is, meaningful) are dependent on how we as spectators are positioned by, and position, the *parergon*. Derrida points out that the *parergon* is not simply the frame however: 'It works the frame, makes it work, lets it work, gives it work to do' (Derrida 1987b: 12). This gives added impetus to the attempts here to discuss a *parergonal* logic of the cinema, for we can comfortably put to one side the frame of the painting, and look to find devices that function as the *parergon* in film.

One way to approach the difficulties of this term in relation to cinema is to consider those elements which problematise the status of the relationship between the film and the spectator. One part of the *parergon* is the space which exists between the spectator and the film; a space which often collapses (in, for example, the appresentation of terror the space is negated in the horror of the image and its forces) in order for the process of *suture* to take effect. Any intrusion into that space, any moment of acknowledging it, necessarily draws attention to the cinematic *parergon*. The self-reflexive moment in comedy when the actor turns to the camera, setting up a complicity between himself/herself and the spectator, functions within the *parergon* because it belongs neither to the inside order of the film nor the outside order of the spectator. Dialogic processes, once acknowledged (or if they function in this self-reflexive manner, such as the *Scream* films), are located in this same region of the liminal. Similarly, the foregrounding of cinematic devices, such as the French New Wave's treatment of montage, operates within the *parergon*. The disconcerting cut in *A bout de souffle* (at the level of the visual and aural) from the kiss of Michel and Patricia in their flat to an aerial sweep of Paris is part of the *parergon*. This is not the kiss nor the shot of Paris, but the diegetically disruptive device of the jump-cut. Running counter to the conventions of narrative in cinema, such cuts end up problematising the status of the structure, as well as presenting points of negotiation in meaning.

This, then, is the first point regarding meaning and the cinematic *parergon*: it suggests a space in which, neither inside nor outside the text, a number of different types of textual devices and processes are located. Often premised on self-reflexivity, these elements operate apart from the diegetic order of things. Their meaning is thus derived not from what has happened in the narrative, but external to that; and not from the act of the spectator, but textually internal to that. The meanings of such devices are distinguished from those derived from the other two 'regions' (the text and the spectator), but are also an integral part of these two. The second point to be made is that such constructions in and by the *parergon* are mobile, sliding in and out of the textual order, and dynamic in their effect to change meanings. This is partly to do with the textual indeterminacy of the *parergon* (that is, it can be located in any number of different parts of the film), and also a consequence of the relationship of the film to the spectator, and vice versa.

These effects of mobility and the dynamic are products of a number of qualities of the *parergon*. Because it is not situated anywhere in particular, and yet also potentially everywhere (a quality especially true in the case of cinema), the *parergonal* aspects of a text are not restricted to specific devices or representations. Its primary attribute in this regard is absence. As Derrida states: 'the *parergon* . . . is called in by the hollowing of a certain lacunary quality within the work' (Derrida 1987b: 128). This is why the operation of the cinematic *parergon* requires the situating of the spectating position in much the same way as was discussed earlier in terms of the gaze and the mirror. This is the *parergonal* process of locating signs and discourses as relative points to one another, as well as the spectator. The lacunary quality of the *parergon* allows it to mutate, transforming common elements of film (such as montage and *mise-en-scène*, characterisation, the narrating point of view) into *parergonal* logic; that is, devices of the frame. Once this takes place then the meaning of these signs becomes foregrounded, for they come to stand for the impossibility of meaning within the film (that is, they cannot mean in the diegetic order like other signs might be able to), as well as the questionable status of meaning outside of (or from) the film of those signs.

An example of this is the whole operation of time and memory in *Last Year at Marienbad*. Signs of time and memory usually have connotative values of reliable or unreliable, each path positioning events and characters in a certain way. When Walter Neff recalls the events that lead up to his death in *Double Indemnity* his memory is not questioned, and works both within the diegetic order, and as a construction of it. This memory is taken to be true because part of its function is a moral one; this is the confession of a man who has been wronged and has done wrong. The memory of the man in *Last Year at Marienbad* is located in the *parergon*, partly because of the *lacunae* which feed into, as well as from, it, and partly because it is so often foregrounded and brought into question. This is also the case of the woman's function, for she is *paregonally* located as she repeats, shifts, and alters time and memory.

Another aspect of the *parergon* is that it contains (puts into operation might be a better phrase for part of its action is very much the catalytic – the work of the text, to recall Derrida) the excesses of the text.[7] This is both those qualities of cinema that are rendered excessive compared to their usual use, and elements that are not normally located within film. To follow up this example of time, the films of Rivette are paced so differently from most other films, with shots going for long periods with gentle repetitions and undulations. This is similar to films by Duras (such as *India Song* (1975) and *Vera Baxter* (1977)) which interplay long dialogues with equally continuous shots of images. Duras's camera will track and trace, flow and explore images for themselves, almost against any narrative requirement. Bergman will do the same thing, only with an intensity invested in representing the workings of the unconscious as they become manifested on and through the body. The long, careful closeups of faces in *Persona* (1966) move the images beyond concerns with either space or time. These are excesses of time of the film. Other examples are those elements which are made excessive though an unusual construction. Examples of this would be: the struck match in *Blue Velvet*, with the sound and image operating within the *parergon*, forcing the spectator to make connections with it because of the repetition, and the emphasis; the excesses of colour in *The Wizard of Oz* (Fleming and Vidor 1939) which, initially at least, shifts the filmic signs into the *parergon* because the framing world order of Kansas cannot possibly sustain such intensity. (This particular example illustrates how the *parergon* can actually function outside of literal frames, but still function as framing devices.) The closing shots of *Blue Velvet*, with their vivid, cartoonesque colours, operate in a similar way. Here the *parergon* operates to unsettle the distinctions made within the film between world orders. The everyday world of middle-class America takes on the same surreal quality as the dark world of Frank. It is the *parergon* which contains these two orders of excess – the excess of violence and the hyper-real excess of the normal. Finally, there is the seemingly impossibly long opening shot in *The Player* (Altman 1992), which seems to signal the excessive self-reflexivity contained through the entire film. As a comparison to this, note De Palma's similar extraordinarily long continuous shot in the opening of *Snake Eyes* (1998). The sequence is so unusually long (and hence contains a fluidity which contrasts with the more common cuts in an opening sequence to establish characters and setting) that the camera becomes foregrounded – a process which continues throughout the entire film. The spectator is reminded of the camera's presence through the breaking of certain conventions (such as the long take) as well as being shown it (the continual use of surveillance cameras, the theme of satellite cameras, photographs, etc.).

The *parergon* also has an unusual status in terms of the relationship between a text (in our case the cinematic) and its socio-cultural and historical contexts. As Derrida points out: 'The *parergon* stands out [*se détache*] both from the *ergon* (the work) and from the milieu' (Derrida 1987b: 61). It does this, Derrida argues, by standing out from the work and its surroundings, but also by merging them. It is, then, both a part of the work and its contexts (defining them, forming them, giving a sense of enclosure, working them into a textual form), and apart from them (by exceeding them, by drawing attention to the very framing process, challenging their history and operations). The *parergon* occupies a distinct site in terms of meaning, for its status of neither in nor out of the work and socio-cultural contexts means that its status of interpretation is foregrounded. The narrating voice of Holly in *Badlands*, because it both confirms and contradicts the actions on the screen, is *parergonal*, and so the spectator comes to question all meaning-forming devices. Derrida's 'metaphor' that the *parergon* is like a figure that stands out from the ground (attached but distinct from) signals that it is something which is attached and recognisable. However, he also points out that it is the efforts to be invisible, to disappear, bury itself, and melt away (Derrida 1987b: 61) that causes the *parergon* to expend its energy. The *parergon* in *The Devil's Advocate* is essential to the narrative, as well as the moral and ethical meditations, yet it buries itself (through subterfuge mostly) quickly, only to resurface at the end of the film.

The final point to be made here on the *parergon* is its relationship to the foregrounding of frames. This framing of the frame operates in many different ways including both a textually derived one as well as the positioning of the spectator, and the inevitable combinations of these. We have already noted that the operation of hypocrisis often involves precisely this critical moment when the spectator becomes aware of his/her position, and actions, in the framing devices. Such frames can be quite literal, such as the frame-tale structure in narrative, as well as more abstract, such as the conceptual investigation of the frames in some films. One of the attributes of this process is that all elements of cinema (which includes the act of spectating) can be imbued with the quality of the frame, and hence *parergon* and liminality. Light in the thriller can operate as a conceptual form because it signals division, difference, generic conventions, and narrative developments; the steady-cam shot can be used to 'step outside' of the frame of camera shots (in, for example, the gunfight scene in *The Quick and the Dead*, any number of shots in *Raising Arizona*, or the final sequences in *The Shining* with the chase through the maze), and in doing so the whole device of camera movement becomes framed and then exceeded. As with other devices of *trompe l'oeil* (such as anamorphosis or the jutting-out effect in Dutch still-life paintings), the intent is to blur the boundaries between image and spectator, as well as challenge the foundations of the frame itself.

8

Seduction: Gender, Genre and Power

> *To seduce is to die as reality and reconstitute oneself as illusion.*
> (Baudrillard)

Seduction encapsulates so many of the themes and practices of cinema. Once more, we find ourselves confronted with a familiar entanglement. Cinema itself is seductive – this is one of its most compelling qualities; and cinema has become well practised and skilled at setting up and devising scenes of seduction. To investigate the sorts of relationships which operate between cinema and seduction we need to bear this aspect in mind. The seductive power of the cinematic apparatus has become one of its defining features. Cinema is seduction, and to watch a film is to be seduced. This is true in the very specific sense of a seductive image (or sound, or sequence, and so on), and it is also true in a much broader sense in that all cinema seduces through the very act of spectating. In this sense the gaze is a relationship of seduction, and the film is what draws it in, luring it by its qualities and its representations. The seduced spectator is constructed by, and constructs, the film. Even from this simple line we can note that much of what follows will trace back through a great deal of what has gone before. Seduction may well be a metaphor here, but it does offer the chance to circle back, and to contemplate some of the essential features of film in terms of the construction of the spectator through the cinema's gaze, the cultural contexts of film, the creation and function of cinematic discourses, and the operation of meaning. In each of these we find seduction.

The themes and processes of seduction surround us. What we tend to experience, however, is much less seduction and more its effects. This is partly because to attempt to describe a unity of seduction, or even a materiality, is an impossibility. Seduction is not limited to certain formal features and textual practices, but rather it is a quality that can be seen to be operating at any number of different levels, both in the broadest sense of the phenomenon, and within specific aspects of film. It is what lies beneath the surface that most often contains the seductive qualities and lures. Seduction that declares itself as such is perhaps the least seductive, for with that comes an overt statement of what is taking place. Seduction is about deception, and as such must always resist truth. To say that something is seduction is really to say that it opposes the truth, resists conclusion: 'To be seduced is to be turned from one's truth. To seduce is to lead the other from his/her truth' (Baudrillard 1990: 81). It could be said that cinema also has a certain investment in such seductions. In order to work towards an idea of how seduction works in cinema, and how cinema itself operates at a level of seduction, we shall commence with a few observations on the elements of the seductive and how they interact. We shall begin by considering the idea of the difference between signs of seduction and seductive signs.

Signs of Seduction and the Seductive Sign

Cinematic signs which operate as the seductive can be divided into two types: the seductive signs and the signs of seduction. The seductive signs are those types which have their seductive quality invested in the signifier, and their primary function is to seduce towards themselves. Such signs have an attraction to the signifier itself. The most obvious examples occur in forms such as propaganda films, where the intent of the signs is to produce a type of political seduction. *Triumph of the Will* does this with its shots of the Nuremberg rallies, where the images of the masses of people are set up to seduce at first the gaze and then the political will of the spectator. That they now have such chilling resonance, totally devoid of any sense of seduction, is a result of history and political knowledge. Similarly, *Battleship Potemkin* attempts political seduction through its recurring seductive signifiers (the masses against the soldiers, and the lone mother and child in the Odessa steps sequence, for example). In both these examples from the right and left of the political spectrum we see seductive signs, where the quality of being seduced is held at the level of the signifier.

The creation of the star system, which invests actors with the attributes of seduction, is a different form of this same process. Certain actors become noted for parts of their body, which work in effect as seductive signs. The voice of John Malkovich, the lips of Bardot, the fetishistic hair of Jane Fonda in *Barbarella* (Vadim 1968), the sculpted muscles of Bruce Willis, the postwar curves (so much a conflation of masculine desire for the sexual and the mother) of Marilyn Monroe, the dark eyes of Gregory Peck in *Spellbound* (Hitchcock, 1945), the generational desires represented in Winona Ryder, are all examples of seductive signs because cinema constructs them to attract the gaze, or some other part of the sensory perceptions such as the ear, of the spectator. They come to signify seduction in themselves and can do this without recourse to other signifying practices. In doing so they have a declarative effect, and once this is established seduction proceeds at the denotative level, with the only question left being as to what the seduction is towards – although with the majority of such signs the answer to this is invariably to the signs themselves.

Such signs contain a direct action within themselves to resist any attempt to look too far beyond the signifying levels of denotation. The reason for this is that seductive signs are emptied of connotative value because they want to signify seduction itself. This is in direct contrast to signs of seduction, for these attempt to resist being seen as seductive at all. Instead, these signs present deceptively simple signifiers and invest the element of seduction in the signified. These signs have an attraction beyond the signifier, and often beyond the sign itself. What comes into play with such signs is that there is a constant questioning of whether or not seduction is taking place; or if it is, to what effect and for what reasons. Signs of seduction are often recognised as such only after their effects have been felt.

Many signs cross over between these two broad types, and it would be wrong to see this as an attempt to categorise in a binary fashion. To return to an earlier example, the images in *Triumph of the Will* and the pout of Bardot do want to seduce, and do declare this (both in themselves and within a broader cultural context). However, the seduction also attempts to take place at a level beyond the signifier – at the level of fascism for one and male sexuality for the other. But what makes these more seductive signs (than signs of seduction) is that there is no real disguising of this, and their seduction operates at the level of complicity. The propositional and modal opacity of these seductive signs is decreased because of this declarative process. Indeed, part of the very seduction is this investment in a self-awareness so that the spectator becomes the willing participant. Signs of seduction, on the other hand, may not even appear especially seductive initially, but usually this quality is revealed at some point. This post-seduced revelation is a common theme in, for example, films of *noir*, thrillers and mystery. The dynamics of the operation of the cinematic signs can be read in terms of these two types, especially when the force of the code is brought into play. Before turning to this let us take a couple of examples to tease out some more attributes of these sign systems.

Seductive signs tend to be heavily invested with a sort of cultural currency. We quickly recognise them because they declare their intent and utilise well-established paradigms, drawn from cultural sensibilities, history, intertextual references, textual conventions, etc. We can take a scene from *Pulp Fiction* to illustrate this, in part because it parodies some of the key aspects of a certain form of cultural and filmic established seductions, and in doing so holds up the devices in a type of *parergonal* logic.

The First Scene of Seduction — Power/Knowledge

The sequence we are most interested in here is the one which commences with the arrival of Vincent at Mia's house to take her out on a date, to the closing scene of their return from the diner and her accidental overdose. This is a set of scenes which draws together a parody of 1950s teenage films of dating, with all their repressed and highly encoded seductions, and a 1990s postmodernist discarding of moral structures and sensibilities of innocence. The setting of the 1950s diner utilises the connotative values of innocence, family life, and sexual clumsiness in direct contrast to elements such as the powerful, dominant figure of the woman (Mia), the open use of drugs (the parodic doubling is well illustrated when Mia uses the euphemism that she has to go and 'powder her nose' only to be shown snorting cocaine in the mirror), and the constant threat of violence. It is this contrast of ideologies and attitudes from the 1950s and 1990s that makes the elements of seduction adhere to and, at the same time, challenge many of the filmic conventions.

This is a scene of seduction which contains both seductive signs and signs of seduction; and one of the clearest seductions is Mia over Vincent. At one level he seems quite incapable of realising the seduction is taking place. Various parts of Mia's body are emphasised in this role of seduction: her hair is vampish Louise Brookes, her fingers impossibly long, her lips are emphasised in shape and colour, and her gaze is direct and constant. All the while Vincent seems oblivious to these elements. One of the key elements of seduction is power, for no seduction can work without it. The power of one person over another can be distilled into any number of different structures; love, sex, desire, and passion are the most obvious and recurring ones, but there are many others. This is the same sort of power that is bound up to knowledge in a Foucauldian sense. Mia's power/knowledge contains many seductive signs to the spectator — it is an inherent part of her character, established long before we meet her, when she is discussed by Vincent and Jules in terms of the throwing of the man out of the window. The first representations of her are located purely within a cultural sense of seduction — the closeup of her lips, a voice which surrounds intimately like a whisper, a gaze (through a surveillance camera) that renders her more powerful because she knows and sees more than others. To this, Vincent's seeming naivety lacks seduction. His wandering gaze, his drug induced semi-stupor, his incapacity to speak (and speech is so often a fundamental part of the seduction process), his childlike mannerisms (the disbelief of a 'five dollar shake' and the use of adolescent expressions for example), all seem to position him outside of the adult world of seduction.

Mia's seductive qualities are based almost entirely on seductive signs — a fairly typical representation of women within a phallocular world order.

Vincent does seduce, but his are more signs of seduction. He does have some seductive signs, most coming in the dance scene where, for the first time, he sustains a seductive gaze equal to Mia's.[1] He is also more aware of the seduction than at first seems likely, or even possible; when they return to Mia's house he stands in front of the bathroom mirror and points out the ethical dilemma he is confronted with, arguing that the safest and most moral line to adopt is to have a quick drink, say goodnight, and then home to 'jerk off' – an action on his behalf intended to defuse the seductive signs. Given this, the power/knowledge of Vincent in the scene of seduction is operating beyond the denotative signifiers, and at a level of the signs of seduction.

Both seductive signs and signs of seduction necessarily operate within a code structure of seduction. The most apparent difference is that the first is more overtly recognisable as part of the code structure, whilst the second relies on this coding process to be recognised as such. In other words, whereas seductive signs have their status confirmed through coding processes, signs of seduction rely entirely on that encoding/decoding process to be understood and recognised. Signs of seduction can be almost any sign, transformed into seduction through the codes of seduction. The model below illustrates this.

Codes of Seduction produce:

Sr (the signifier becomes an agent of seduction)
Sd (the signified has the function of seduction)
Sn (the relationship of Sr–Sd relies on a seductive process)

The first part of this model (the sign, represented as Sn) presents us with the idea that any sign exists *in potentia* as seductive, and it is often embedded in certain conventions which contribute to, or resist, this attribute. Remembering that part of the agenda here is to consider how cinematic signs (that is, all films as they come to constitute the cinematic apparatus) themselves are seductive, as well as those film signs involved in the particular representation of seduction, there are certain confluences which cannot be readily represented on so schematic a diagram. We then see the three parts of the sign – its signifier (1), signified (2), and the *glissading* bar (3) which represents the various relationships which exist between these other two. Each of these elements (and combinations of one, two or all three elements can do this) passes through the code of seduction to produce different effects and ways of interpreting them. The signifier which is read in terms of such a code is most like the seductive sign, for its active agency is to seduce, or to represent the seduction, or, as is most often the case, a conflation of the two. Mia's lips and Vincent's innocence are signifiers which, read through the code of seduction, become seductive signs for each other and the spectator.

In signs where the signifier is not positioned as seductive (its materiality resists this, or the context is not as clearly established) the signified can have the function of seduction, almost running counter to the operation of its signifiers. In these cases the code of seduction not only 'categorises' such signs, it provides a system for making sense of them, and linking them to other seductive moments. In *The Piano* there is a whole series of elaborate seductions operating at the level of the signified, but resisted within the signifiers. The piano itself is a seduction – of civilisation in a colonial world, of romantic love, of speech/communication and its rejection, of the choice between the seduction of death and the possibility of happiness in life. The exchange of keys for flesh is more clearly a series of seductive signs, whereas Ada's fierce sense of her self becomes a sign of seduction to both Stewart and Baines. At another level there are cultural seductions, with Baines physically representing a white person seduced to the Maori culture with his facial tattoos, and Stewart, with his anomalous European dress and mannerisms, representing the resistance to one form of cultural seduction (the Maori), but giving in to another (the European). But to read almost any of these signs in this way requires us to track the signified through the code of seduction, and then to reassess the signifier.

The third passage we find in this model is when the bar of the sign passes through the code of seduction. In this process it is the relationship of the signifier and the signified which is reread in terms of seduction. In other words, the bar binds the two other elements together as being seductive. In this sense the *glissement* of the bar, its sliding qualities, becomes fixed through the cinematic *point du capiton* of codes of seduction. A sign becomes understood as representing seduction not necessarily in itself, but by being fixed at that moment through the codes of seduction. The most obvious example of this is where either the signifier or the signified (or indeed both) seem openly resistant or oppositional to a reading of seduction. Evil as seductive, which is so deeply embedded in a great many film representations, relies on this sort of structure. (This is the same argument used against cinema as having the capacity to seduce its audience into immorality.) The binding of a potentially abject signifier with an equally abject signified can only produce a seductive quality if the bar itself has been positioned in terms of a code of seduction. Michael Corleone's turning towards violence in *The Godfather* is construed as seductive at the level of the bar (with its feature of *glissement* momentarily fixed by this reading of seduction.

Codes of seduction, to sum up, have three primary functions. Firstly, they establish signifiers as seductive in their materiality. The film conventions of pouting female lips and chiselled male jaws are signifiers of seduction because of these codes. Secondly, they provide interpretations of the signified which relocate the entire sign within a context of seduction. Thirdly, they allow a binding of the elements of the sign so that it

necessarily functions in terms of seduction. In order to observe more fully
these operations, and engage in more detail with some of the processes of
seduction, we will now consider how different genres utilise and adapt the
codes and signs of seduction.

Seduction and Genre

We have already noted that one of the primary attributes of seduction is
power/knowledge. But this does raise a number of difficulties. Is all seduction about power? If the participants in seduction know what is taking
place (that is they have supposedly equal knowledge), is it still seduction?
What happens to things like power and knowledge after the seduction has
taken place? To consider these more fully this section will consider how
seduction operates across a number of different film forms, commencing
with the one that has one of the greatest amounts of investment in seduction, film *noir*.

Film *noir* operates with a continuous undercurrent of seduction. Its
entire narrative propulsion, character development, ideological perspective, and created world order circle around the one fundamental quality
that people are seductive and are seduced. These sexual, seductive relationships are quite different from those represented in erotic films, where
there is not so much seduction as just stated sexual intent. Sexual fulfilment
in *noir* is never the compulsion, but rather it is the power of the sexual over
people. This is what gives *noir* its darkest moments, because the actions of
the seducer (more often than not the female) are derived from an investment in power/knowledge. So heavily invested in seduction are the signs
of *noir* film that almost anything can acquire this attribute. The codes of
seduction permeate all actions, objects and exchanges; but for this to operate effectively there is also an unequal distribution of knowledge. Men are
generally shown to be unaware of the seduction until it is too late. They
recognise the seductive signs, but not the signs of seduction, which are the
ones more clearly imbued with power/knowledge. In *Double Indemnity*
the spectator's first view of Phyllis Dietrichson is from a first person perspective of Walter Neff. We, like him, clearly recognise the seductive signs
as she walks down the stairs, picking up from the closeup of her anklet, her
bare legs, her almost too blond hair, the sensual clothing. This is a male
perspective of what seductive signs look like, with all power seeming to be
located in this scopophilic gaze. Of course the code of seduction reverses
this, and the signs of seduction are flowing in the opposite direction; he is
not being seduced by the seductive signs, but by the *noir* ones that are operating beyond the materiality of the signifier.

This double play of signs filtered through the code of seduction is a recurring theme in *noir* – so much so that it is one of the defining qualities of the genre itself. Even the neo-*noir* films of the 1980s and 1990s, such as the remake of *The Postman Always Rings Twice*, *The Last Seduction* and *The Big Heat* (Kasden 1981), observe this process of layering seductive signs which are stated, with signs of seduction which contain the elements of power/ knowledge. It is this interplay which helps define the signs as such, and locates the characters and events within certain sexual politics. One of the biggest shifts between the original sequence of *noir* films and the neo-*noir* versions is that the women are often positioned as positive in their powerful attributes, even if there are still senses of masculine paranoia of the seductive woman. Once this takes place we begin to witness what Baudrillard describes as a seduction which has 'an ironic, alternative form, one that breaks the referentiality of sex and provides a space, not a desire, but of play and defiance' (Baudrillard 1990: 21). In these terms, and in this space, *noir* films, both the originals and the later versions, provide a *parergonal* logic of seduction. The spectator both knows and understands the function of seduction in this film form, but occupies a site outside of this knowledge in order to let the seduction operate. This is a good example of hypocrisis, for the spectator is seduced not simply at the level of a represented seduction, but as part of the power/knowledge structure of seduction. (We shall return to Baudrillard's reading of seduction later in this chapter and explore these ideas further.)

A different type of seduction takes place in the Western and the Gangster genres, but with very similar gender politics. The sorts of seductions which operate are almost invariably not sexual in both these forms, for they are located firmly within deeply conservative and repressive sexual politics. Instead the seductions in the Western and Gangster films come primarily from two sources – violence and territory. The seduction of violence operates in a similar way to the *femme fatale*. The knowledge of the threat of death, the compulsion to return, the impossibility to resist, the ubiquity of the seductive signs as they come to define the social order, are as true of violence in the Western and Gangster films as they are of the woman in *noir*. The seduction comes in at various levels, often with initial resistance, then acceptance and deep involvement, before a tragic ending. Signifiers such as guns in *Winchester 73* (Mann 1950) and the knife in *The Iron Mistress* (Douglas 1952) represent how the 'good' man is seduced into violence. Similarly, the past and revenge operate in some ways as part of the seduction in, for example, *High Noon*. *Unforgiven* represents a self-reflexive turn on precisely this narrative device in the Western, just as *Miller's Crossing* does the same in terms of the Gangster film. Both films employ characters who openly discuss the seductions (and ethics) of violence, the past, and vengeance, and both find resistance is impossible. Territory, be it land in the Western or a city in the Gangster film, is positioned as equally seductive. For it is the playing out of masculine desires to possess and control that is manifested in the need for territory. In *noir* this masculine desire for 'territory' is the body of the woman.

Seduction in the romance genre is different from *noir* in that it follows two broad possibilities, each derived from a certain position of power/ knowledge: it can be positive seduction and leads to love; or it is negative seduction and leads to tragedy. As with *noir*, the code of seduction preexists any films of this form, so the signs can be substantially different from film to film and the spectator can still be aware of their operations. The sustained and polymorphic attributes of these codes means that the seduction can be found in quite diverse contexts; the comic becomes part of the seduction in screwball and romantic comedies, working at this level in, for example, Hepburn and Tracy in *Adam's Rib* (Cukor 1949), Gable and Colbert in *It Happened One Night* (Capra 1934) and Hepburn and Grant in *Bringing Up Baby* (Hawks 1938). Once more we can see a sort of reflexivity of this in films that push the conventions much further as the comic stands in for seduction, and in doing so operates as part of it. What the comic allows, at the same time, is both an acknowledgment and denial that seduction is taking place. The humour of the situation places the seduction on to the comic, and vice versa. In this way the sexual repression, of which seduction is an essential part, that humour attempts to avoid is played out at the level of the comic. This displacement of the signs and codes of seduction represents a different inflection of the power/knowledge involved.

The Scene of Seduction: The *Urphantasie* of Cinema

The Second Scene of Seduction – Freedom and Phantasy

In a scene in *Easy Rider* a family man leans out of his car window, gazes longingly at Wyatt and Billy on their motorbikes as they pause in the traffic. Gazes meet, a few words are exchanged about how lucky they are in their freedom, and then they separate. The scene sets up a reversal of the positioning of the spectator in the film's intentionality of seduction. This man comes to represent what the spectator (especially those in the film's contemporary audience who could possibly think that the dream of motorbikes and freedom might exist in the latter part of the 1960s) does not want to be, and yet is. His car, like the seats of the cinema, distinguishes him from the phantasy presented by the two on the bikes. The seduction is presented as possible, but unlikely, desired yet destructive. This is a phantasy heavily invested in a (Western) cultural order, made more ironic in the cinema of Wenders (such as *The American Friend* (1977) and *Paris, Texas* (1984) where the freedom of the road is revealed to be a circuitous trip of introspection and non-arrival), or Antonioni's *The Passenger* which ends with a 360-degree panning shot, representing the impossibility of escape and resolution.

Psychoanalysis has a difficult relationship to seduction, stemming largely from a theory that Freud devised, supposedly abandoned, and then seemed to keep circling around. This is his 'scene of seduction' in which he initially argued that everyone experienced, during childhood, an attempt of seduction by an adult, which was then followed by a second scene of seduction which takes place after puberty (see Freud's *Studies on Hysteria*). He appears to abandon this theory, replacing it with the theory of the Oedipus complex as an explanation of the sexual development of the individual, but parts of it came to be invested in his later ideas on the development of child sexuality. Laplanche and Pontalis point out that 'it is Freud's first and sole attempt to establish an intrinsic relationship between repression and sexuality' (Laplanche and Pontalis 1986: 10), and as such retained a significant point in his theories. The other part to Freud's theory of seduction and sexual development is what he called the primal scene. This is the child's discovery of sexuality by catching the parents in the act of sex. The child, Freud argues, mistakes this as an aggressive act, and misreads orgasmic pleasure as violence. More significantly, this is the moment where adult sexuality becomes known/experienced by the child, and signals the child's movement into the Symbolic.

When Freud introduced the term *Urphantasien* (primal phantasy) he did so in order to negotiate these twin difficulties of the chronological developments of phantasy, and the different types of reality involved in the conscious and unconscious. As Laplanche and Pontalis point out: 'Since it proved impossible to determine whether the primal scene is something truly experienced by the subject, or a fiction, we must in the last resort seek a foundation in something which transcends both individual experience and what is imagined' (Laplanche and Pontalis 1986: 16). This should also provide some invaluable material in understanding how cinema operates as a scene of seduction for both the spectating subject and the cultural order.

What is important for us here is contained in two related propositions: the first is the general idea that seduction works at an unconscious, as well as conscious, level; the second is that cinema has its own formations of a primal phantasy (*urphantasie*) from which scenes of seduction are constructed and made sense of, as well as providing a type of link to the cultural order of things. Part of this order is psychoanalysis's distinction between realities – 'reality' and psychical reality (discussed earlier) – and cinema's capacity to move across the boundaries, producing signs and effects that operate in both realms.

One of the more direct ways we witness a relationship between these ideas and cinema is film's role in negotiating repression and sexuality through a playing out of seduction scenes. This is quite literally a sense that cinema replicates various *urphantasie* in its own scenes of seduction, providing a release from some of the cultural and psychical repressions. This is providing cinema with a function that Freud attributes to all phantasy (daydreams, imaginings, etc.) – a filling in of the gaps that are made through the acts of restriction. Not many people get seduced in the ways shown in cinema, but the scenes presented in films provide material that is demanded from the lacunae of both cultural and individual repressions (that is, the experienced and the imagined). This does raise the issue of whether we should see cinema as an *urphantasie* or a secondary phantasy (the latter being more clearly part, and product, of the imaginings of daydreams and such like). However any clear-cut answer to this is unlikely and unnecessary, as all phantasy is constituted of a heterogeneous mix from the two, and teasing them apart is a seemingly impossible task. The cinematic *urphantasie* is constituted of that reservoir of material we witnessed above, including the interplay of the spectator and individual films, certain cultural practices, generic formulations, and the manipulation of the corporeal to become seductive – in short, the cinematic apparatus itself. Secondary phantasy, on the other hand, is more clearly a part of the text that is actually produced in the combination of these elements. Seduction is a primal phantasy in itself, as is cinema, and the combination of these, along with the spectator's own elements of phantasy, produces secondary phantasies. This is the case of watching scenes of seduction represented in a film, and the actual experience of watching cinema overall.

The role and function of the spectator in all this can be correlated to a point that Laplanche and Pontalis make in closing their account of phantasy and sexuality. They argue, via Freud, that phantasy has a strong auto-erotism, produced largely through this quality of an inmixing of realities as well as an investment of the self within the experienced phantasy. Furthermore, they postulate that this auto-erotism provides 'the connection between fantasy and desire' and that 'fantasy is not the object of desire, but its setting' (Laplanche and Pontalis 1986: 26). This is clearly derived from Lacan's own position when he states: 'phantasy is the support of desire; it is not the object that is the support of desire' (Lacan 1986: 185). Cinema, we would argue, produces a site for the spectator to engage in a type of auto-erotism through this connection and setting of desire. The auto-erotism in cinema is derived from the spectator's own *urphantasie* meeting that of cinema's. Such a meeting draws the spectator into the scenes of seduction, whilst the spectator attempts to posit his/her own elements of phantasy into this. In other words, there exists in the Symbolic order of cinema a structure of phantasy which provides the settings of desire, but has certain lacunal qualities (from, for example, censorship, repression, cultural differences, and, for individual spectators, a lack of correspondence with their own phantasies). Part of the seduction of cinema is derived precisely from these gaps, because it is here that the spectator releases his/her own *urphantasies*. This also equates to some feminist (film) theory which argues for the lack of female desire – which is both female desire seen as lack, and a lack of a space for that desire – in phallocentric culture. The seductive qualities of a phallocular cinematic practice are directed towards men, but this does not mean that all cinema has to be as such.

Baudrillard offers tangents and inflections on these issues, and even if some of his ideas are unpalatable because of their curious sexual politics, there is still much to be gained by examining these points. Seduction for Baudrillard operates at the level of appearances (thus feeding into his theories on the simulacra[3]), and nowhere is this better illustrated than in and through the body. This is a relationship of struggle and revolution, of resistance to the gendering of the body in the Symbolic. As he puts it: 'seduction alone is radically opposed to anatomy as destiny. Seduction alone breaks the distinctive sexualization of bodies and the inevitable phallic economy that results' (Baudrillard 1990: 10).[4] One of the difficulties of Baudrillard's argument, however, is his division of the masculine and feminine in terms of seduction and production. When he argues, for example, that the masculine is the power to produce, whilst all the feminine has is the power of seduction (a negativity of the masculine power[5]) there are difficulties in resolving the gender politics and implications. Baudrillard is, admittedly, giving a negative twist to the processes included in the masculine production values, and a subversive, revolutionary quality to that of feminine seduction; but the tying of the feminine to seduction is somewhat problematic given the history and ideological connotations which already exist.

The part of Baudrillard's analysis that is of greatest relevance here is when he discusses the relationship of the mirror and reflection. It is through this that we can continue to examine the idea of cinema as seduction, and the auto-erotism of the spectator. Baudrillard's example of the *trompe l'oeil*, with its missing dimension, is comparable to the ideas being developed here. The *trompe l'oeil* provides an absence within the text-image which invites the gaze of the viewer. At the same time, it is the very nature of this trick which seduces, for its enigmatic qualities pull the gaze towards it. It is these absences and enigmas which allow the interplay between seduction and phantasy, and also provide the space for seduction to operate. Baudrillard sees these gaps as actually performing like a mirror, reflecting the spectator's own sense of self in terms of seduction – the seduction of the self's image. For him, 'true seduction proceeds by absence' (Baudrillard 1990: 108), for the absences are both creative points and liminal sites.

In terms of the cinematic spectator, seduction operates at a number of
levels, but what is fundamental is the seduction of the spectator's gaze by
the film, and the seduction of the film by the gaze. This recalls an earlier
discussion on the *passe partout*, the *parergon*, and tain of the mirror. In these
terms the tain is the seductive element of film, the glass the translucent and
slight distance between spectator and desire. What seduces most is the self
positioned within the frame, reflected back *through* the cinematic apparatus. Seduction can only work within this frame of reference – of the self
seducing the self through the images and events in the film. This brings us
to the important point of the intentionality of seduction, for it is here we
witness further issues of power and meaning.

The Seduction of Light

When we are seduced, we are seduced towards something as well as by
something/someone. There is always an intentionality involved. This suggests a number of things, including that there are two orders of seduction:
one where the act of seduction is primary over the reasons for the seduction, and another where this is reversed and seduction itself is disguised by
the other factors. In the first there is an acknowledgement of the seduction
but not its intentionality; in the second the seduction may not even be
apparent until long after it has taken place. Clearly power and knowledge
determine much of this situation, but the intentionality, and directional-
ity, of seduction underpins much of how this is played out. But one of the
enfolding aspects of all this is that we are often seduced by the lack of
power/knowledge, and we participate with an expectation of gaining
some insight, some power and control over knowledge and the Other.
The seduction of light here works at the level of power/knowledge (the
seduction of light is to be able to reveal) as well as the lights of cinema
itself – the images that flicker and glow in seductive qualities.

The Third Scene of Seduction – Obsession

Antonioni's *Blow Up* is constructed almost entirely along what might be
described as classical seduction scenarios. There are a number of different
types of seduction, each operating differently, but having the same sorts of
outcomes, often culminating in a type of spiritual desolation. There are
sexual seductions represented initially in the fashion shoots, where the
lens of Thomas's camera is not too subtly represented as both phallus and
penis. This is also shown in the sexual encounter with the two teenagers
who invade Thomas's flat and work-space. But both these seductions are
really only used to contrast the real seductions which are derived more

fully from *trompe l'oeil*, mirrors, enigmas, and light. It is in these that we witness a representation of the intentionality of seduction, as well as the film's capacity to seduce the spectator. (These other two scenes of seduction if anything repel the spectator from being seduced into the scene because of their masculine arrogance and phallocentric qualities.)

One of these seductions is based around the relationship of Thomas, Jane, and the man in the park. At first the power and interest of the photographer are derived from a voyeurism that yields control over other people's lives – a theme continually represented in his character. Jane's attempt to obtain the photographs back from him results in the same sort of overt seduction we see in those other images of the fashion shoot and the teenagers. It is stated as a seduction intended to gain an entirely differentiated goal. But there is another seduction which operates beyond this, derived this time from enigma. It is the seduction based on the questions and mystery as to why the film is so important to Jane. This, in turn, leads to the primary seduction which underpins the entire film.

This is the seduction of light. This is the blowing up of the photograph so that light and dark become smudged and the question of the existence of the body is raised. Thomas's need to know becomes the spectator's seduction, because it also becomes our need to know. This seduction is pure seduction because it overrides all else, even allowing the spectator to become interested in a character that had so far been shown as arrogant, self-obsessed, uncaring in his feeling towards others, and sometimes brutal. As a metaphor for seduction, the photographs work well. The more we look for clues, the more we peer at the light and dark areas trying to shift them into shapes, the more the answer eludes us – so much so that the seduction has taken place before we know it, transforming itself into one of the corollaries of seduction – obsession. These are the same sorts of obsessive seductions and unanswered gazes we find in other Antonioni films – the vanishing of people in *L'Avventura* (1960) and the journey for a new identity, and to keep that pretence alive, in *The Passenger*. Furthermore, the blowing up of the photographs – this seductive gaze over the grainy images – reveals another quality of seduction. There are no answers to be derived from it, for seduction provides its own legitimation. The power/knowledge of seduction is not in solving the riddle of the image, but of moving the gaze outside of its usual perspective. Seduction produces more seduction, just as it produces more images within the image.

The seduction of light operates in this twofold fashion. It promises answers (the seduction of power through knowledge, and knowledge through power) but only produces this blinding effect; it pulls the gaze towards something that is absolutely compulsive, but not satisfying in itself because intentionality lies elsewhere. To see how this works we can consider a few more examples.

The Fourth Scene of Seduction – Subjectivity

In *Blade Runner* all the characters are driven by the need to know about their status of life, of its duration and its relationship to the qualifications of the human and non-human. It may seem odd to describe this as seduction, for it would appear to be more about existence. But the way life itself is established in the film makes it a seduction rather than a necessity of subjectivity. The idea of authentic Being informs a great deal of philosophy, and Sartre's *pour-soi/en-soi* and Heidegger's idea of *Dasein* provides us with an explication that can be read in the same way of life and subjectivity as seduction. Here the seduction is not simply to live, but to have a sense of beingness, of authentic subjectivity. The replicants are more human than human; more powerful, intelligent, and, as is revealed in the final scenes of Batty's death, more compassionate. Yet still there is the seduction of subjectivity which is both more than what they have, and less. This seduction drives the narrative, and once more we can see different levels of its operation. The scene where Deckard meets Rachel is straight out of classic film *noir* – it is Walter meets Phyllis all over again – and operates within those parameters of seduction. The woman represents danger and sexuality because she is so unknown. This becomes problematised in a later scene with the virtual rape (or at the very least violent sexual force) of Rachel by Deckard. If this first encounter posits seduction, this later one replaces it with force. In these terms the subjectivity (of Deckard and Rachel, seemingly human and non-human) is negotiated and determined in the first scene, but undercut and questioned in the second.

In the roof-top scenes which close the film we are offered the replicant's explanation for their seduction towards the human. Batty's speech which ends 'Time to die' is a complex discourse on self-reflexivity because it reveals such a depth of knowledge on the intentionality of his actions and the processes of seduction. It is also the same sort of reversal of empathy that we see in *Blow Up*, for the spectator now becomes located within a seduction towards this very act. Batty's search for subjectivity comes at that very moment when life expires and an understanding takes place. The white dove which flies from his arms becomes the metaphor for the soul he and the other replicants so strongly desired. It stands for a seduction that destroys and creates at the same moment. It is as light as the blurred photographs in *Blow Up* are dark – but both seduce.

The Seduction of the Dark

If cinema's light seduces, then there is also that other order of seduction – the darkness that surrounds us. And if there is a seduction towards the knowledge that light promises, there is an equally seductive quality to the dark recesses of the unknown and unknowable. This is, of course, also the area of immoral seduction, of those things which seduce and then prove to be the darker side of things. And yet, both light and dark can seduce in the same way, at the same time, towards the same objective. Seduction is ultimately beyond good and evil, but what happens after seduction can often be placed within this moral climate. For this reason the seduction of the dark should not simply be seen as the evil counterpart of the seduction towards the good – for in the seductive moment they are the same thing.

The Fifth Scene of Seduction – Betrayal and Revelation

One of the ways light and dark become entwined in the structure of power/knowledge is the revelation of betrayal at the end of the seduction. The knowledge gained is a dark one, revealing the intentions of the characters, the answers to various mysteries placed throughout the events, and often a reversal in the characteristics of the protagonists. In *Les Diaboliques* Christina is seduced into killing her husband, and the spectator is seduced into thinking this is an appropriate course of action – his brutality contrasted with Nicole's (relative and seeming) tenderness allows for the idea of legitimate murder. This is a theme of ethical cause and effect that drives a great many films. But both Christina and the spectator are duped through a much greater seduction based on betrayal, of which this expressed version is but a small part. The darkness that motivated the stated seduction overrides that sense of legitimising the actions of escape and freedom through murder. This is an example of the intentionality of the seduction being disguised and repressed by the very act of being seduced; seduction in such scenes overcomes its intentionality.

The reverse of this also operates in these scenes of betrayal, and the sense of seduction can be repressed through an overstated intentionality. In such cases the knowledge of what is taking place disguises the fact of any seduction. Michael Corleone knows he is being seduced by violence – this is its intentionality and its light; but Mike, in *The Last Seduction*, only thinks he knows he is being seduced. The seduction is, like in *Les Diaboliques*, premised on betrayal rather than escape or sex. The other inflection of this is where there is no sense of seduction at all, this quality only being revealed later. This can take place at the level of representation (as in the twists of film *noir* and a great many thrillers) and it can also take place at the level of the cinematic apparatus. The killing of Marion a third of the way through *Psycho* is a form of seduction and betrayal because the spectator, through narrative traditions, is led to believe that she is the central protagonist. We are seduced by the usual expectations of narrative

cinema, and then are betrayed by her death. The revelation of this seduction comes after the shower scene when we realise that the narrative is not
about her and we have been seduced into investing these attributes into
that character. Certain film genres depend almost entirely on this relationship of seduction and betrayal of the spectator to construct their narrative
and produce their effects. The horror genre seduces and betrays constantly
in order to terrify, and the spectator is a willing participant in this whole
process, acknowledging and denying the seductions from one moment to
the next.

Cinema's seductive qualities are invested in all of its elements, in part
because it takes the attributes of the everyday (vision, colour, sound, the
body, space and time) and presents them in an excessive and intensified
form. The very rarefied economies of cinema become seductive because
there is in them more than themselves. Cinema presents seduction, and
seduces, as a site of resistance, as negotiations of power and knowledge, as
systems of desire; in doing so seduction becomes part of the very materiality
of cinema itself.

Notes and References

1 The Gaze: Masochism, Identification and Phantasy in the Spectator

1. The standard translation for this is 'Instincts and Their Vicissitudes'. However it has become increasingly acknowledged that the rendering of *Trieb* as 'Instinct' is quite misleading. A more appropriate term might be 'drive' or, in French, *pulsion*. I have returned to the original to avoid any further difficulties of translation.
2. The term 'economic' in this title refers to Freud's concept of the topographical division of the mind. The most well known of these is the conscious, preconscious and unconscious. However, Freud also spoke of the operation and relations of the mind in other terms, including the economic and dynamic. In these he emphasised the flow and balance of energies, and the effect these had on the interplay between the unconscious (and hence repressed) and the conscious (and the censored).
3. In summary, Freud's argument is that women are restricted by culture from showing their desires in an active way. Subsequently, narcissism develops as a type of release because it avoids the usual repressive devices. In Freud's theory, desire for the self escapes the repression of phallocentric control because it is either a form of disguise, or not acknowledged as desire.
4. For a curious variation on this sort of cycle of masochistic relationships, compare *La Bombola* (Lunas 1994), where violence masquerades as love firstly in terms of the mother and then the lover. Both are killed in the same way and within the same violent contexts.
5. It is noteworthy that the Oedipal complex is not simply about the male child's relationship with the parents. For Freud it is about all individuals' entry into the social order. In this sense it is part of the formation and prescription of the subject (both male and female) into the Symbolic.
6. Writerly and readerly are concepts Barthes develops in *The Pleasure of the Text* (1975) to make a distinction between a more passive act of reading (the readerly text) and the active interplay of the reader in the making of the text (the writerly). These ideas are discussed elsewhere in this book.
7. We will take up this issue of Lacan's theories of subjectivity in further detail in Chapter 3.
8. See glossary for a definition of this term as well as discussion in the following chapter.

9. However, as Metz points out, cinema does, culturally, sanction the viewer. It is accepted that films will be watched, and in doing so the gaze of the audience slides between being that of the unknown and unacknowledged, to the accepted and expected.

10. This theme of phantasy will be returned to in the final chapter of the book when we consider the relationship between seduction and cinema.

11. See especially Freud's essays on sexuality, for example *Three Essays on the Theory of Sexuality* (1977).

12. In Freud's theories the primal scene is that moment where the child catches (literally or through some intellectual abstraction) the parents in the sexual act. For Freud this is a universal phenomenon, playing a key role in the psycho-sexual development of the subject. Freud argues that the child interprets the sexual scene as one of violence by the father against the mother, and so a sadistic and masochistic relationship.

13. Barthes does speak about cinema, notably in the essay 'Diderot, Brecht, Eisenstein', (Barthes 1977) and with passing references elsewhere ('The Face of Garbo', in *Mythologies*), but it would be fair to say that he could never be considered a major figure in terms of film theory.

14. Both these issues will be discussed in more detail later.

2 Dangerous Supplements and the Envy of the Gaze

1. For definitions of the Mirror Stage see the glossary.

2. In the formula the *a* stands for the French *autre*, that is, other.

3. Later we shall also consider how Foucault's ideas present ways of reading both in terms of and counter to this scenario.

4. A brief synopsis of some parts of the story may be of some use here. There are four main characters: Lola Valérie Stein, her friend Tatiana Karl, a mysterious woman called Anne-Marie Stretter, and two men – Lol's one-time fiancé, Michael Richardson, and Jacques Hold. There are many twists in the story's convoluted narrative of frames within frames, but basically ten years before the setting of the events Lol and Tatiana have gone to a ball with Lol's partner Michael Richardson. Anne-Marie Stretter comes to the ball, dances with, and then leaves with, Lol's fiancé, leaving her in the state of *ravissement*. Lol then persuades Jacques and Tatiana to re-enact this scene, as well as the seduction, whilst she hides and watches them.

5. Parallel to this, so much of Lacan's theorising of the gaze originates from Sartre's ideas in *Being and Nothingness*. In this book, Sartre describes the power of the gaze of the Other, using the example of someone caught looking through a key-hole. Not caught in a literal sense, but the abject guilt and feeling of what it is to be caught in such an act.

6. See, for example, Bazin (1967 and 1971) or Nichols (ed.)(1976) *Movies and Methods* contains useful articles on these issues and a wider bibliography.

7. For psychoanalysis – particularly Freudian and Lacanian – the subject is a fragmented and divided subject. This split starts at the mirror stage, but continues
   throughout the subject's life. The splits include those from the Symbolic order,
   within himself/herself through the division of the ego, id and super-ego, and the
   repression of the unconscious drives and desires.
8. This term carries with it a great deal of critical currency, particularly in terms of
   the writings of Baudry. We will consider it in more detail in a later section, but its
   meaning here, and throughout, is the formation and operation of the *cinematic* itself.
9. It is noteworthy that recent critical writings in Queer Theory took as one of
   their starting points the representation of the vampire; see, for example, Sue-Ellen
   Case's essay 'Tracking the Vampire' (1991).
10. Later it will be important to consider some of the points made by Lacan on the
    supplement and the feminine.
11. To extend this discussion even further, in Kracauer's schema anything that did not
    contribute to the effect of realism would be seen as a supplement –and a dangerous
    one at that! Kracauer's theories are founded on the idea that it is the photography
    which forms the underlying material of film. Once more, we see that in much of his
    (somewhat extreme) theory everything else in film – including editing – is a sup-
    plement to the realism of the photographic image.

3   The Shattering Pluralism: Film and Its Discourses

1. See, for example, works by Eco and Pasolini, for investigations on cinema and
   semiotics.
2. The lineage of Metz's work also demonstrates this. From the structuralist/semiotic
   early works of *Film Language: A Semiotics of the Cinema* (1974) to the blend of semiotics and psychoanalysis in *The Imaginary Signifier: Psychoanalysis and the Cinema*
   (1985), there is a recurring theme of film language and how we might read it.
3. Kristeva's Symbolic is derived from Lacan (via Lévi-Strauss) and, generally
   speaking, means the social/cultural domain, the operation of the sign in a coded
   language structure, and the processes of communication. Her sense of the poetic
   language is far broader than a literary model, and involves those disruptive elements which challenge, change and collapse those signifying practices of the Symbolic. In some ways the idea of a cinematic language derived from such a 'poetic'
   discourse parallels what Pasolini describes theoretically as a cinema of poetry
   (Pasolini 1976: 542–58) and is evident in his film practice.
4. This idea has been developed, most notably, by Baudry in, for example, 'The Apparatus: Metapsychological Approaches to the Impression of Reality in the Cinema'
   and 'Ideological Effects of the Basic Cinematographic Apparatus'.
5. Our principal concern here is with the relationship of these concepts to filmic discourse; however, in Chapters 4 and 5 we will consider the cultural contexts and
   implications of such ideas. For this reason tackling this particular issue will be
   taken up at a later point.
6. This point will be taken up in more detail in the following chapter.

7. The question arises as to why we should focus on *The Archaeology of Knowledge* when Foucault himself later points out the problems of some of these strategies, leading him to develop what he termed a genealogical approach to these issues and problems. The answer is twofold. Firstly, Foucault never actually abandons his archaeological ideas and methods, but he does refine them considerably. There is much to be gained by considering the ideas he posits in this book both in terms of understanding Foucault's opus, and applying his ideas to film. Secondly, to develop some ideas on film and discourse, and filmic discourse, it is important to engage in the ideas from the archaeology approach. In doing so we gain, at the very least, the possibility of mapping out some concepts on what a Foucauldian approach to film might look like. It is also important to recognise the position of this work in terms of Foucault's own development. Coming after the 'historical studies' on madness and medicine, and following *The Order of Things* (1970) as a type of development of technique, *The Archaeology of Knowledge* is Foucault's own self-reflexive turn, just as he asks us to adopt such a position ourselves. In the following chapter Foucault's ideas on power and discourse in terms of film will be developed more fully.

8. The ensuing examples are intended to serve as notional pieces until a more extensive analysis and set of examples is taken up in the following chapter on the body and discourse.

4 Flesh Into Body Into Subject: The Corporeality of the Filmic Discourse

1. See Freud's essay 'The Uncanny' in *Art and Literature*.
2. See *The Four Fundamental Concepts of Psychoanalysis* (1986), particularly the conclusion where, with one eye fixed on the role of the analyst, Lacan works his way through the relationship of transference in terms of love.
3. This is a more suitable translation of the German *Trieb* than 'instinct' as it allows for a distinction between this psychical sense and a biological one.
4. I have discussed the centrality of desire in Lacan's theory elsewhere (Fuery 1995) and refer the reader to this.
5. We will not take up another of the major forms of body fluids here – that of tears – in part because their representation is usually self-evident. Categories such as the fearful tear, that of sorrow, and of joy, are all culturally established and mostly operate within well-defined parameters.
6. This is an idea we shall return to in Chapter 7 with a discussion of the *lacunal* orgasm.
7. Foucault's notion of power is directly related to knowledge. For him 'power produces knowledge' and 'power and knowledge directly imply one another' (Foucault 1987a: 27).
8. The related idea of the abject body will be taken up in the next section of this chapter, and for this reason perhaps the most obvious examples of altered bodies, their desirability and threat, which take place in horror and thriller films will not be developed here.
9. Buñuel even uses two different actors to play the same character. This altered body is never questioned by any of the characters in the film.

10. See *History of Sexuality* (three volumes); *Madness and Civilisation* (1987b); *Discipline and Punish* (1987a); *The Birth of the Clinic* (1975).

11. It is interesting to note, in terms of the scopic drive being so essential to cinema, that Freud positions the visual central to libidinal economies: 'Visual impressions remain the most frequent pathways along which libidinal excitation is aroused' (Freud 1977: 69).

12. Briefly, the panopticon is an idea derived from Bentham's 1840s plan for a prison where the buildings of the cells surround a central tower. The guard can see into the cells, but the prisoners cannot see if the guard is in the tower or not. Thus there is no need even to have someone in the tower as the prisoners will always have to assume that they could be being watched. Foucault takes this as a model for the larger processes in a culture which produce self-surveillance. The gaze becomes the efficient system for the manifestation of power and control. For Foucault it is a fundamental element of our social order: 'We are much less Greeks than we believe. We are neither in the amphitheatre, nor on the stage, but in the panoptic machine, invested by its effects of power, which we bring to ourselves since we are part of its mechanism' (Foucault 1987a: 217).

13. In this sense what Lacan means when he talks about the symptom works equally well in terms of cinema: 'When deciphered, it appears as self-evident, imprinted upon the flesh, the omnipresence for the human being of the Symbolic function' (Lacan 1985: 127).

5 The Ideology of Love: Film and Culture

1. Dividing the drive up in this manner is in keeping with the idea found in Lacan's theory of partial drives. This is the operation of the drive(s) in psychical reality; and for our concerns it is also the conflation of film and spectator, as well as culture.

2. This issue is discussed in greater detail in Chapter 8 on seduction.

3. Cixous, in 'Laugh of the Medusa', counters this, saying that it is men who are incapable of the gift, and women are always producing gifts outside of the system of exchange that Derrida describes. It is interesting to consider this in terms of the above discussion of Ilsa's gifts of the two letters.

4. This combination of love and violence is found throughout the films of the New Wave, not in an exploitative manner, but often in an explorative one. Examples include the post-war lovers in *Hiroshima, Mon Amour* (Resnais 1959) and the sense of personal suffering, cultural devastation, and love; the two women in *Les Biches* (Chabrol 1968) where there is such a fierce sense of overwhelming personalities; and even the sexually and socially disruptive Bardot in *Et Dieu Créa la Femme* (Vadim 1956) who seems to continually confuse sexuality and love, or cause such confusions.

6 The Carnivalesque: Film and Social Order

1. The terms 'ontologies' and 'ontological orders' are used in the phenomenological sense here: that is, the formation of 'realities', such as a textual ontology where

events, identities, subject positions, histories, etc. have a specific currency and legitimacy within that order, but (potentially) lack this in another ontology (such as the wider social order).

2. This is a scene to which we shall return later in this chapter.

3. In this context it is well to recall Kristeva's point that parody is not part of the carnivalesque. As she points out: 'The word "carnivalesque" lends itself to an ambiguity one must avoid. In contemporary society, it generally connotes parody, hence a strengthening of the law. There is a tendency to blot out the carnival's *dramatic* (murderous, cynical, and revolutionary in the sense of *dialectical transformation*) aspects' (Kristeva 1984a: 80). This must certainly also hold true for carnivalesque cinema.

4. See Heath, articles in Rosen (ed.), *Narrative, Apparatus, Ideology* (1986) for further readings on this topic.

5. As with all these orders of reality, this is a complex issue. To witness how someone like Freud dealt with such a notion the reader is referred to his essay 'The Loss of Reality in Neurosis and Psychosis' (1984).

6. Of course the whole history of the theories of simulacra reaches back at least as far as Plato's model of the cave; and it is this history that Baudrillard is a part of. In a different way Baudry (1986) makes use of this history to analyse cinema's relationship to the outside world.

7. It is through this line of argument that Lyotard is able to assert that 'everything is a sign or mark, but that nothing is marked or signified, in that in this sense, signs are signs of nothing, not in the sense that they refer to a zero which would be what causes them to signify' (Lyotard 1993: 69). Lyotard argues that each sign sets up a complex network of references to other signs. So it is not that there is nothing, but that there is no singularity to the sign, and hence the sign's relationship to reality is one of plurality.

8. Kristeva defines this discourse as originating from those texts which have a lineage back to Menippus of Gadara, a third-century philosopher and satirist, but which historically extends further back. For more on this, see Kristeva 1984a: 82.

9. Many of the film examples given below contain a number of the attributes; however, rather than limit the examples to a few, the following show the qualities of the Menippean across a wide range.

10. See especially *The Ethics of Psychoanalysis* (1992) which contains some of Lacan's most important writings on this issue.

7 Film and Meaning

1. A key model for this originates in the works of Roman Ingarden, whose concerns were to investigate what makes literature literature, what gives it its *literariness*. See *The Literary Work of Art* (1973).

2. See Chapters 1 and 2 for further discussion on the splitting of the gaze.

3. This has been discussed in an earlier chapter on cinema and discourse. Basically Foucault radically reinterprets concepts such as the episteme when he attempts to devise a genealogical method, or the analysis of systems of knowledge and power.

The discussion here is informed by that genealogical method, noting how the episteme signals an early attempt by Foucault to deal with these issues.

4. Clearly one of the fundamental difficulties here is approaching the issue of film and
meaning via the ideas of Lacan and Foucault, when both theorists had quite independent agendas and motivations. The ensuing discussion is not meant to imply a
homogeneity between the conceptual points of Lacan's *point du capiton* and Foucault's power/knowledge. Rather this section is driven by the continuing ideas on
how meaning can be seen to operate within cinema, and both Lacan and Foucault
provide excellent points of departure for this.

5. Hence Derrida's consideration of the *parergon* of his own book as part of the circle of
investigations. It is noteworthy that Derrida is constantly caught up in these issues
of analysis as *parergon* as he negotiates his way through Kant, the source and insti-
gator of Derrida's arguments. At one point Derrida asks if what Kant is doing is
parergonal – a question he also addresses to his own work (for example, Derrida
1987b: 63–4; 9–10).

6. This construction of meaning/truth, like power/knowledge, is both helpful and
ambiguous. We adopt it here to signify that part of the function of the *parergon* is
to produce just such a relational context. This whole string of power/knowledge/
meaning/truth encircles itself so that formations of 'truth' become signifiers
of power.

8 Seduction: Gender, Genre and Power

1. Which suggests an intertextual reference to the younger, physically seductive body
of John Travolta in *Saturday Night Fever*.

2. This is a line that runs remarkably similar to the ways in which Freud discusses the
operation of the comic/wit in the unconscious. See especially his *Jokes and Their
Relation to the Unconscious* (1983).

3. As he puts it at one point: 'For seduction, desire is a myth. If desire is a will to power
and possession, seduction places before it an equal will to power by the simula-
crum' (Baudrillard 1990: 87). Later he adds: 'Seduction lies in the transformation
of things into pure appearances' (p. 117); and within Baudrillard's complex notion
of appearance and simulacra, this can also be seen as an operation of cinema.

4. In another book, Baudrillard argues the same ideas in even more clear-cut terms:
'If sex and sexuality ... are really a mode of exchange and production of sexual rela-
tions, seduction on the other hand is contrary to exchange, and close to challenge'
(Baudrillard 1982: 90).

5. See, for example, Baudrillard 1990: 14–15. To be fair to Baudrillard, he does
return to this issue through *Seduction*, cleansing some of the binarism implied here.
However, the problem of aligning the masculine with the power of production, and
the feminine with seduction – its opposite – is never fully resolved.

Glossary

Lacan, in a typical poststructuralist gesture, argued that his terms should not be defined, rather their meaning should be arrived at within the context of their usage, the processes of analysis, and the working out of the problems. This is part of the reason why we find so much fluidity and play within the terms themselves. Within such a sense it is always difficult to provide a standard sort of glossary of the terms, and the following is intended as a guide to some of the key theoretical terms discussed throughout the book. Most of the terms are notoriously slippery and caution must always be exercised in such summaries. The following is framed with a sense of open-endedness and the reader is encouraged to follow up the concepts in the primary texts from which they originate. (Wherever possible the relevant text is given in the definition.)

Abjection   Through Kristeva's book *Powers of Horror* (1982), this term has passed from its anthropological origins (especially Mary Douglas) into the areas of psychoanalysis specifically and poststructuralism generally. From this perspective, the term has taken on both a cultural and psychical sense, thus becoming an important development in theorising subjectivity. The abject, for Kristeva, is both a cultural force and a part of the psychical apparatus, notably the unconscious. As such it is seen as a crucial factor in understanding how these two complex processes operate and interact. In abjection the sense of the self is threatened by those things that can cross, and so defy, the imagined sense of the body and its boundaries. One such example is bodily fluids – blood, urine, semen, tears – which mark the transgression of the body as whole and perfect. A consequence of this is that anything associated with these signs of abjection comes to threaten subjectivity itself. Part of cinema's role is to allow the acting out of abjection, both at the cultural level and in the subject's psychical processes. It is the power of abjection to challenge and disrupt, to place the known into the liminal and on the borders, that gives its cinematic manifestations so much potency.

Aphanisis   A key term from Lacan (1986) who shifts its original psychoanalytic meaning so that it comes to represent a particular process in the subject's interaction with the Symbolic order. Along with alienation, aphanisis represents a fear of the loss of those signifiers which have come to represent subjectivity. Lacan argues that the subject invests certain signifiers with immense psychical value, so that their loss (or even potential for this) represents a loss of identity within the Symbolic order.

Appresentation (see also *Lacunae*)   This term, derived from phenomenology, refers to the idea that all phenomena are presented as incomplete and part of the act of consciousness is involved in adding further information and details. Where such information comes from will depend on the particular object or sensation, but certainly memory, cultural conditioning, and, in the case of texts, the contextual fields, all play a part. Appresentation can be seen as both a fairly mechanical process (the adding to of signs and representations to make them seem complete) as well as the more abstract and complex – such as how ideology operates to make certain constructions seem more valid.

Codes   In semiotics the role of codes is complex (see, for example, Eco's discussion in *Theory of Semiotics* (1976)) and the relative simplicity of some of the descriptions can be deceptive. Codes order signs, as well as provide rules of exclusion, combination, and hierarchy. As such they are fundamental to the ways in which meanings are produced and signs interpreted.

Peter Wollen's early work *Signs and Meaning in the Cinema* (1969) provides an example of some rudimentary issues in cinematic codes and how they operate. In one sense they are comparable to the operation of generic conventions, but it is also necessary to consider how they operate beyond the textual boundaries. Barthes's (1977) work on codes of fashion and food, for example, demonstrates the wider cultural implications and operations of codes. Metz (1973, 1974) offers a sustained examination of codes in cinema, utilising complex semiotic theory to argue for a language of film.

Différance   From Derrida, a term emphasising the indeterminate nature of meaning and interpretation. The neologism is derived from the meaning being made up of deferral and difference: all acts of meaning and interpretative gestures involve deferring the arrival at a particular meaning; and within every act of interpretation there is the process of difference. In many ways this term has become representative of deconstruction as a method, demonstrating how the issue of meaning itself is central to its investigative field.

For Derrida the term represents a critique of how Western philosophy has devised systems of analysis and the production of meaning. In this sense it is as much a philosophical stance as any analytic tool. His principal concern is how philosophy as a discipline has attempted to establish itself within a privileged position of interpretation. This is what he calls the white metaphor of all systems of truth (see, for example, *Margins of Philosophy* (1986)), as certain hermeneutic positions argue that they are more insightful, more truthful, than others. Derrida then extends this examination to all systems of knowledge, cautioning against any such privileging. *Différance* is one of his strategies to deconstruct the very idea of a central, single, and universal truth.

Episteme   We take a particular inflection given to this term by Foucault here. This is the formation of knowledges through power, and the study of them in terms of such a context. However, Foucault is quite explicit that epistemes are not simply knowledge as it is socially constructed, but rather emphasises the relationships between knowledges as they produce discursive practices. It is these relationships that form the epistemes (see especially Foucault, *The Order of Things* (1970)).

Epistemocine   We coin this term to speak of the ways in which the Foucauldian idea of power/knowledge as it operates in the formulation of meaning is devised within cinema. These, then, are units of meaningful 'utterances' (sounds, images, segments of action, lighting, etc.), formed within a film, operating through a power/knowledge process – which can include the textual, cultural, sexual, and so on. This is also in keeping with Foucault's ideas on relationships and meaning (see above).

Glissading bar   From Lacan, referring specifically to an interpretation of the structure of the sign. Lacan draws on semiotic theory to present a model of the unconscious, where meaning is derived from the slippage between the signifier and the signified; or between the representations in the conscious and the repressed drives and desires of the unconscious. The sliding (glissading) bar is part of the mechanism which allows for the disguising of such unconscious ideas (see Lacan, *Four Fundamental Concepts of Psychoanalysis* (1986)). Because it is a critique of how meanings are formulated, this notion of the sliding bar ties in with a great many other poststructuralist and postmodernist projects. See, for example, Derrida's notion of *différance*.

Imaginary; Symbolic; Real   Lacan developed three terms – the Imaginary, the Symbolic, and the Real – over a period of years, and they have become wedded in a system of concepts on subjectivity, the unconscious, and the social order. The Imaginary has its emphasis on the image (rather than a sense of fantasy as first seems to be the case in the use of such a term) as it forms a self-reflexive moment of the subject. This idea stems from Lacan's theory of the Mirror Stage. At around 18 months the child becomes aware of his/her social position, and is forced to move from the egocentric position into the social world of language. This, according to Lacan, causes considerable trauma and represents a splitting of the subject's sense of the self, from which we never fully recover. The Imaginary is the moment of this realisation of the self as split (the *Ichspaltung*).

The Symbolic is Lacan's term for the social order (organised through the signifier). It is the large and complex social structures into which the subject must enter. It is also the site where the signifier – that is, all systems of communication and representation – is produced, struggled for, and lost. It is noteworthy that the Mirror Stage also marks the sexualising of the subject, and the demands to operate within culturally determined gender positions. This means that, for psychoanalysis, the entry into the Symbolic order also marks a repression of certain sexual drives (Freud's notion that we are all bisexual to begin with), the assertion of the Oedipal complex, and a demand to represent desires within a particular cultural order.

The Real is perhaps the most difficult of the three terms to tie down. It certainly holds the other two within a relational context, but also stands outside of them. At one level it is what we might also consider to be the unconscious, with its antisocial drives and desires. The Real, as Lacan once said, is the impossible; it is that which is lacking in the Symbolic order. Lacan terms it the Real because it relates not to social reality, textual realism, or the reality of objects and things; rather it is the real of the psyche, and all that operates within it.

Lacunae   From phenomenology and developed extensively in reception theory (see especially Roman Ingarden and Wolfgang Iser). *Lacunae* (also known as spots of indeterminacy) are the 'missing' parts of the text, requiring the participation of the reader/spectator. They are defined as key elements in the active construction of the text by the reader, and as such became a fundamental part of the death of the author idea. Part of this process is what phenomenology terms concretisation. This is the reader's necessary act of completing the text which is full of these indetermined moments.

Mirror Stage (see Imaginary)

Objet petit a   A term from Lacan that denotes the formation of objects of desire. Lacan distinguishes these little objects of desire (the '*a*' stands for the French term *autre*, other) from the big A Other as a type of cultural register of desirable moments. The Other itself remains elusive and always beyond the subject.

Phallocentrism and Phallocularism   From feminist theory, phallocentrism was seen as central to masculine discourse and its assertive control not only over material possessions, but also language and cultural formations. As such it was seen as actually shaping the psychic apparatus as well as having this wider social sense to it. Feminist theory distinguishes the phallus (this idea of masculine power and domination) from the biological penis, and thus men themselves are subjected to a type of power relation to phallocentrism. We have coined the term phallocularism here to suggest the idea of a masculine gaze constructed precisely out of this socio-economic and psychical site of subjectivity.

Readerly and Writerly   From Barthes, the idea that there can be different levels of participation by the reader in the text. Although Barthes's description sometimes seems like a system of textual classification, the emphasis is very much on the idea of the active (writerly) and passive (readerly) acts of the reader/spectator. It is important to recognise that Barthes never prescribes the qualities of the readerly and writerly to specific texts, for what may seem to be a passive encounter with a particular text in one instance, may subsequently operate at a much more creative and active level. It is the role and function of the reader, along with factors such as textual histories, interpretative models, even reading fashions, that transforms texts from one type to another. These terms parallel another set of ideas developed by Barthes, the work and the text.

Real (see Imaginary)

Scopophilia   Most simply put this is the pleasure of looking. According to Freud it is, along with exhibitionism, an essential part of the normal formations of the socialised subject. However, scopophilia becomes more problematic when it replaces the development of adult sexual relations and becomes the primary form of interaction. It became a crucial term in film theory in the 1970s (through Mulvey's work), but more recently there has been a re-evaluation of how this term might be best employed. Mulvey and others emphasised the idea of the power in the male gaze and how it makes women seem to be passive objects. In this sense scopophilia is part of the phallocentric discourse, forming moments in cultural operations of the image. However the pleasure of the gaze is never simply masculine because there is also an incitement of power against it. In these terms – especially from Foucault and some of the French feminists – pleasure is a much more destabilised, and destabilising, process.

Subjectivity One of the largest and most complex issues of critical theory, discussions of subjectivity are part of every major theoretical idea from poststructuralism and postmodernism. This is because from all the different aspects – such as psychoanalysis, feminism, cultural studies, deconstruction, semiotics – there has been a radical rethinking of the subject and how he/she operates within cultural and textual systems. The dominant model of the subject in Western thought came from the eighteenth century's Enlightenment where it was seen as whole, stable and at the centre of all things. This has been replaced with ideas that the subject is never whole, but rather fragmented and split, constantly driven by unconscious desires and demands. The subject is also split from the cultural order by its lack of control of the signifying practices. In these terms there is little stability in the subject, instead a constantly changing and charged entity.

Symbolic (see Imaginary)

Filmography and Synopsis

The following is offered as a guide and reference to the films referred to. Because some films are dealt with in depth, or are referred to more than once, whilst for others only a passing mention is made, the following is divided into two parts. The first part contains fuller information and a short comment on the films referred to in more detail; the second is further reference material on the second type.

Major References

Belle de Jour (dir. Luis Buñuel, Italy–France, 1967)

Buñuel's versions and interpretations of surrealism are always present in his films, but often it is the subtle parts of them that carry the most power. Combining this aesthetic style, biting social commentary (often Marxist in intent), and the ironic, Buñuel's films often attack both thematically and stylistically cultural institutions and our positions within them. *Belle de Jour* tells the almost parodic sexual fantasy of the bored, affluent wife who becomes a prostitute. Her various sexual encounters with the bizarre, the perverse and the violent are always posited as commentary on, and parody of, sexual relations (a theme Buñuel deals with in other films, notably the earlier *Diary of a Chambermaid* (1964) and returns to in *That Obscure Object of Desire* (1977)), and in particular masculine constructions of them. *Belle de Jour* is ambiguous in its politics of control (another common theme in Buñuel's films –compare the almost literal loss of control with the wandering camera in *The Phantom of Liberty* (1974) and the unsuccessful party guests in *The Discreet Charm of the Bourgeoisie* (1972)), and the sexual fantasies of Severine/Belle oscillate between a lack of control and a reassertion of her desires. The idea of the double existence is also played out in this film, which in turn becomes a reflection of the conscious and repressed (Severine) against the expression of the unconscious and free-flowing desire (Belle).

La Belle Noiseuse (dir. Jacques Rivette, France, 1991)

In *La Belle Noiseuse* we find one of the recurring themes of Rivette's cinema – the impact of art (such as painting, as is the case with this film, as well as drama, literature, and cinema) on people's lives and emotions. *La Belle Noiseuse* uses painting as a metaphor for the investigation of creativity, and the unease at which we cope with close scrutiny of our lives and being. A painter, Frenhofer, has been unable to paint for years. He is persuaded to try again by a visiting student, and agrees to paint Marianne, the student's girlfriend. The film (some four hours long) is made up almost entirely of watching Frenhofer attempt to paint the body of Marianne, which is constantly contorted, manipulated and exposed. The gaze of the painter, like that of the photographer in *Blow Up*, is positioned as more than just seeing; it exposes. And like the subject of the photographs, the film's spectator is always left in doubt as to what is actually finally shown on the canvas. In this way both films demonstrate the idea that part of the spectating position is the act of looking, rather than the act of arriving at a complete image.

Betty Blue (dir. Jean-Jacques Beineix, France, 1986)

The representation of Betty's slide to madness is compulsive because the film circles around the events in much the same way as Betty's mind does. There is a certain seductive element to the way Betty acts, at least up until the point where her madness becomes violent and destructive. The film offers little explanation as to what causes her actions, and there is a sense that she enters the narrative filled with passion that always threatens to tip over. The spectator is certainly thrown straight into a scene of sexual intimacy with Betty and Zorg naked on a bed, moments before orgasm. Contrasted to Betty's passions is Zorg's semi-comatose acceptance of the world and all it throws at him. It is only when he must participate in helping Betty, and then eventually killing her to end her suffering, that he is seen as active. The film plays with the idea of merging the two in the last part of the narrative. Zorg dresses as Betty, acts with a sense of madness we have only seen so far in Betty, and then hears her voice after she is dead. In this sense it is a film as much about crisis of identity as about madness and sexual passions.

Blade Runner (dir. Ridley Scott, USA, 1982)

Scott's film mixes the genres of film *noir* and science fiction, in both their formal features and themes. The pursuit by Deckard, the *noir* private eye (complete with his voiceover), of a group of escaped replicants (sophisticated 'robots' who have come to question their existence, and who act and seem human) becomes one of personal re-evaluation; at the heart of this detective work is the question of what constitutes subjectivity, first theirs and then his own. The figure of Deckard is interesting because he follows so many of the archetypes of the hero of these genres, yet also breaks them. His morality is constantly brought into question (he shoots people in the back, is violent towards women), as, eventually, is his status as human. His double is Batty, the leader of the replicants. For all that Deckard represses, Batty manifests, including the search for the father, the questioning of death, and violence towards others and the significance of these actions.

Blood Simple (dir. Coen Bros., USA, 1984)

This film is so effective in twisting its plots and subplots that its narrative structure, like the *noir* film *The Big Sleep*, threatens to fold in on itself. The title is somewhat ironic, as there is really nothing simple that comes from the blood of the violent acts committed. Deception and misreadings are the primary forces of the narrative and we find many variations of them. The deceptions committed by the detective with the photographs, the misreadings by Ray and Abby of the events, the faked killings and double-crossings, all lead up to a black comic ending. The style of the film is claustrophobic and dark.

It locks the spectator into a small-town world that is ordered by brutal violence – nowhere better shown than in the mopping up of blood scene, and the killing of the body three times over.

Blow Up (dir. Michelangelo Antonioni, Italy–UK, 1966)

This film has a familiar sense of Antonioni's cultural commentary, this time with Italian eyes investigating England in the 1960s. The simple story of an egocentric photographer – Thomas – stumbling across a man and woman in a park, and then taking their photograph, becomes a type of metaphysics of the gaze, the subject, and meaning. The closer Thomas scrutinises the photograph from the park (a film desperately sought by the woman, Jane) the less clear things become. There is always a question as to whether there actually is a body in the bushes, as we only ever gain evidence of it from Thomas's eyes – no one else sees it. These questions of perception and our capacity to interpret the world (mostly through vision) is metaphorically represented in the closing scenes when Thomas watches a group of mimes pretend to play tennis. When they hit the imaginary ball over the fence the camera seems to follow it, and then Thomas is invited to throw it back. His participation in pretending to pick up the ball and throw it back aligns him even more fully with the Imaginary (in Lacan's sense) world of the camera.

Bonnie and Clyde (dir. Arthur Penn, USA, 1967)

Penn's version of the story of the two gangsters is significant in a history of this genre because it marks a point at which sympathy is both constructed and withdrawn at various points throughout the film. This structure of utilising audience (and generic) expectations in order to subvert them informs the whole film, both in style and theme. The sepia-infused shots of 1930s America give the film a certain style that is undercut by some of its treatment of the two main characters. For example, the sense of romance between Bonnie and Clyde is created at one level, and then undermined by the representation of Clyde's impotence (rather than his homosexuality, which is the more likely cause). They, and their gang, are presented less as heroic and more as social misfits, which again runs counter to much of the Gangster genre. The final scene of their death is famous for its graphic, unrelenting violence – but more than this it effectively captures this interweaving of opposites of the generic expectations and the different inflections given to them.

A bout de souffle (dir. Jean-Luc Godard, France, 1959)

One of the key films of the French New Wave, *A bout de souffle* was Godard's first feature film. The simple story of a young thief wanted by the police for murder, and the American student who loves and fears him (and eventually informs on him), is rendered complex and innovative through Godard's highly experimental use of cinematic conventions. Lighting, editing, dialogue, camera use, and narrative pacing are all challenged and usurped throughout the film. It has a rawness about it that eventually becomes what the film is about. The centrality of the film to the development of modern cinema means that it is often viewed as a piece of history. This, combined with the fact that it is also a remarkable thesis on film-making, sometimes makes us overlook the significant point that it does actually work as a narrative. Even its own self-reflexivity does not totally take away the qualities of romance that drive the characters.

Casablanca (dir. Michael Curtiz, USA, 1943)

Eco argues that the popularity of this film is because it is so full of clichés that everyone knows its mythology. It is so familiar that, so he argues, the audience overlooks its over-sentimentalising and is trapped within the narrative. The story is classically romantic, of lost love that is refound and then lost again. Set during the Second World War, Rick runs a bar in Casablanca, rejecting his and the world's politics, until Ilsa, the woman he loved and lost in Paris, comes back into his life. She is married to Victor Laslo, a freedom fighter against the Nazis. With only one set of stolen transit letters available for escape, the choice comes between Rick and Ilsa leaving (and so selfish love) or Victor and Ilsa leaving (sacrifice of personal love for the world's salvation). The final scene of Rick and Captain Renault walking into the mist, with the lines that it is the beginning of a beautiful friendship, resonate with homoerotic feelings. It would seem Rick's choice still left him the capacity to find love.

Cat People (dir. Jacques Tourneur, USA, 1942)

Tourneur collaborated with producer Val Lewton for a series of films in the 1940s with a supernatural theme. *Cat People* is striking for its use of *lacunae* to create the terror of the film. We never see the 'monster', except through suggestion and the characters' responses. The film also explored the relationship between pleasure and horror at a number of levels; the most overt is in playing with the spectator's sense of pleasure at imagining the abject; there is also the narrative's theme of sexual pleasure and repression, with the main character of Irena Dubrovana representing the dangers – and unknown – of women's pleasure within a masculine world order. The idea that sexual desire transforms the body is a line of thought in the development of hysteria, and the narrative can be seen as presenting the feminine attributes of Irena (along with her 'foreign-ness') as cause of her changes.

Chien andalou, Un (dir. Luis Buñuel, France, 1928)

This collaborative film (with Salvador Dali) is one of the few true surrealist films, in as much as it was made during the time when surrealism was a coherent artistic movement, and attempted to remain true to that aesthetic. Rather than plot, the film presents various images of dream-like events, using the film medium to enfold the images into one another. In this way it approaches the idea of filmic metaphor, as well as exploring cinema's potential to represent the unconscious (which is always an impossible dream). The film did intend to shock with both its images – with razor-sliced eyes, ants emerging from hands – and themes. It is perhaps an indicator of the critical culture, and the operation of the spectator, that we attempt to mesh the images and sequences into a narrative – often succeeding! The overwhelming nature of desire as both a creative and destructive force permeates all the images and sequences. Desire – especially the masculine – is the andalusian dog here.

Citizen Kane (dir. Orson Welles, USA, 1941)

Welles's film is a fine example of the domination of form over story, where the narrative is slight (the rise and fall of a media magnate) but the technical aspects are complex and often startling. There are many moments in the film that demonstrate a keen self-reflexivity of both filmic narrative and the spectator's role in the film processes. As such, *Citizen Kane* demonstrates how a film can turn the spectator's own gaze back on to them, forcing a reflection on the complicity of their role in the creation of images and fictions. It is a film that surrounds the spectator so that he/she becomes embedded into its very existence and operation. The story itself reflects these twists of film-making, as it sets frames within frames. The idea of a reporter investigating the death of the media magnate Charles Kane, and in particular his final words of 'Rosebud', carries with it an ironic tone. This pursuit of what is positioned as a profound truth (but turns out to be a simple toy from childhood) allows the film to use a variety of forms (flashback, voice-over, news footage, character's memories, etc.) in telling the story. What begins as a reporter's investigation of the final utterance of Kane (and so setting up the idea of a mystery/detective theme), turns into a critique of story-telling and biography.

Crash (dir. David Cronenberg, Canada, 1997)

One of the most interesting aspects about *Crash* is that it depicts the cultural fascination with violence and death in such a detached manner. The story of two couples who are inexplicably drawn into a morbid attraction to car crashes is presented in part as a slide towards madness, but more as a depiction of their inability to satisfy needs and desires. We may well spend the entire film waiting for a voice that speaks out against their actions, offering a site of reason against the destructive urges – but such a voice never appears. There is a certain conflation of Freudian motifs – the film could easily have been renamed the death drive – with an outsider's analysis of the American car culture. As such the car becomes a metaphor for a number of different objects and processes: it is seen as an extension of the body; a manifestation of fragmented subjectivity; a culturally displaced object of desire; a type of social destruction. Cronenberg's films demonstrate a recurring theme of the merging (usually in a destructive fashion) of the human body and technology. We see this in his remake of *The Fly*, the body as machine in *Videodrome* and *Naked Lunch*; and in different forms of alien-ness (such as parasites) in *Rabid* and *Shivers*.

Les Diaboliques (dir. Henri-Georges Clouzot, France, 1955)

Clouzot's works, from 1942 with *L'Assassin Habité au 21* to 1968 with *La Prisonnière*, covered a range of material, but the subjects and treatments tended to have a familiar feel of oppression and entrapment. This is nowhere more true than in *Les Diaboliques*, with its destructive story of two women's plot to murder the brutal husband of one of them. The film constructs systems of power across gender (the two women colluding against the man, but also the betrayal of that relationship between the women) and class. There is also a type of perversion of the family structure, not only in the film's setting (a school), but also a sense of mother and daughter against the father. The plot and style have strong connections to Hitchcock.

Double Indemnity (dir. Billy Wilder, USA, 1943)

The seemingly perfect crime is plotted between Phyllis Dietrichson and her lover, Walter Neff, to kill her husband and make it look like a train accident. In doing so they would claim the double indemnity for the insurance claim. The crime is solved not by the police, but by an insurance claims investigator, thus positioning money and business as the heroic elements, and passion and women as corrupt outsiders or as the dangerous supplement to happy innocence. This supplementary quality is positioned as the unethical, with the woman being a primary cause of it. This moral tale is further positioned as a cautionary one through the use of the flashback technique.

The Godfather (dir. Francis Ford Coppola, USA, 1972)

The Godfather (and its sequels) demonstrates cinema's power to position the spectator as accomplice. It moves beyond a black and white morality in that it evokes empathy and revulsion for the violent acts of gang wars and the Mafia. It does this in a number of different, yet interlinked, ways: it takes long sequences of the family as a unit (including the wedding and Don Corleone's death with his grandson in the vineyard), suggesting that this is about these issues rather than gang wars; it provides the family with history and cultural roots; it sets up family motivations for all the acts. Once it has done all this it systematically undoes the sense of the familiar, culminating in the turning of Michael into the villain, and, metonymically, presenting a sequence of intercuts between the family at a baptism and the killing of enemies.

High Noon (dir. Fred Zinneman, USA, 1952)

This film is a good example of the way films can devise political commentary and social allegory in a popular genre (and it paved the way for a number of similar Westerns in the 1970s). The first of these, political commentary, by its analysis of the effects of McCarthyism; the second, social allegory, in its representation of social abandonment. It is not just the townspeople's refusal to help retiring Marshall Will Kane confront the outlaw gang, but also their treatment of Amy Kane's Quaker beliefs and Helen Ramirez's sexual past. In terms of narrative development, *High Noon* is surprisingly slow in its pace. The build-up to the gunfight takes the bulk of the film, the shoot-out only a few minutes. Yet it is this careful and measured structure that translates so much of the emotional tension. Will Kane is presented as a vulnerable man, rather than demonstrating the forceful heroics of other Western heroes; and it is this quality that carries much of the allegorical force because this is the presentation of the individual as ordinary.

Last Seduction, The (dir. John Dahl, USA, 1993)

The uncompromising *femme fatale* in this film, Bridget, uses both body and mind to out-manoeuvre the men who come across her path. She uses masculine desire against them, and in this demonstrates a trait lacking in a great many of the women in earlier *noir* films – a knowledge of the phallocentric discourses, including business power and homophobia. Her other quality is the ability to cover all the possible tracks that might go wrong. Whereas the unravelling of the plan in classic *noir* often rests on a simple slip or an unpredicted turn, Bridget knows them all, including the sliver of paper she burns in the final moment of the film. It is knowledge rather than her sexuality that delivers up the power she has – an attribute that demonstrates Foucault's power/knowledge process in both negative and positive ways.

Last Year at Marienbad (dir. Alain Resnais, France, 1961)

Resnais demonstrated his interests in the slippage of time and memories in his earlier film, *Hiroshima Mon Amour*. However, in *Last Year at Marienbad* he attempts to go even further into an interior world of the mind. A man tries to persuade a woman – and even himself at times – that they have met before, and that their relationship goes far beyond a superficial meeting. The qualities of the film are often dream-like, with extraordinarily composed shots and fluid sequences. The woman (played by Delphne Seyrig) is presented as a figure half real, half imagined, and the man who pursues her often seems on the brink of madness. As an analysis of time, the film works beautifully not only in terms of cinematic time (and the ways in which Deleuze speaks of it), but the time of memories, and the memories of the spectator. Interestingly, one of the ways the film does this is through its use of space, for it is the sensual tracking shots that come to represent the passage (or cycle) of time.

Manon des sources (dir. Claude Berri, France, 1986)
This is the sequel to *Jean de Florette*, taking up the story of his daughter. Manon lives the life of a wood spirit, part of the *parergon* of the social order. She is a constant reminder to the villagers of the guilt they share over the tragic life and death of her father. Ugolin, the nephew of the key conspirator against Jean, falls in love with her, and is slowly driven mad by this love, and desire. Manon discovers the truth about the past, stopping the water to the village, before returning it in a curious ritual that is incorporated into the religious beliefs of the people. As such, Manon's gift of water not only socialises her into the Symbolic order; it also incorporates a sort of pantheistic order into the Christian system.

Miller's Crossing (dir. Coen Bros., USA, 1990)
The Coen Brothers effectively combine popular cinema with innovation, particularly in their inventive use of the camera. Their films often employ the camera to convey psychological states, as well as a perverse first-person narrating position. *Barton Fink* arrests the spectator's capacity to resist nightmares through the sweeping camera and claustrophobic settings – qualities it shares with *Blood Simple*. Similarly, *Raising Arizona* employs the same sorts of camera devices to achieve great comic effect. *Miller's Crossing* uses the conventions of the gangster genre to meditate on how moral issues become for-mulated in film forms. The central character, Tom, is an individual caught between violent factions of gangsters and police. What continually saves him is his speech. Although violence occurs and is always imminent, Tom demonstrates the good heart – that is, the morally correct. This is not the morality of the Symbolic order, but a sense of the good (in Lacan's sense).

My Beautiful Laundrette (dir. Stephen Frears, UK, 1985)
Along with a number of other small budget films financed by Channel 4 (including, significantly, Mike Leigh's *High Hopes* (1988)), this film represented a revival of sorts in independent British cinema. From this point in the early to mid 1980s we witness a diverse and rich set of films emerging from Britain (including the works of Greenaway, Potter, and Jarman). Frears, like many of his counterparts, moved to Hollywood, and to a certain extent *My Beautiful Laundrette*, along with *Sammy and Rosie Get Laid* (1988), represents a deceptively sharp insight into British culture and politics in the Thatcher years that is lost after that move. The story of gay love, interracial affairs, and class difference works as much as a critique of sexual politics as it does as a reflection of a culture coming to terms with a post-colonial agenda. The two main characters of Johnny, the violent working-class punk, and Omar, the middle-class Anglo-Indian, have so many complexities to their relationship that it is not surprising that the even-tual points of negotiation are about power and outside interventions.

Nightmare on Elm Street (dir. Wes Craven, USA, 1984)
Craven's vision of the horror genre is almost always invested in the self-reflexive. *Night-mare on Elm Street* marks an important point in the reinvention of the horror film because

it is part of a series of films produced by directors who merge the mainstream of Hollywood production, with the historical legacy of exploitation films from the 1960s and 1970s. Craven, along with people such as Cronenberg, Tobe Hooper, Lynch, and Abel Ferrara, freely draw on the small-budget, independent productions from the late 1960s and early 1970s to make films that are technically and visually smooth, but seldom socially safe. So often these films appear to be one thing (Hollywood) but end up challenging that status. The meta-cinematic devices (and we find these in, for example, Hooper's *The Texas Chainsaw Massacre* (1973) with its reference to Freak shows, and *Lifeforce* (1985) with its exploitative nudity) of these films operate at a beyond to the more straightforward acknowledgements of generic conventions. Instead, something like *Nightmare on Elm Street* emphasises the known in order to reveal just how much we can accept the strange. The story of a vengeful Freddy Kruger, who invades the dreams of a group of middle-class teenagers, creates the horror within the everyday, but ensures its terror by cutting off all avenues of escape. The horror exists within the known (the suburbs, middle America, and the world of dreams) in order to make everything a potential threat.

Passion (dir. Jean-Luc Godard, France, 1982)
In *Passion* we witness the recurring motifs of Godard's work (self-reflexivity, Marxist politics, innovative use of cinema's devices) combined with his more recent interests in contemplations on art. The entwined stories of a film-maker who cannot complete his film about painting, the workers' struggles in a factory, and the difficulties of romantic love, allow the film to posit a common emotion across a range of quite different contexts. It would be too simplistic to say that *Passion* is about the inability to complete/ produce because of factors beyond our control, but this is certainly one of the elements that is used to bind the film together. As a cinematic text, *Passion* is perhaps one of Godard's most beautiful films, so often slipping into rich images that exist because they are extraordinary to look at, much less than as part of the narrative development. In these images of paintings we also witness how Godard continues to investigate the relationships between movement, composition, and framing – all features essential to the make-up of his cinema.

The Piano (dir. Jane Campion, New Zealand, 1993)
Campion's film about Europeans in the strange land of colonial New Zealand reflects on emotional trauma and family structure. Ada and her daughter travel to the wildness of New Zealand from England, keeping with them the unlikely object of a piano. Ada's insistence on this piano, and how it is used in the emotional play between her husband, Stewart, and eventual lover, Baines, carries much of the film's force. The haunting qualities of *The Piano* can be traced to a number of levels in the film, one of the primary ones being how it locates the main characters outside of different cultural orders. The narrating character, Ada, refuses speech and communicates through her daughter; Baines is a part of, and apart from, the cultural orders; Stewart mentally exists in a different world – a European culture that he has not left. Such a collection of personalities means that people defined through lack effectively inhabit the narrative. Baines's love for Ada, their affair, the brutal revenge of Stewart, her husband, and the romantic ending (which takes the film from wild beaches and woodlands, to a highly cultivated yard and house) move Ada and Baines from this status of lack to one of socialised

presence. The piano itself ties these three into a system of power and desire. It is an instrument of control, with each using it as a device of manipulation. The images and themes are consistent with other films by Campion: *Sweetie* (1989), for example, combines a surreal representation of suburbia with a darkly comic version of female relationships.

The Postman Always Rings Twice (dir. Tay Garnett, USA, 1946; remade Bob Rafelson, USA, 1981)

Garnett's version of this film became one of the key texts in film *noir*. Its composition of a dysfunctional married couple and the intervention of a drifter has the sort of economy which allows for subterfuge and double-dealings. It contrasts the sense of the family unit – albeit an unhappy one – with the single person. In keeping with *noir* ethics, the woman is the active agent, prompting murderous acts from the lover. The level of mistrust between the characters is overcome through passion – sexual desire overrides not just the moral and ethical structure of marriage, but also any sense of betrayal. It is passion that both motivates, legitimises and transgresses the different relationships. Rafelson's version has a more tragic feel about it, tending towards the romantic. Interestingly, Visconti's version of the Cain novel (on which these films are based), *Ossessione* (1942), was seen as an early part of Italian Neo-realism. From the same source we witness three films with quite different critical surroundings. *Noir* is rarely considered part of a realist tradition, yet Visconti's film is seen as that because of its treatment of greed and malice – the same qualities that make the other two part of *noir* cinema.

Psycho (dir. Alfred Hitchcock, USA, 1960)

Psycho is Hitchcock's exercise in manipulation and deception. Almost every element in the film is devised to lead both characters and audience in the wrong direction. This is part of its function – to declare manipulation only to reveal that as yet another variant on manipulation. When all is revealed the film quickly falls into a narrative, and it is at that moment where the film works least well. Marion Crane, whom we encounter in the opening scene in bed with her lover, steals money from her company. She plans to use that money so that Sam, her lover, and herself can be together. Pangs of doubt and remorse mean that she intends to return the money, but she meets up with Norman Bates, who runs a small hotel. Bates's strange mannerisms quickly become overtly mad, but for much of the time the viewer is led to believe the killer of Marion, and the other characters, is Norman's mother. He is eventually caught by Sam and Marion's sister and locked away in a psychiatric ward. The film closes with a report from a psychiatrist and voice-over from Norman. So no matter how the psychiatrist explains Norman Bates's actions, there must always be a wariness because of all that has gone before. Of course all horror films work on the premise of manipulation, but *Psycho* structures itself as a *mise-en-abyme*, each layer working counter to the others. That it is a film infested with seemingly meaningful signs only adds to this creeping paranoia and deception.

Pulp Fiction (dir. Quentin Tarantino, USA, 1994)

Tarantino's film employs a populist sense of postmodernism, with its collapse of temporal structures, flawed spatial dimensions, stock characters playing warped versions of themselves, and a seeming lack of distinction between different textual forms. One of the strengths of *Pulp Fiction* as a narrative film is its capacity to hold the many disparate elements simultaneously as parody and narrative. It is the entwining of the subplots that brings the film together, so that the audience begins to work towards figuring out how characters and events meet, more so than with the usual narrative processes of film. This may well be a consequence of the spectator's sense of how narratives are supposed to act. As such, the film is made up of a series of interconnected short narratives about gangsters and lovers.

Rome, Open City (dir. Roberto Rossellini, Italy, 1945)
Rossellini's film of a city at the closing period of the Second World War has long been held as a seminal piece in film realism generally, and the development of Italian Neo-realism in particular. The film is more than simply an exercise in style, however, and weaves a complex plot of love and betrayal into the events. The freedom fighter Manfredi and priest Don Pietro continually try to outwit and undermine the Gestapo. Both are eventually captured (Manfredi is betrayed by his lover Marina in a series of images economical in structure yet multi-layered in their effect) and killed by the Nazis. Much of the power of the film is derived from this interweaving of the individual's sense of the war and tragedy within the much larger scope of a social order in the state of collapse. The harsh and barren cityscape (so antithetical to the post-war constructions of Rome as a city of romance) works at the level of both social commentary and ideas of realism.

Silence of the Lambs (dir. Jonathan Demme, USA, 1991)
One of the most powerful attributes of this film is its constructions of power and gender, played out through a binarism of corporeality and the psychical. Clarice Starling, the slight, nervous-looking FBI agent, is introduced through her diminutive size as she struggles on the obstacle training course. Her position within the playing out of serial killers and violent men is almost continually defined through this fragility of body. As Hannibal Lecter, the killer who consumes his victims, acknowledges, her strength is the capacity to cover and disguise the past. The irony of this is that of all the characters, including Lecter, she is the one least well known. The story of using one serial killer to catch another, and using Starling as the intermediary, positions the spectator in a difficult point. All knowledge must be derived from the criminally insane; so madness becomes the interpretative gesture. Lecter becomes an embodiment of Descartes' idea of the malign genie – only this one must be continually addressed as a source of interpreting the world.

Taxi Driver (dir. Martin Scorsese, USA, 1976)
As with *Silence of the Lambs* (see above), Scorsese's film does not give the spectator an interpretative position outside of madness. Travis Bickle's mind moves closer and closer to obsessive behaviour, violence and self-destruction. The fact that the social order ends up reading his actions as heroic inserts even greater cynicism into the film. Bickle's mental instability is continually thwarted in his attempts to find release. There is the seeming love of the political worker (who becomes offended when, on their first date, he takes her to a pornographic film), the desire, and unsuccessful attempt, to assassinate the politician, and the need to save Iris, the child prostitute. Each fixation is undone as Bickle struggles to make sense of his world through sex and violence.

***Unforgiven* (dir. Clint Eastwood, USA, 1992)**
Eastwood's film is a careful study on the Western genre, particularly as it moves between a type of mythic cultural status and the reworkings of this in the latter part of the twentieth century. It is the self-reflexive turns of this story about William Munny drawn back into a type of violence associated with his past (initially because of money, and then for revenge) that makes *Unforgiven* both true to the Western form and a challenge to it. The whole playing out of events is produced within a context of the return of the repressed, and a demand to confront that which constitutes a person's subjectivity. Added to this is the whole issue of morality – is someone capable of changing their morality, or will past events always make escape impossible?

***White Heat* (dir. Raoul Walsh, USA, 1949)**
The almost excessive Oedipal themes of Walsh's film make this story about Cody Jarret, petty gangster haunted by paranoia and congenital psychosis, a curious piece in the gangster genre. It is the rawness of Jarret, with his hatred and mistrust of everyone except his mother, that drives much of the narrative. This quality allows the character to swing between the calculating gangster and an insane, destructive ego incapable of any rational thought. He befriends an undercover policeman in prison, who becomes a mother substitute (as well as presenting scenes of homoerotic closeness). The symbolism of this is complete when the policeman betrays him, just as Ma did in contributing to Jarret's madness.

***Withnail and I* (dir. Bruce Robinson, UK, 1987)**
The story of two out-of-work actors, living in abject conditions in 1960s London, who plan their escape with a weekend in the country, works in part through the contrasts (of a certain wide innocence of 'I' to the excess of Withnail; the country to the city) and in part through the development of unusual and ambiguous relationships. The absolute comic excesses of this film provide much of its force, from the Rabelaisian to the surreal to touches of Ealing comedy, and the film crams in styles of humour as well as the comic itself. Whenever it approaches pathos, for example, it does so almost as an experiment in style rather than simply to achieve an effect.

Other Films Referred to

Adam's Rib (dir. George Cukor, USA, 1949)
Adventures of Baron Von Munchausen, The (dir. Terry Gilliam, UK, 1988)
Alien (dir. Ridley Scott, USA, 1979)
Alien 2 (dir. James Cameron, USA, 1986)
Alien Resurrection (dir. Jean-Pierre Jeunet, USA, 1995)
All That Jazz (dir. Bob Fosse, USA, 1979)
American Friend, The (dir. Wim Wenders, Germany, 1977)
Angel (dir. Robert Vincent O'Neil, USA, 1984)
Apocalypse Now (dir. Francis Ford Coppola, USA, 1979)
Armageddon (dir. Michael Bay, USA, 1998)
Avenging Angel (dir. Robert Vincent O'Neil, USA, 1885)

Bad Girls (dir. Jonathan Kaplin, USA, 1994)
Badlands (dir. Terrence Malick, USA, 1973)
Baisers Volés (dir. François Truffaut, France, 1968)
Barbarella (dir. Roger Vadim, Italy–France, 1968)
Basic Instinct (dir. Paul Verhoeven, USA, 1992)
Battleship Potemkin (dir. Sergei Eisenstein, Russia, 1925)
Beyond Good and Evil (dir. Liliana Cavani, Italy, 1977)
Biches, Les (dir. Claude Chabrol, France, 1968)
Big Heat, The (dir. Fritz Lang, USA, 1953)
Bitter Tears of Petra Von Kant (dir. Rainer Werner Fassbinder, Germany, 1972)
Blood and Roses (dir. Roger Vadim, Italy, 1961)
Blood of a Poet (dir. Jean Cocteau, France, 1930)
Body Double (dir. Brian De Palma, USA, 1984)
Boston Strangler, The (dir. Richard Fleischer, USA, 1968)
Brazil (dir. Terry Gilliam, USA, 1985)
Bringing Up Baby (dir. Howard Hawks, USA, 1938)
Butcher Boy, The (dir. Neil Jordan, Ireland, 1997)
Butterfly Kiss (dir. Michael Winterbottom, USA, 1995)

Cabinet of Dr Caligari, The (dir. Robert Wiene, Germany, 1919)
Camille (dir. George Cukor, USA, 1937)
Canterbury Tales (dir. Pier Paolo Pasolini, France–Italy, 1971)
Caravaggio (dir. Derek Jarman, UK, 1986)
Chinatown (dir. Roman Polanski, USA, 1974)
City of Lost Children (dir. Jean-Pierre Jeunet and Marc Caro, France, 1995)
City of Women (dir. Frederico Fellini, Italy, 1981)
Clockwork Orange, A (dir. Stanley Kubrick, UK, 1971)
Close My Eyes (dir. Stephen Poliakoff, UK, 1991)
Cook, the Thief, His Wife and Her Lover, The (dir. Peter Greenaway, Netherlands–France, 1989)
Crying Game, The (dir. Neil Jordan, UK, 1992)

Dark City (dir. Alex Proyas, USA, 1998)
Daughters of Darkness (dir. Harry Kumel, France–Belgium, 1971)
Decameron, The (dir. Pier Paolo Pasolini, West Germany–France–Italy, 1970)
Delicatessen (dir. Jean-Pierre Jeunet and Marc Caro, France, 1991)
Deliverance (dir. John Boorman, USA, 1972)
Desert Hearts (dir. Donna Deitch, USA, 1985)
Devil's Advocate, The (dir. Taylor Hackford, USA, 1997)
Dirty Harry (dir. Don Siegel, USA, 1971)
Discreet Charms of the Bourgeoisie, The (dir. Luis Buñuel, France, 1972)
Do the Right Thing (dir. Spike Lee, USA, 1989)
Domicile Conjugal (dir. François Truffaut, France, 1970)
Dr No (dir. Terence Young, UK, 1962)
Drive, He Said (dir. Jack Nicholson, USA, 1972)
Drowning By Numbers (dir. Peter Greenaway, UK, 1987)
Duck Soup (dir. Leo McCarey, USA, 1933)

Easy Rider (dir. Dennis Hopper, USA, 1969)
Elephant Man (dir. David Lynch, USA, 1980)
Eraserhead (dir. David Lynch, USA, 1978)
Et Dieu Créa La Femme (dir. Roger Vadim, France, 1956)
Even Dwarfs Started Small (dir. Werner Herzog, Germany, 1970)
Existenz (dir. David Cronenberg, Canada, 1999)
Eyes Without a Face (*Les yeux sans visage*) (dir. Georges Franju, France, 1959)

Fallen (dir. Gregory Hoblit, USA, 1998)
Fatal Attraction (dir. Adrian Lyne, USA, 1987)
Fifth Element, The (dir. Luc Besson, USA, 1988)
Fisher King, The (dir. Terry Gilliam, USA, 1991)
Fly, The (dir. Kurt Neumann, USA, 1958)

Germinal (dir. Claude Berri, France, 1993)
Go Fish (dir. Rose Troche, USA, 1994)
Golden Balls (dir. Bigas Lunas, Spain, 1993)
Grease (dir. Randal Kleiser, USA, 1978)
Grifters, The (dir. Stephen Frears, USA, 1990)

High Heels (dir. Pedro Almodóvar, Spain, 1991)
Hiroshima, Mon Amour (dir. Alain Resnais, Japan–France, 1959)
How To Make An American Quilt (dir. Jocelyn Moorhouse, USA, 1995)
Hunger, The (dir. Tony Scott, USA, 1983)

I Know What You Did Last Summer (dir. Jim Gillespie, USA, 1997)
I Married a Monster From Outer Space (dir. Jean Fowler, Jr., USA, 1958)
India Song (dir. Marguerite Duras, France, 1975)
Invasion of the Body Snatchers (dir. Don Siegel, USA, 1956)
Iron Mistress (dir. Gordon Douglas, USA, 1952)
It Happened One Night (dir. Frank Capra, USA, 1934)

Jean de Florette (dir. Claude Berri, France, 1986)
Jettée, La (dir. Chris Marker, France, 1963)

Kika (dir. Pedro Almodóvar, Spain, 1993)
Killer Tongue (dir. Alberto Sciamma, Spain, 1996)
Killing of Sister George, The (dir. Robert Aldrich, UK, 1968)
Kiss of the Spider Woman (dir. Hector Babenco, Brazil–USA, 1985)
Klute (dir. Alan J. Pakula, USA, 1971)

L'Amour à Vingt Ans (dir. François Truffaut, France, 1962)
La Bombola (dir. Bigas Lunas, Spain, 1992)
Last Tango in Paris (dir. Bernardo Bertolucci, Italy–France, 1973)
L'Avventura (dir. Michelangelo Antonioni, Italy, 1960)
Lawrence of Arabia (dir. David Lean, UK, 1962)

Les 400 Coups (dir. François Truffaut, France, 1959)
Lianna (dir. John Sayles, USA, 1983)
Lipstick (dir. Lamont Johnson, USA, 1976)
Live Flesh (dir. Pedro Almodóvar, Spain, 1998)
Lock, Stock and Two Smoking Barrels (dir. Guy Ritchie, UK, 1998)
Lolita (dir. Stanley Kubrick, USA, 1962)
Lost Highway (dir. David Lynch, USA, 1997)

Mad Max (dir. George Miller, Australia, 1979)
Man Bites Dog (dir. Rémy Belvaux, André Bonzel, Benoit Poelvoorde, Belgium, 1992)
Man Who Shot Liberty Valance, The (dir. John Ford, USA, 1962)
Marnie (dir. Alfred Hitchcock, USA, 1964)
M*A*S*H (dir. Robert Altman, USA, 1970)
Missouri Breaks, The (dir. Arthur Penn, USA, 1976)
My Fair Lady (dir. George Cukor, USA, 1964)

Naked (dir. Mike Leigh, UK, 1993)
Name of the Rose, The (dir. Jean-Jacques Annaud, France–Germany–Italy, 1986)
Nanook of the North (dir. Robert Flaherty, USA, 1922)
New York, New York (dir. Martin Scorsese, USA, 1977)
Newsfront (dir. Philip Noyce, Australia, 1978)
Night Porter, The (dir. Liliana Cavani, Italy, 1974)
$9\frac{1}{2}$ Weeks (dir. Adrian Lyne, USA, 1986)
North by Northwest (dir. Alfred Hitchcock, USA, 1959)

Once Upon a Time in the West (dir. Sergio Leone, Italy–USA, 1968)
Orlando (dir. Sally Potter, UK, 1993)

Paris, Texas (dir. Wim Wenders, USA, 1984)
Passenger, The (dir. Michelangelo Antonioni, Italy, 1975)
Peeping Tom (dir. Michael Powell, UK, 1960)
Perdita Durango (dir. de la Iglesia, USA, 1998)
Performance (dir. Donald Cammell, UK, 1970)
Persona (dir. Ingmar Bergman, Sweden, 1966)
Personal Best (dir. Robert Towne, USA, 1982)
Player, The (dir. Robert Altman, USA, 1992)
Prizzi's Honour (dir. John Huston, USA, 1985)
Prospero's Books (dir. Peter Greenaway, Netherlands–UK, 1991)
Public Virtues, Private Vices (dir. Miklos Jancsó, Hungary, 1976)

Quick and the Dead, The (dir. Sam Raimi, USA, 1995)

Raging Bull (dir. Martin Scorsese, USA, 1980)
Raising Arizona (dir. Coen Brothers, USA, 1987)
Rambo (dir. George Cosmatos, USA, 1985)
Ran (dir. Akira Kurosawa, France–Japan, 1985)

Rear Window (dir. Alfred Hitchcock, USA, 1954)
Reservoir Dogs (dir. Quentin Tarantino, USA, 1992)
Romper Stomper (dir.Geoffry Wright, Australia, 1992)

Salo, or The 120 Days of Sodom (dir. Pier Paolo Pasolini, Italy, 1975)
Samourai, Le (dir. Jean-Pierre Melville, France, 1967)
Saturday Night Fever (dir. John Badham, USA, 1977)
Saving Private Ryan (dir. Stephen Spielberg, USA, 1998)
Scream (dir. Wes Craven, USA, 1996)
Searchers, The (dir. John Ford, USA, 1956)
Seven (dir. David Fincher, USA, 1995)
Shaft (dir. Gordon Parks Jr., USA, 1971)
Shane (dir. George Stevens, USA, 1953)
Sheltering Sky, The (dir. Bernardo Bertolucci, USA, 1990)
Shining, The (dir. Stanley Kubrick, USA, 1980)
Simon of the Desert (dir. Luis Buñuel, Spain, 1965)
Single, White Female (dir. Barbet Schroeder, USA, 1992)
Sirens (dir. John Duigan, Australia, 1994)
Sisters (dir. Brian De Palma, USA, 1973)
Sliding Doors (dir. Peter Howitt, UK, 1998)
Snake Eyes (dir. Brian De Palma, USA, 1998)
Some Like It Hot (dir. Billy Wilder, USA, 1959)
Spellbound (dir. Alfred Hitchcock, USA, 1945)
Spiceworld (dir. Bob Spiers, UK, 1997)
Straw Dogs (dir. Sam Peckinpah, USA, 1971)
Strictly Ballroom (dir. Baz Lurhman, Australia, 1992)
Swept Away (dir. Lena Wertmuller, Italy, 1975)

Tampopo (dir. Juzo Itami, Japan, 1986)
Ten Commandments, The (dir. Cecil B. de Mille, USA, 1923 and 1956)
Terminator, The (dir. James Cameron, USA, 1991)
Terminator 2: Judgement Day (dir. James Cameron, USA, 1991)
That Obscure Object of Desire (dir. Luis Buñuel, Spain–France, 1977)
Thelma and Louise (dir. Ridley Scott, USA, 1991)
Them (dir. Douglas, USA, 1954)
They Died With Their Boots On (dir. Raoul Walsh, USA, 1941)
Thin Red Line, The (dir. Terrence Malick, USA, 1998)
Three Colours Red (dir. Krzysztof Kieslowski, Poland–France, 1994)
Tie Me Up, Tie Me Down (dir. Pedro Almodóvar, Spain, 1998)
Tit and the Moon (dir. Bigas Lunas, Spain, 1994)
Titanic (dir. James Cameron, USA, 1998)
Trainspotting (dir. Danny Boyle, UK, 1996)
Triumph of the Will (dir. Leni Riefenstahl, Germany, 1936)
Twelve Monkeys (dir. Terry Gilliam, USA, 1996)

Ulzana's Raid (dir. Robert Aldrich, USA, 1972)
Usual Suspects, The (dir. Bryan Singer, USA, 1995)

Vampire Lovers, The (dir. Roy Ward Baker, UK, 1971)
Vanishing Point (dir. Richard Sarafian, USA, 1971)
Vera Baxter (dir. Marguerite Duras, France, 1977)
Videodrome (dir. David Cronenberg, Canada, 1983)

What (dir. Roman Polanski, Italy, 1973)
When Night is Falling (dir. Patricia Rozema, Canada, 1995)
White Line Fever (dir. Jonathan Kaplin, USA, 1975)
Wickerman, The (dir. Robin Hardy, UK, 1973)
Wild at Heart (dir. David Lynch, USA, 1990)
Wild Bunch, The (dir. Sam Peckinpah, USA, 1969)
Winchester 73 (dir. Anthony Mann, USA, 1950)
Wizard of Oz, The (dir. Victor Fleming and King Vidor, USA, 1939)

Z (dir. Costa-Gavras, France, 1969)
Zed and Two Noughts, A (dir. Peter Greenaway, Netherlands–UK, 1985)

Bibliography

Barthes, Roland (1973) *Mythologies*, trans. A. Lavers, London: Jonathan Cape
—— (1975) *The Pleasure of the Text*, trans. R. Miller, New York: Hill & Wang
—— (1977) *Image–Music–Text*, trans. S. Heath, Glasgow: Fontana
—— (1982) 'The Reality Effect', in T. Todorov (ed.), *French Literary Theory*, Cambridge: Cambridge University Press
—— (1984) *Camera Lucida*, trans. R. Howard, London: Flamingo
—— (1990) *A Lover's Discourse: Fragments*, trans. R. Howard, Harmondsworth, Middlesex: Penguin
Baudrillard, Jean (1982) *In the Shadow of the Silent Majorities*, New York: Semiotexte
—— (1983) *Simulations*, trans. P. Beitchman, New York: Semiotexte
—— (1990) *Seduction*, trans. B. Singer, London: Macmillan
Baudry, Jean-Louis (1986) 'Ideological Effects of the Basic Cinematographic Apparatus', and 'The Apparatus: Metapsychological Approaches to the Impression of Reality in Cinema', in P. Rosen (ed.), *Narrative, Apparatus, Ideology*, New York: Columbia University Press
Bazin, André (1967) *What is Cinema? (Volume One)*, Berkeley: University of California Press
—— (1971) *What is Cinema? (Volume Two)*, Berkeley: University of California Press
Case, Sue-Ellen (1991) 'Tracking the Vampire', *Differences: A Journal of Feminist Cultural Studies*, vol. 3, no. 2. pp. 1–20
Cixous, Hélène (1986) *The Newly Born Woman*, trans. B. Wing, Minneapolis: University of Minneapolis Press.
Deleuze, Giles (1972) *Un Nouvel archiviste*, Paris: Fata Morgana
—— (1987) *Cinema 1: The Movement Image*, trans. H. Tomlinson and R. Galeta, London: Athlone Press
—— (1989) *Cinema 2: The Time-Image*, trans. H. Tomlinson and R. Galeta, London: Athlone Press
Derrida, Jacques (1973) *Speech and Phenomena and Other Essays on Husserl's Theory of Signs*, trans. D.B. Allinson, Evanston: Northwestern University Press
—— (1976) *Of Grammatology*, trans. G.C. Spivak, Baltimore: Johns Hopkins University Press
—— (1978) *Writing and Difference*, trans. A. Bass, London: Routledge & Kegan Paul
—— (1981) *Dissemination*, trans. B. Johnson, London: Athlone Press
—— (1986) *Margins of Philosophy*, trans. A. Bass, Sussex: Harvester Press
—— (1987a) *The Post Card: From Socrates to Freud and Beyond*, trans. A. Bass, Chicago: University of Chicago Press

—— (1987b) *The Truth in Painting*, trans. G. Bennington and I. McLeod, Chicago: University of Chicago Press

—— (1990) *Memoirs of the Blind*, trans. P.A. Brault and M. Naas, Chicago: University of Chicago Press

—— (1994) *Given Time: 1. Counterfeit Money*, trans. P. Kamuf, Chicago: University of Chicago Press

—— and Marie-Françoise Plissart (1989) 'Droit de regards', trans. D. Wills, *Art and Text*, 32, pp. 19–97

Eco, Umberto (1976) *A Theory of Semiotics*, Bloomington: Indiana University Press

—— (1979) *The Role of the Reader*, Bloomington: Indiana University Press

—— (1984) *Semiotics and the Philosophy of Language*, Bloomington: Indiana University Press

Foucault, Michel (1970) *The Order of Things*, London: Tavistock

—— (1975) *Birth of the Clinic*, trans. A.M. Sheridan Smith, New York: Vintage

—— (1979) *The History of Sexuality, Vol. 1*, trans. R. Hurley, New York: Vintage Books

—— (1980) 'Confessions of the Flesh', in C. Gordon (ed.), *Power/Knowledge: Selected Interviews and Other Writings by Michel Foucault, 1972–1977*, New York: Pantheon Books

—— (1982) *I, Pierre Rivière . . .*, trans. F. Jellinek, Lincoln: University of Nebraska Press

—— (1983) 'Interview with Michel Foucault', in H. Dreyfus and P. Rabinow, *Michel Foucault: Beyond Structuralism and Hermeneutics*, Chicago: University of Chicago Press

—— (1986a) *The Archaeology of Knowledge*, trans. A. Sheridan-Smith, London: Tavistock

—— (1986b) *The Foucault Reader*, ed. P. Rabinow, Middlesex: Penguin

—— (1987a) *Discipline and Punish: The Birth of the Prison*, trans. A. Sheridan, London: Allen Lane

—— (1987b) *Madness and Civilisation: A History of Madness in the Age of Reason*, trans. R. Howard, London: Tavistock

Freud, Sigmund (1977) *On Sexuality*, trans. J. Strachey, Harmondsworth, Middlesex: Penguin

—— (1983) *Jokes and Their Relation to the Unconscious*, trans. J. Stinchey, Harmondsworth, Middlesex: Penguin

—— (1984) *On Psychopathology*, trans. J. Strachey, Harmondsworth, Middlesex: Penguin

—— (1985) *Case Studies 1: 'Dora' and 'Little Hans'*, trans. J. Strachey, Harmondsworth, Middlesex: Penguin

—— (1986) *The Interpretation of Dreams*, trans. J. Strachey, Harmondsworth, Middlesex: Penguin

—— (1987) *On Metapsychology: The Theory of Psychoanalysis*, trans. J. Strachey, Harmondsworth, Middlesex: Penguin

—— (1988) *The Psychopathology of Everyday Life*, trans. J. Strachey, Harmondsworth, Middlesex: Penguin

—— (1990) *Art and Literature*, trans. J. Strachey, Harmondsworth, Middlesex: Penguin

Fuery, Patrick (1995) *Theories of Desire*, Melbourne: Melbourne University Press

Hillier, Jim (ed.) (1986) *Cahiers du Cinéma*, Cambridge, Massachusetts: Harvard University Press

Ingarden, Roman (1973) *The Literary Work of Art*, Evanston: Northwestern University Press

Irigaray, Luce (1985) *Speculum of the Other Woman*, trans. G. Gill, Ithaca, New York: Cornell University Press

Klein, Melanie (1988) *Love, Guilt and Reparation*, London: Virago

Kristeva, Julia (1982) *Powers of Horror: An Essay on Abjection*, trans. Leon S. Roudiez, New York: Columbia University Press

—— (1984a) *Desire in Language*, trans. T. Gora *et al.*, Oxford: Basil Blackwell

—— (1984b) *Revolution in Poetic Language*, trans. M. Walter, New York: Columbia University Press

—— (1986) 'Ellipsis on Dread and the Specular Seduction', in P. Rosen (ed.), *Narrative, Apparatus, Ideology: A Film Theory Reader*, New York: Columbia University Press

Lacan, Jacques (1983) 'God and the *Jouissance* of The Woman', 'Intervention on Transference' and 'A Love Letter', trans. J. Rose, in J. Mitchell and J. Rose (eds), *Feminine Sexuality: Jacques Lacan and the École freudienne*, London: Macmillan

—— (1985) *Écrits: A Selection*, trans. A. Sheridan, London: Tavistock

—— (1986) *The Four Fundamental Concepts of Psychoanalysis*, trans. A. Sheridan, Harmondsworth, Middlesex: Penguin

—— (1987) 'Homage to Marguerite Duras, on Le ravissement de Lol V. Stein', in *Duras by Duras*, California: City Lights

—— (1988a) *Freud's Papers on Technique*, trans. J. Forrester, ed. J-A Miller, Cambridge: Cambridge University Press

—— (1988b) *The Ego in Freud's Theory and in the Technique of Psychoanalysis*, trans. S. Tomaselli, ed. J-A. Miller, Cambridge: Cambridge University Press

—— (1992) *The Ethics of Psychoanalysis*, trans. D. Porter, ed. J-A. Miller, London: Routledge

—— (1993) *The Psychoses*, trans. R. Grigg, ed. J-A. Miller, London: Routledge

Laplanche, Jean and Pontalis (1986) 'Fantasy and the Origins of Sexuality', in V. Burgin, J. Donald and C. Kaplan (eds), *Formations of Fantasy*, London: Methuen

Lyotard, Jean-François (1984) *The Postmodern Condition: A Report on Knowledge*, trans. G. Bennington and B. Massumi, Manchester: Manchester University Press

—— (1993) *Libidinal Economy*, trans. I. Hamilton Grant, Bloomington: Indiana University Press

Metz, Christian (1973) *Language and Cinema*, trans. D. Umiker-Sebeok, The Hague: Mouton

—— 1974) *Film Language: A Semiotics of the Cinema*, trans. M. Taylor, New York: Oxford University Press

—— (1976) 'On the Notion of Cinematographic Language', in B. Nicols (ed.), *Movies and Methods, Volume 1*, Berkeley: University of California Press

—— (1985) *The Imaginary Signifier: Psychoanalysis and the Cinema*, trans. C. Britton *et al.*, Bloomington: Indiana University Press

Mourlet, Michel (1986) 'In Defence of Violence', in J. Hillier (ed.), *Cahiers du Cinéma*, Cambridge, Massachusetts: Harvard University Press

Mulvey, Laura (1986) 'Visual Pleasure and Narrative Cinema', in P. Rosen (ed.), *Narrative, Apparatus, Ideology*, New York: Columbia University Press

Nichols, Bill (ed.) (1976) *Movies and Methods*, Berkeley: University of California Press

Nietzsche, Friedrich (1964) *Complete Works*, ed. Oscar Levy, New York: Vintage

Pasolini, Pier Paolo (1976) 'Cinema of Poetry', in B Nichols (ed.), *Movies and Methods (Volume 1)*, Berkeley: University of California Press

Riviere, Joan (1986) 'Womanliness as a Masquerade', in V. Burgin, J. Donald and C. Kaplan (eds), *Formations of Fantasy*, London: Methuen

Rosen, Philip (ed.) (1986) *Narrative, Apparatus, Ideology*, New York: Columbia University Press

Ruthrof, Horst (1992) *Pandora and Occam*, Bloomington: Indiana University Press

Sartre, Jean-Paul (1966) trans. Hazel Barnes, *Being and Nothingness*, New York: Washington Square Paress

Wollen, Peter (1969) *Signs and Meaning in the Cinema*, Bloomington: Indiana University Press

Index

207